Twins in the World

Twins in the World

The Legends They Inspire and the Lives They Lead

Alessandra Piontelli, M.D.

TWINS IN THE WORLD
Copyright © Alessandra Piontelli, 2008.

First published in 2008 by
PALGRAVE MACMILLAN®
in the US—a division of St. Martin's Press LLC,
175 Fifth Avenue, New York, NY 10010.

Where this book is distributed in the UK, Europe and the rest of the world,
this is by Palgrave Macmillan, a division of Macmillan Publishers Limited,
registered in England, company number 785998, of Houndmills,
Basingstoke, Hampshire RG21 6XS.

Palgrave Macmillan is the global academic imprint of the above companies
and has companies and representatives throughout the world.

Palgrave® and Macmillan® are registered trademarks in the United States,
the United Kingdom, Europe and other countries.

ISBN-13: 978–0–230–60597–8 paperback
ISBN-10: 0–230–60597–4 paperback
ISBN-13: 978–0–230–60596–1 hardcover
ISBN-10: 0–230–60596–6 hardcover

Library of Congress Cataloging-in-Publication Data

Piontelli, Alessandra, 1945–
    Twins in the world : the legends they inspire and the lives they
lead / Alessandra Piontelli.
        p. cm.
    Includes bibliographical references and index.
    ISBN 0–230–60596–6—ISBN 0–230–60597–4
        1. Twins—Psychology. I. Title.

HQ777.35P56 2008
306.875—dc22   2008005347

A catalogue record of the book is available from the British Library.

Design by Newgen Imaging Systems (P) Ltd., Chennai, India.

First edition: October 2008

10 9 8 7 6 5 4 3 2 1

Printed in the United States of America.

*In fondest memory of
my beloved father.*

Contents

List of Figures

Acknowledgments

Many people have accompanied me in my inquiries into the world of twins. For reasons of privacy, I can mention only a few. Nevertheless, my deepest gratitude goes to all the twins and their families who so patiently and generously allowed me to conduct this study. I am also grateful to all the colleagues and institutions who supported my work and asked me to work with them.

Virginia La Plante has been the most wonderful and skilled editor always willing to offer me help and support. Luba Ostashensky at Palgrave has been of invaluable help, offering me her precious advice. Joanna Mericle, also at Palgrave, patiently helped me deal with the in-house style. Martyn Anderson has struggled with my English and the Latin construction of many of my phrases. Angela Von Der Lippe at Norton first suggested writing this work in a narrative form. Gabriella Veggio of Porta d'Oriente, Turin, helped me smoothly organize my journeys to the remotest corners of the earth. Parts of this work were presented at various meetings and conferences. I am particularly grateful to Giannis Kugiumutzakis for inviting me to Crete, to Diane Garcia for asking me to lecture in LA, to Professor Karl Heinz Brisch for inviting me to Munich, and to Cristina Cristobal for asking me to go to Spain. All were wonderful arenas for testing out some of my thoughts. Some very special friends have been of enormous support. I particularly want to thank Lou-Mariè Kruger for all our intense discussions in South Africa, Carol Gilligan for the endless times we spoke about motherhood and all the fun we had, Luis Verrier for teaching me so much, not only about twins, but also about life, Anayke Chux, Jim Penagin, Sadou Aboubacar, and Abu Fofana for all their advice, Jasuhito Kassai for his exquisite kindness, Maria Teresa Gallo and Giuliana Norsa for being so patient with me, and Silvano Ponzi for his ever-present support. Jerome Bruner, Colwyn Trevarthen, Dan Stern, Liz Spillius, Libby Bryan, Richard and Marisa Katz, Roberto Moro-Visconti, and the late Mauro Mancia have all been marvellous friends. I am also greatly indebted to all the staff at maternal/fetal medicine unit of the University of Milan for their endless support, and particularly to Alessandra Kustermann, Umberto Nicolini, Elena Caravelli, Laura Villa, Chiara Boschetto, Cinzia Zoppini, Luisa Bocconi, and Sara Salmona. Maran Elancheran and the whole team of Newgen Imaging Systems, Chennai (India) have been extremely helpful and competent throughout the various stages of production. Finally my husband Luigi, as usual, has lovingly been by my side throughout, and my sons Filippo and Roberto have put up with a busy mother too often talking about twins.

The responsibility for what I have to say in this book is entirely mine.

Introduction: A Personal Journey

Most people who have written about twins are themselves twins or parents of twins, but I am not. I am a doctor, specializing in neurology, psychiatry, and psychoanalysis, with a long training in obstetrics. Most books on twins also deal broadly with behavioral genetics, the psychology of twins, or their upbringing. This work does not fit into any of these categories. Instead it describes and compares how various cultures, including the developed world, deal with twins. In doing so, it mixes anthropological, cultural, medical, psychological, and personal facts. This combination of interests is somewhat unusual, and I arrived at it by a circuitous path.

My interest in twins came about initially for the same reasons that everyone is fascinated with twins. Identical or monozygotic twins are seen as two distinct human beings, but we are unable to distinguish the one from the other because they look startlingly the same. Human origins are also a source of curiosity to everyone, and twins, having shared the same pregnancy and interacted unseen in the womb, would seem to possess superior knowledge about where we all came from. Additionally, twins are reputed to be united by a special link, which resembles the fantasy of romantic love that it is possible to find a perfect "twin soul" or "twin mate" with whom to communicate even without words. Paranormal communication is in fact often ascribed to twins.

Scientific developments have lately brought some of these notions about twins into the spotlight. The first clone, for example, the famous sheep Dolly, led to the futuristic scenario of parthenogenesis. People imagined the possibility of having a life after death by creating a human replica. While reincarnation turned out to be a fallacious dream, monozygotic twins, who are the closest one can get to human clones, were associated with this fallacy. People began to wonder what it means to live with a double, not in eternity, but in the here and now.

My own interest in twins emerged not from such developments but gradually from my work. After completing the specialties of neurology and psychiatry in Italy, my native country, I moved to London in order to deepen my psychoanalytic education. During my English years I worked and taught at the Tavistock Clinic, where I came into contact with leading psychoanalysts; one in particular, Esther Bick, influenced me deeply. She taught me to observe the interactions of infants with each other and with their caregivers on weekly visits to them at home, in their natural surroundings. Like many anthropologists, I became a participant observer, fitting in as far as possible with the routine and subculture of the household, while also noting the reactions to my presence of all those family members who happened to be present at a visit. While developmental psychologists and others have provided more accurate views of infant behavior, I was drawn to Bick's naturalistic approach. By following her teachings, I learned how to deal with foreign communities as well as with the intricacies of family life.

My first observations came as a bit of a shock when I visited Irish families who at that time in London were being seriously marginalized because of the regular bomb attacks carried out by the IRA. In retaliation, Irish homes were burned down and stones were thrown at their young children. My hosts were at first suspicious of me, but they soon accepted me on the assumption that Italian inevitably meant Catholic, putting us all in the same boat. They became extremely gentle and kind to me, while the retaliatory attacks on them continued. I was victimized as well. When I parked my car in the district, its windows were regularly smashed. For the first time in my life I came into direct contact with racial hatred and violence.

While living in England, I expected that clinical work and research with mothers, children, and infants would remain my occupation for life. Then one day an 18-month-old boy, whom I shall call Jacob, was brought to me for a consultation by his parents, whom he was driving mad with his restlessness and lack of sleep. While his parents talked, I noticed about Jacob's restlessness a peculiar quality. He was exploring every possible corner of my consulting room, seemingly obsessed by a vain search for something. Occasionally he also shook various objects on my book shelves and desk frantically. When I commented on this behavior, saying simply that Jacob seemed to be looking for something he had lost and could not find anywhere, he immediately stopped and looked at me intently. I then observed that he seemed to be trying to shake all the objects to life, as if their stillness meant something terrible to him, like death. His parents suddenly burst into tears and explained that Jacob was in fact a twin, whose co-twin had died two weeks before his birth. Jacob had therefore spent almost two weeks in utero with a dead, unusually unresponsive co-twin. The simple verbalization of this event brought about an incredible change in Jacob, who stopped moving restlessly about and smiled. It in turn facilitated a process of intense mourning by his parents, who until then had been unable to grieve. And the event aroused in me a desire to know more about the mysterious link that unites twins. Jacob's loss, though clearly mediated through his parents' grief, seemed to date back to his own experience before birth.

Upon my return to my own country, when my second son was on the way, ultrasounds had become available, bringing revolutionary changes to the field of obstetrics. I decided that research on fetal behavior was my next logical step, for just as "the child is the father of the man," as pointed out by the poet William Wordsworth,[1] so is the fetus the "father of the infant." I began to work in the biggest maternity hospital in my country, where I learned to perform ultrasounds, and after about one year I was assigned to a special unit for twin pregnancies. My interest at first centered on the twins' intrauterine life, but gradually broadened to include the reactions to twins by both their parents and their obstetricians. During an ultrasonographic session, people would ascribe different motives to the behavior of each twin fetus, much as one does to the behavior of babies in ordinary life. The comments ranged from, "He is a nervous type. The other is calm," to "This one will become a ballet dancer, the other a truck driver. Look how big he is!" to "Oh, look, how they fight! They will give us a tough time!"

This tendency to "anthropomorphize," "adultomorphize," and attribute meaning to the motions of twin fetuses, which was universal among all those not closely acquainted with fetal life, led me into research that helped to dispel it as a myth. Meaning-attribution, for example, is fundamental to postnatal life, helping us in caring for our infants and in facing the complex nuances of social interaction, but it is neither appropriate nor functional when applied indiscriminately to fetal behavior. Fetal motions, save possibly for short spells in the latest stages of pregnancy, are not equivalent to wakefulness and even less to intentionality and consciousness. A social dimension is absent from prenatal life.[2] Fetuses are indeed gradually preparing to enter a social world, but twin fetuses can hardly be regarded as highly interactive partners engaged in complex social and emotional interactions on their own.

The marked increase in twins that occurred at this time as a result of fertility treatments drew my attention to another phenomenon. Initially twins are ardently desired, but with advancing gestation the pregnancies turn out to be extremely taxing, and the idealization of twins often changes into ambivalence or even hatred. In one case an intelligent young woman who had recently given birth to John, a single child, came to me for a consultation because she was worried about her twin boys, who were five years old at the time. She said, "The twins seem to be doing all right, but it was all so different with them than it is now with John. I am afraid that they may have suffered from my behavior." When I asked her to describe her behavior with the twins, she said, "Relating to two is quite different from relating to one. You always feel disconnected. You look at one and hold the other. You talk to one and look at the other. My facial expressions, hand movements, breast-feeding, rocking, cuddling, and stroking all felt disconnected. With John I can concentrate all my senses, actions, and feelings on him. I can play and have one-on-one conversations. I find this closeness delightful. It was never possible with the twins. There was no energy or space left over for savoring their joys. I was in the middle of a maelstrom and could live only from one day to the next. I regret having been too busy fighting for survival to enjoy them fully when they were babies."

When I asked how the twins were doing, she first replied, "Actually they are doing very well. Their teachers are enthusiastic. They are bright, sociable, and well-behaved." Then she became lost in thought and looked distressed. I suggested that she probably had something else on her mind that worried her but was difficult to talk about. She started crying and said, "When I was told I was expecting twins, I felt elated. But then my pregnancy was complicated—all sorts of complications, from excess amniotic fluid to high blood pressure, uncontrollable itch, liver problems, sickness, varicose veins, diabetes, breathlessness, and sleeplessness—you name it. It was torture. I felt invaded and overwhelmed. I started hating them. I did not care any more about their health and growth. I just wanted to get it over. When they were born, I loved them, but frequently I also continued hating them. It was such an ordeal. I was alone in their care. My husband had to work in another town and was rarely there. I felt like screaming and hitting them. Now I feel awful about it. I am always afraid that my initial hatred may have damaged them." She then asked me to see the twins for a consultation. When I subsequently confirmed that they were doing well and that ambivalence and hatred are emotions that even the best mothers feel at times, she was greatly reassured.

The intensity of the contradictory feelings expressed by this mother, as well as by many of my other patients in the twin unit, led to new questions about whether the many difficulties twins present before birth continue after birth, and in what form.

I set out by observing the behavior of 30 pairs of twin fetuses with ultrasounds, and I continued following their development after birth. Despite public enthusiasm for twins, it turned out that twins upset family life to an extraordinary degree. During the first few years, twins were far from nice, and in private they could be hell. Past the initial stages, most parents doted on their twins and most twins grew up well.

While observing the turbulent growth of twins, I also had the chance to observe the special bond developing between them. Adult twins often claim that their bond is stronger and more long-lasting than any other tie, including that of marriage. We all yearn for a perfect match with another person, and in the initial stages of falling in love we often deceive ourselves into believing that we have found the ideal. Yet, once the illusion of the honeymoon period is over and the partners confront a real, as opposed to an ideal, person, unions can break. Twins are the closest one can ever get to the ideal of a permanent soul mate. Though their bond can be fraught with many more conflicting feelings than is generally thought, it is always lifelong and is always experienced as having primary importance.

During my research, major social changes took place that profoundly affected my work. Most developed countries faced a dramatic drop in birthrates, and a large part of Europe, notably Germany and Italy, reached zero growth. At the same time, Europe witnessed a substantial new wave of immigration, ending its five centuries of exporting human resources. In Italy, immigration was an especially new phenomenon, for the poorest strata of the local population had still been migrating abroad through the 1960s. Now immigrants were needed to solve problems involving the need for more workers in some sectors of the labor market. Those who immigrated did not necessarily come from the lower strata of their countries, yet they often found themselves having to accept low jobs. Many who started off illegally were able to join an already formed network of family, friends, and acquaintances. Despite concerns of politicians and the public, these immigrants rapidly changed Italy's face and are here to stay.

Immigrants became an increasingly familiar presence in my twin unit, because they reproduced earlier and more frequently than Italians as a result of spontaneous rather than artificial conception. Because I love talking to mothers and because immigrant mothers are only too pleased to be shown any interest soon after their delivery, I began visiting them in their homes and in communities that ranged from Peruvian, Philippine, and Sri Lankan to nationalities from all over Africa.

During my visits to these different women, the conversation naturally revolved around their twins. Soon entire neighborhoods joined in the conversation, and all were willing to inform me about the customs surrounding twins in their countries of origin. Chilling scenarios emerged, in which twins were not at all the object of universal fascination. Such scenarios were usually projected onto some remote ethnic minority, with phrases like, "They do that only in the jungle," "They do that only in the bush," or "Only some primitives behave like that." These immigrants understandably wanted to be seen in a good light and to blend with the dominant culture, but their descriptions were so detailed and realistic as to arouse my suspicion.

Surprisingly, immigrant mothers generally coped with twins better than did Italian women. Depression, when present among immigrants, was due to isolation, poverty, out-of-wedlock pregnancy, and nostalgia for homeland, not to postpartum depression, which seemed to affect Italian women alone.

Working with immigrants reminded me of a dream I had harbored since childhood. When I was 12, my parents had taken me along to spend several months in Africa, which I consider to have been one of the happiest periods of my early life. I dreamed of returning to Africa one day to work as a doctor, having in mind a romantic notion of Dr Schweitzer, busy all day with his patients and in the evenings making the jungle resonate with classical music on his piano.

My first long stay abroad as a doctor, however, had not been in Africa but in India, where I had completed my residency by working in a hospital in Delhi for one year, caring for neurological and psychiatric adult patients who were accompanied by entire families. Their poverty was appalling. Male psychiatric patients were surprisingly few, because most of those whom I would have diagnosed as suffering from severe psychiatric disorders were living out on the streets and were treated like holy men. Women, on the contrary, were plentiful, and their madness seemed to be aggravated by social circumstances. They had been cast out by their families and society for all sorts of reasons, from being no longer virgins, being widowed or childless, to being overaged child prostitutes. Their plight reinforced my embryonic desire to work with mothers and children abroad.

After returning to Italy, I had to set aside my dream of working abroad as a doctor for years, well past a second marriage and a second son. But as I am a restless type, and also persevering, traits that my husband accepts and perhaps even likes, once more I took up my old dreams and began to work overseas periodically. My assignments took me to many countries in Africa, Asia, South America, and the Pacific.

Although my work abroad centered on medical issues, from time to time I also made inquiries about twins. Knowing the ordeals that western parents go through during the early years of their twins, I wondered how people living in less fortunate circumstances could cope. It turned out that twins elicited extreme ambivalence, the same as back at home. The chilling scenarios that had been only hinted at by immigrants in my own country materialized before my very eyes.

Although this book describes the customs related to twins in various populations, it makes no claim to the depth of an anthropological or ethnological inquiry. Anthropologists usually spend years in the field, while physicians generally leave after only a few months. Working as a doctor, however, has other advantages for social research. Regardless of background, people like to receive as well as to give, and health matters to everyone. Being offered medical care is especially appreciated in areas of the world where it is nonexistent, limited, difficult to obtain, or unafford-able. A doctor is also expected to ask questions, and when they are asked in a nonjudgmental manner, they are often answered in a straightforward way. A doctor is also generally exposed to matters that are otherwise considered private or at least are kept out of the public eye. Finally, working for brief periods in many places makes it possible to explore more than one ethnic group. My work gave me an overview of how twins are regarded across many continents and cultures.

Working with people from different cultural backgrounds can nevertheless stir up mutual anxieties and irrational emotions. Initially I naively assumed that as a do-gooder, I would be automatically accepted in any community, and could develop with its members the same straightforward, rational alliance as I did back at home. Most people I encountered were indeed exquisitely kind, hospitable, and welcoming. But this was not the rule. Once abroad, I was now "the other." When confronted with strangers, people sometimes react with diffidence, insecurity, or fear. They try to wall off or even eliminate the stranger. In my work, some communities were actively hostile and even dangerous. In addition, a local history of colonialism, oppression, and racism could also not be easily erased by my desire to help. As a doctor, I held precious medicines and the power to cure, but not everyone accepted my healing methods or welcomed my presence. From time to time people grabbed my medicines and then asked to be left alone.

As a result of these reactions, I often felt isolated and lonely. These emotions are difficult to deal with, especially when one is far from home, tired, living in discomfort, alone, or accompanied by difficult coworkers. My psychoanalytic training helped me to cope with my feelings without being overwhelmed by the complex interactions involved in any community work. I came to see many of the negative exchanges as projections onto me of the feelings of helplessness, misery, oppression, and naked impotence that my patients and their families were themselves experiencing. Such feelings had a long history in an abominable past and often an equally intolerable present.

Contrary to my encounters with immigrants back home, people abroad wanted to know a lot about me. Their curiosity centered mainly on racial differences as manifested in the pale color of my skin, on national characteristics and Italian way of life, and on religion. My lack of any religious beliefs disconcerted people so much that I sometimes avowed a belief in God but not in the religious apparatus usually connected with it. More difficult to tolerate were some questions about personal matters, such as my sexuality, marriage, falling in love, and love for my children. I often felt quite naked in front of all the questioners. Yet my nakedness taught me a lot about myself and I soon realized that my acceptance of feeling naked was a prerequisite to establishing an open interchange with others.

From the very first moment in which our mothers set eyes upon us, we begin to live in a social world that largely shapes our identity and behavior. Seeing myself mirrored in the eyes of others made me aware of aspects of myself I had previously ignored. My body language was accurately and minutely scrutinized. We all have our little foibles and quirks, and mine were all pointed out to me. My laughter, tone of voice, posture, gesticulations, smiles were commented upon, and my moods were accurately perceived.

Neutrality and detachment were impossible for me, if not altogether fictional. Only when I was alone in the evenings could I take a more reflective stance in trying to understand my encounters during the day.

One day, for instance, when I was engaged with a line of patients, the local shaman came up to me, looked at my chin, touched it, and said, "You have a facial hair." I was surprised and annoyed. My skin is so smooth that I don't even need to shave my legs, so why was he interrupting my work to ridicule me? Reflecting over this small episode in the evening, I came to understand that the shaman had rather tried to convey two different meanings and emotions to me. On one hand, he was jealous of my success with his patients and wanted to mock me in front of everyone by pointing out one of my blemishes. On the other, by hinting at a beard, which only he was allowed to wear in the village, he paid me a compliment. My "beard," albeit minimal, marked me as belonging to his kind. Having understood this, I was able to overcome my irritation and made a joke of it. From then on our relationship became one of mutual trust and genuine warmth.

Each encounter resulting in a dialogue was charged with strong emotions that left both participants changed. Dialogue is the essential precondition for understanding and accepting "the other," as only dialogue and mutual comprehension can bridge differences of skin, nation, and religious belief. As the cultural anthropologist Clifford Geertz says, "[when meeting the other] We are not seeking either to become natives or to mimic them. Only romantics and spies would seem to find point in that. We are seeking, in the widened sense of the term in which it encompasses very much more than talk, to converse with them, a matter a great deal more difficult, and not only with strangers, than is commonly recognized."[3] Conversing did not always come effortlessly to me, and I remember, on many of my evenings abroad, feeling exhausted, emptied, and anxious for silence. Despite such difficulties, all my encounters left me enriched and even more curious about the world of "the others," with its different ways of coping and interpreting nature. Often a simple question about twins opened up a fascinating and unknown universe. The approach to twins in different cultures has much to tell us about their broader beliefs about children, reproduction, pregnancy, motherhood, and gender.

In recounting my experiences, I have followed a Dantesque path in reverse. The initial chapters concentrate on the ascending steps toward the idealization of twins. Subsequent chapters deal with the progressive descent to the inferno to which countless twins are led. The last chapter brings the reader up to the adult experience of twins. And finally the conclusion highlights the qualities of motherhood that are uniquely exposed by twin births.

Reports are rendered more difficult and debates more heated when they focus on members of our own species. We inevitably respond emotionally and often irrationally. When it comes to studying the sacred subject of motherhood and the bleak destiny of many children, we can expect even greater emotional turmoil and controversy. My report lacks the aseptic quality that might render its findings both scientifically and emotionally more acceptable and less grievous.

Many of the findings reported here are highly traumatic. To protect the privacy of the people involved, in all but a few instances, I have not identified, or have given fictitious names to, the ethnic groups concerned, and changed the regions where they lived, the institutions with whom I worked, and the various individuals with whom I came into contact. Any details that might reveal their identity have also been omitted or changed.

Finally the events described here belong to a particular moment in time. All societies undergo changes, and developing countries often change at a dazzling rate. Governments are upturned, urbanization grows, wars cease, international interventions occur, and incredible human resources are tapped. What was true only a few years back may today no longer be the case. Should someone else happen to visit many of the places where I stayed in the past, he or she will hopefully find that twins there are finally thriving.

Chapter 1

Our Twins

Only a few years ago twins were rare in Central Park. Whenever I spotted a pair, I felt a special thrill. All this has changed dramatically. My thoughts today have turned from a thrilled, "Look! Twins!" to a dismayed, "Oh, my...more twins." In the 1980s twins accounted for about one in 105 births among the white race. In the last decade the developed world has witnessed a striking rise in twinning rates. According to the CDC National Vital Statistic Report, the birthrate for twins has undergone a 38 percent rise since 1990 and a 65 percent jump since 1980. Twins currently account for one in 70 births, and the numbers are constantly escalating.[1]

I am often in New York, where one of my sons works, and I have longstanding professional contacts. While there, I like to sit on a bench in Central Park and engage in "twin-spotting," as my friends call it, observing young twins freely in a natural setting. The mothers strolling through Central Park with twins are chiefly in their mid- to late thirties or even early forties. The average child-bearing age is now 29.3 years in the United States,[2] but it is much higher in urban areas such as Manhattan, because the national average includes people of all races and nationalities, some of whom reproduce early but are unlikely to be represented in the area around Central Park. Not so long ago a woman expecting her first child in her early thirties was considered "old" and looking for a "baby to change her life." Most women married early and had children in their twenties or even in their late teens. This tendency changed in the mid-1970s when there was a widespread postponement of child-bearing age owing to a combination of factors, such as completing an education and establishing a career first, trying out different partners before settling into a stable relationship, lengthened life spans, an increased emphasis on standards of living, and the possibility of prenatal diagnosis of genetic defects like Down syndrome.

Maternal age has a positive impact on twinning rates, which triple in likelihood by age 37 and then sharply drop off.[3] At the same time, age has a negative impact on fertility, defined as the ability to achieve a pregnancy. The decline begins at the age of 30, becomes more obvious between 35 and 40 years, and drops dramatically thereafter. After the age of 35, 25 percent of women are infertile as compared to 7 percent at age 20, and 15 percent between the ages of 30 and 34. The age of 41 is considered to be the point when fertility stops and sterility starts.[4] The drop is due to a mixture of factors. Principally the ovarian reserve of eggs decreases with advancing age. In addition, the quality of the ova deteriorates, increasing the incidence of chromosomal defects. The endocrine function of the ovary also declines, making it unable to sustain the necessary hormonal changes that allow pregnancy to continue.

Though an increasing number of couples decide not to have children under these circumstances, the social stigma against childless women, who are regarded as "dry," spinsterish, and incomplete, is still strong. The age-old ideas of sterility as a disease and of sterility in a couple as evil and abnormal still lurk beneath the surface of enlightened modernism. While marriage is increasingly considered less of an essential status for women, motherhood continues to be regarded as the indispensable fulfillment of femininity. Maternal desire is closely linked with these cultural factors, so that when the biological clock starts ticking fast, many women are unable to resist the ancient societal pressure and decide to reproduce at an age when their mothers would have already been grandmothers.

Women deciding to postpone child-bearing to the limit increasingly have to resort to assisted reproduction in order to give birth. In more than half of successful assisted reproductions the outcome is twins, triplets, and occasionally more.[5]

The dramatic rise in twinning rates is due overwhelmingly to these ever newer and more sophisticated fertility treatments. Twins can now be induced by hormones not produced by the body of the woman giving birth. The eggs can be fertilized artificially in aseptic laboratories. Fertilized eggs, no matter how obtained, can be frozen, thawed, and implanted at will, rendering fertilization independent of the initiation of pregnancy. Once the embryos are frozen (or cryopreserved), gestation can be started at a later, more convenient date. Embryos of twins can be implanted at different times and even born through different pregnancies. In other words, one twin may actually be older or younger than its co-twin. And for the first time in the history of mankind the old dictum *mater semper certa est* (you always know who the mother is) no longer proclaims a universal truth. Egg donation creates a split between the genetic and nurturing mothers. Surrogate motherhood produces a division between the egg donor and the hosting uterus. The future will certainly bring about further un-imaginable developments.

The success rate of fertility treatments for either men or women is not high. The success of insemination oscillates around 4–30 percent, even when performed in optimal physical conditions and at the peak age for fertility, but failures do not make the news.[6] Popular opinion remains convinced of the omnipotence of medicine in the realm of reproduction: everyone can reproduce if given the right treatment. Some couples are prepared to go to any length to obtain the desired result.

Our mothers bore children without this element of choice and often without any yearning. They were told that people did not desire children; they simply had them. Up until the 1950s it was estimated that five out of every six children were not the consequence of an act of will but the chance by-product of a variety of acts, ranging from resignation, duty, love, or sheer sexual appetite.[7] Only at the beginning of the 1960s did the so-called reproductive revolution, with the introduction of reliable birth control and legal abortion, make motherhood largely an option. Birth control pills, condoms, vaginal gels, spermicidal foams, diaphragms, relatively safe means of abortion, and widespread access to information and medical care all contributed to determining when our children would be born by choice. The number of children per family declined.

Various socioeconomic reasons also accounted for the drop in children. Children are no longer considered a family asset and source of cheap labor. The costs of bringing up a child have steadily increased since laws on child labor and mandatory education were introduced toward the end of last century. The dramatic decrease in infant and child mortality and the massive increase in urbanization, industrialization, and women's education and employment accelerated the reduction in child-bearing. Working parents in urban areas could bring up and educate only a few children. A changed mentality was also of paramount importance in the reproductive revolution. With the moral acceptance of birth control, marriage, repro-duction, and sexuality were no longer inextricably linked and 'sanctified.' An individualistic mentality emerged, rendering the self-fulfillment of in-dividual family members more important than the well-being of the family as a whole.

Aside from these socioeconomic considerations, the magnitude of the drop in children indicates per se that maternal desire is not a straightfor-ward, inbuilt core of a woman's life but is rather a conflicted, ambivalent psychological force. As soon as they were given a chance, women repro-duced less and less. Assisted reproduction has brought about another revo-lution in conflict with the birth control revolution. Motherhood is no longer seen as merely a planned option, but is increasingly experienced as a right, as something due, or as an essential element for the fulfillment of one's basic desires.

No matter how ardently pursued, more often than not, twins do not bring about the craved-for fulfillment and happiness as symbolized by the ever-growing parade of twins in Central Park in their double-sized prams. No parent of a singleton would invest in such a cumbersome, quickly outgrown item. The cost of raising any child to the age of 17 in middle-class American families is estimated to range between $165,000 and $233,530.[8] The cost doubles for twins. From the start, twins are a weighty economic burden. Considering the neonatal period alone, twins require twice the amount of clothing, diapers, formulas, bottles, baby creams, medical treatment, and even living space. Some families are stretched financially to the limit.

The costs are not solely financial. Depression ranks high among mothers of twins, 37 percent of whom at four months post-partum experience depression serious enough to warrant professional help, in contrast to 10 percent of all mothers.[9,10] Quality of life has also been found to drop dramatically, or 80 percent for mothers of twins compared to 20 percent for all mothers.[11] Sleepless nights, relentless round-the-clock feeding, twice as much yelling, and not a minute's privacy or any chance to read a book, take a bath undisturbed, or just go for a walk alone can all account for the increase in maternal depression.

Twins as toddlers are especially taxing, suggesting the relative unfitness of the human species to care for two children simultaneously. In Central Park, twins dash in every possible direction, usually opposite ones, have twice as many temper tantrums, fight ferociously, and get into all kinds of danger at the same time, such as one twin swallowing stones while the other leans over the pond. In one afternoon survey six out of ten mothers had tied their toddler twins to reins.

Fathers too are worn out by twins. Another afternoon survey of 20 double strollers revealed that seven were pushed by men. Whereas men are increasingly involved in the care of all children, paternal involvement in twins is especially urgent and inevitable. Fathers participate from the very beginning in the whole taxing endeavor. As one exasperated man commented, "This is no longer a marriage or a family but a business enterprise." Often fathers flee from the entire business. According to a survey published by the National Organization of Mothers of Twins, women reported a decline in their mate helpfulness/supportiveness from 88 percent during pregnancy to 66 percent at 1–5 years after pregnancy.[12] When both parents were observed together in Central Park, they often ignored each other, did not seek physical contact, looked tense, resentful and angry, and engaged in verbal fights. All these behaviors are considered by marriage counselors to be "relationship warning signs" potentially leading to marital breakdown and separation. Marital tensions escalating to divorce are in fact frequent amongst parents of twins: 35 percent report serious marital problems.[13]

The attitude of the public to twins is quite different. Twins break down some of the rules dominating our daily social contacts, such as keeping a safe distance and respecting each other's space. People turn around to stare at twins. Even perfect strangers feel entitled to go and look at or touch twins and talk to their parents or whoever is accompanying them.

Parents are usually tolerant and even pleased by these moments of "fame." Few can resist the lure of drawing attention to the twinship in their children by some display, such as matching hats or shirts, which have an immediate visual impact even when the twins are far from "identical." Often twinship is more than hinted at by clothes that are not only identical but also noticeable in themselves, as when twins are dressed like flowers, bunnies, or bumblebees. Twins dressed alike appeal irresistibly not only to strangers but also to the parents themselves. This minor compensation to parents for their private ordeals is not so insignificant, for studies have shown the visual appeal of infants and young children to be an important element in fostering parental care. Nature is unfair, and beautiful children have an advantage magnetizing everybody's attention and grabbing parental interest. By dressing twins alike, parents gain support and encouragement in their difficult upbringing.

For dealing with the enormous physical and psychological strains connected with the care of young twins, parents turn to the manuals on twins from conception onward that are now ubiquitous in bookstores and proliferating at a dazzling pace. Manuals on how to raise twins were noticed in 18 strollers out of 20 one afternoon. Having become a multimillion business, manuals cover the most disparate aspects of our lives and have the same rationalistic approach analyzing different points and are dominated by a soothing motto: every problem can be solved. Manuals have to reinforce positive thinking, and the difficulties involved in bearing and raising twins are in most cases glossed over in an over-optimistic, "Don't worry" tone. As it said on the cover of one of these manuals, "This delightful book is intensely practical. It can help you chart a way through all the excitement and the joys of coping with twins."[14] Twins are described as the ultimate parental dream, with an aura of religiosity often bordering on the miraculous. Some manuals go overboard in an attempt to infuse enthusiasm in overwhelmed parents. As another stated, "Congratulations, you're going to have twins, triplets or more! Are you still dazed from hearing those words? Have all your thoughts suddenly turned to mountains of diapers, limousine strollers, and stereo babies? You are not alone! The experiences of multiple pregnancy birth and parenting are unique making you and your babies very special!"[15] Envy of twins is even attributed to parents of singletons, who apparently tend to see twins as the embodiment of their own yearning for an ideal soul-mate.

Manuals, books, magazines, various forms of media, and increasingly the net are all replacing the advice, wisdom, and support younger generations traditionally received from their elders. Few grandparents take care of twins. On two consecutive afternoons in Central Park I noticed 35 pairs of twins, and only two grandmothers and one grandfather were attending to them. Various reasons underpin the fading of this age-old network of support. Twins are particularly tiresome and elderly grandparents do not feel up to caring for two infants. On the other hand average life expectancy has undergone a 30-year increase during the twentieth century and this expanded life span has turned healthy grandparents into relatively young adults, who still work and have the prospect of embarking on a second or even third life. Nowadays only one-third of our entire life is spent in the active care of children, and grandparents want to enjoy their newly found freedom once their children have left home. Additionally, nuclear families often live far from their close relatives, making concrete help and the passing on of experience down the generations largely impossible.

For more scientific explanations, parents may turn to behavioral genetics. Sir Francis Galton, Darwin's cousin, opened up the field in 1875 with a paper titled, "The history of twins as a criterion of the relative powers of nature and nurture."[16] Francis Galton was only marginally interested in evolution. He set out to discover how much individual difference among human beings is derived from the intrinsic nature of the individual and how much from the characteristics of his or her environment. Twins seemed to be particularly suited for his purposes. Galton was the first scientist to notice and describe the two fundamental types of twins, based on differences in fertilization. Twins can originate either from two different ova fertilized by two different sperms or from a single fertilised ovum. Monozygotic or so-called identical twins are derived by the splitting of the same fertilized egg and thus carry the same genome. Dizygotic twins, on the contrary, coming from different eggs fertilized at the same time are, genetically speaking, just like ordinary siblings, sharing on average 50 percent of their genes. Since monozygotic twins are usually reared together and hence share not only the same nature but also the same nurture, their similarities may in part be explained not only by their genes but also by their shared cultural environment.

Behavioral geneticists focus mainly on monozygotic twins, considered to be "experiments in nature" or "living laboratories," from which they hope to tease out the relative strength of the genetic, inherited makeup and the various environmental components in determining different characteristics of an individual. Particularly sought after for study are those rare twins who were given out for adoption separately and thus "reared apart." The fact that these twins share only their genes emphasizes the possible impact of their different environments. Studies on twins have provided no unequivocal results whether applied to pathology, especially schizophrenia and multiple sclerosis, or normality. Behavioral geneticists incline toward genetic explanations of even complex behavioral manifestations, such as intelligence, personality, love styles, happiness, and marital satisfaction.[17] Behavior, even in its simplest form, is inextricably controlled by a multitude of genes as well as by an infinity of environmental factors, including the intrauterine environment, which is overwhelmingly ignored. Many scientists also no longer consider genes as implacable blueprints. Concepts of plasticity, interaction, and expression, to name but a few, are all replacing the former inflexible associations between genes and ineluctable destiny.

The "findings" of behavioral geneticists have nevertheless led to a widely popular view of twins as photocopies of each other. The most illustrious example is possibly that of the first pair of monozygotic twins to have been separated at birth and later reunited, the Jim twins. Each married twice. Their first wives were named Linda; their second, Betty. Each twin had a son with the same name, but spelled differently: James Alan and James Allan. As children, each twin had a dog named Toy. Both twins smoked Salems, and both savored an occasional Miller Lite beer. Both bit their fingernails. Both scattered love notes to their wives around the house. The popularization of these inconsequential and widespread habits has indirectly supported the general stereotypical view of twins as "different" Barnum circus oddities to be watched with intense curiosity. More to the point, frantic parents having to deal simultaneously with two screaming infants do not find it helpful to be told that a given trait of their twins may be 60 percent inherited and 40 percent environmental.

Psychology is the other branch of science that parents avidly read. Psychologists in turn have come up with two questionable key concepts in the development of twins: individualization and de-twinning. A "Decalogue" compiled by a group of eminent psychologists on the Web site of the World of Twins Association presents "essential commandments" for bringing up healthy twins, such as "Provide separate sleeping arrangements and if possible separate rooms," "Organize different programs for each twin," "Have different desks for doing their homework," "Never dress them alike," "Never call them twins or allow anyone else to do so," and "Choose separate classes starting from the crèche." The underlying suggestion here is that twins should be adapted to impossible singleton standards, which are considered to be the norm. In other words, in order to function properly, twins basically would have to be reared apart and live different lives.

Other specialists in the field of psychology have found twins to be prone to various developmental impairments. Language development in twins has been found to be "vulnerable to delay," intellectual development to be "slow," and twins are said to be at risk of developing a condition called "secret language," whereby they communicate in a private jargon that is comprehensible only to each other. Especially during adolescence, twins may "gang up" in committing illicit activities, such as confusing others through their similarity or switching clothes and identities to pass exams or even commit robberies and become drug dealers.[18] Yet these scenarios have to be put into perspective. The incidence of a true "secret language" is so rare that it has not been evaluated statistically. When learning to talk, twins may just go through a transitory phase of gibberish communication, which only they seem to share. Although language is frequently delayed in twins by an average of six months, the overwhelming majority learn to talk. Most studies of twins have shown their IQ to be on average seven points lower than that of singletons. Yet by school age there is no significant difference between twins and singletons. Most twins complete school, reach higher levels of education, are good citizens, and do not turn out to be truants. Many twins are high achievers in all sorts of professional realms.

Parental anxieties do not stop at adolescence. Studies have found that twins, and especially monozygotic twins, marry less. One-fourth of all monozygotic males and nearly a half of all females remain single. However, this fact should also be put in perspective. Twins often claim that their living together supplies them with joys unknown to the rest of us. Their link is very special. Some may not want to split up for the sake of marriage, even though age-old conventions still portray marriage as the ultimate indicator of a healthy and happy lifestyle.

As a result of all the above-mentioned studies, parental anxieties skyrocket. Parents fear that their twins may turn out to be mentally defective, low achievers, solitary loonies, criminals, and truants. Such parental fears are concentrated in a bestseller, "*The Silent Twins*," by Marjory Wallace, which tells the true story of twin girls who refused to talk to anyone save each other.[19] Their secret language was incomprehensible to everyone outside the pair. At school they were isolated and refused to learn anything, and in the end they stayed home. At adolescence the twins became addicted to both alcohol and promiscuous sex, and finally were sent to prison for ganging up to commit vandalism and arson. The twins were mutually dependent and extremely entwined, but also hated each other. Just as the gates of the prison were being opened after they spent 11 years inside, one twin suddenly and mysteriously died. The survivor, though feeling "freed," continued to miss her sister and spent the rest of her life living in confinement at home.

Psychological studies of twins have had an unfortunate influence on education. As soon as twins enter school, they are in a double limelight. Teachers on the look out for problems often exert the full force of their therapeutic zeal on twins. In countless conversations and meetings with overzealous teachers, they diagnosed "secret language" when twins where just whispering something to each other, or antisocial behavior when twins picked up the odd swear word. All this extra attention makes their peers even more curious, so twins feel like oddities and, if anything, end up sticking even more closely together. Ultimately many twins are referred for treatment to the same psychologists who initially ignited the fears. When describing gloomy scenarios professionals recommend early intervention, and overanxious parents frequently seek advice for any trivial concern. In my country I have been referred twins for uttering one single wrong word, being average school achievers, crying when first separated at nursery school, and even for refusing to be toilet-trained at three months. In my practice, only very few cases warranted treatment. Despite initial difficulties, most twins do well and, after the early stages, become a great joy for their parents.

Besides scientists, high forms of literature, ranging from Shakespeare[20,21] to Musil[22] or Joyce Carol Oates,[23] have always shown a deep interest in twins. However, twins have nowadays become key players in science fiction, thrillers, horror stories, and the movies made from them. Two otherwise remarkable works currently fill parental nightmares. "*Dead Ringers*" is a film produced in 1988 by David Cronenberg depicting the perverse relationship of monozygotic twin gynecologists.[24] The symbiotic balance between the brothers is suddenly upset by the arrival into their lives of a woman. As always the twins share everything, including her. When one twin realizes that he does not want to share this object of love with his co-twin, they are both ultimately confronted with the deadly threat of separation. Both twins are eventually sucked into an inexorable vortex of mutual destruction. "*On the Black Hill*" is a novel written by Bruce Chatwin in 1982 describing the secluded life of monozygotic twin men.[25] The now 80-year-old twins recollect their bachelor lives in which any chance of joy, possibilities of romance, and ultimately of separation were stifled by the barrier their union created and the stiffnecked pride and bigotry characterizing their temperaments. This dark "neo-gothic" side of twinship contrasts sharply with the widespread "how nice!" societal view.

Given their visual impact, twins also figure frequently in photographic books, which parents keenly buy. Especially popular are the pictures by Ann Geddes, an Australian-born photographer, who depicts babies in idyllic, cute, angelic tones.[26] Twins feature prominently in her books and in the innumerable products derived from her work, ranging from cards to bookmarks and mugs. Twins are portrayed as delightful, sweet, peaceful, chubby little cherubs embracing each other and all beaming in smiles. Her images fit and enhance the popular "nice" view of twins. Several years ago, in 1989, I carried out a research in my country, which involved home visits to families of young twins whom I had followed throughout pregnancy. Before and immediately after pregnancy, Ann Geddes' books and pictures were in every household. However, by two months after the twins' birth, they had disappeared. As a mother commented, "This is sickening. Twins are no angels. I love my twins, but they give me hell. My life is far from idyllic at the moment. It feels like a nightmare."

Other photographic books also enhance popular views about twins. In a beautiful and acclaimed book, "Twins: Photographs and Interviews by Mary Ellen Mark" published in 2003, all the photographs portray twins according to established age-related conventions: infant twins are cute, prepubertal twins are funny, postpubertal duos are sexy, middle-aged ones are pathetic.[27] These pictures are disquieting. Not only are all the twins dressed alike, often in outrageous gear, but they also move in perfect synchrony or display the same physical defects such as protruding teeth. We are back again to twins as Barnum circus phenomena. The most striking element of the 34 interviews with twins aged over 20, is that twenty three interviews revolved around their sexuality. After reading this book, I once entered the words "twins" and "porn" on the Internet and found 8,710 entries for twins, catering to every whim and fancy. Twins were portrayed as fulfilling the wildest sexual fantasies, all conjured up in sync: homosexuality, incest, threesomes, and voyeurism. Prurient curiosity about the sexuality of twins is extremely common.

On the net, one can find all sorts of other information about twins, from where to buy second-hand strollers to simplified lessons in biology. Parents increasingly turn to it for all sorts of requirements. Chat lines for parents and twins wanting to exchange their experiences are also proliferating at a startling rate. The net has reestablished in a wholly new way a lost network of knowledge, support, and company.

Twins also feature prominently in the media, where they are marketed as brand names just because they are twins. As with photography, their striking appearance makes them particularly media-friendly.

The most illustrious example is the Olsen twins, a pair of nonidentical girls who began their acting career when one year old on a television series called "Full House." According to their official Web site the show achieved a popularity second only to Bill Crosby. By age ten the twins had become "the youngest self-made millionaires in American history." When 17, they were rated the second most popular teenage female stars, and their total financial worth was estimated to be $ 300 millions. In order to reach such astronomical figures, the Olsen girls were made to adhere to all the above-mentioned age-related conventions about twinship, ending up the cycle by becoming just plain sexy. The unhappy conclusion to this huge success story is that in June 2004 one of the twins entered a rehab program, suffering from anorexia nervosa. The girl has now recovered, but the strains of being in the limelight since the age of one and the pressures of having to fulfill age-related standards had taken their toll.

Other disquieting media phenomena include "psychic twins," who are said to have paranormal qualities. The most famous examples are the identical twins Terry and Linda Jamison, who claim on their Web site to have predicted the May 2000 stock market crash and the terrorist attacks on the World Trade Center and Pentagon, as well as to have assisted police in solving murder cases and reuniting families across national borders. Terry and Linda have made a fortune out of their special "gifts," which they declare to be enhanced by their twinship.

Twins may truly be prone to greater sensitivity to each other's moods and physical states, even at a distance. Many uncanny coincidences have been reported, such as twins sensing the death or malady of a co-twin living miles apart. For now, telepathy is a pseudo-science and simply too difficult to prove or disprove among any of the three most telepathy-prone groups, namely mothers and newborn babies, dogs and their owners, and identical twins.

The mind-reading qualities attributed to twins have made them central to another pseudo-scientific field, the New Age Movement. According to this belief, twins are an essential element of human nature. In attaining collective enlightenment and reunion with God, each of us receives help not only from angels and other spiritual guides, but most poignantly from our own twin. In the beginning of time there were only twin souls, and at the fall of mankind these souls were separated from each other and have ever since been searching for their other half.

Besides these dubious concepts, one modern branch of medicine is taking a disquieting interest in identical twins. To settle an aesthetic debate about plastic surgery, four plastic surgeons decided in 1992 to use their favorite techniques on the faces of two sets of identical twins. From time to time the four doctors have subsequently gathered to compare pictures of the twins and to discuss about how each face is "holding up" under the different procedures. Monozygotic twins may help someone choose the best face-lift.[28]

Another plastic surgeon, Dr Darrick Antell, found that some twins in their middle-age were still very much alike, whereas others differed a lot because of differences in their lifestyles. Avoiding sunbathing, smoking, drinking, and stressful events, for example, all made one twin more youthful-looking than the other. Comparing adult twins teaches us about correct lifestyles. However, since then Dr Antell has moved a step forward. When he met a pair of 71-year-old female twins, who had come to look less and less like doppelgangers as they got older and ardently desired to look alike again, he offered to re-twin them. The sisters visited the doctor's Park Avenue office and came out hours later bandaged and bruised, but quite pleased, as they declared, to be back "on the road to sameness." Since then the physician offers his services free to any twins he selects for study. People resorting to plastic surgery have different motivations, ranging from remedying physical defects that impair them socially, to wanting to feel rejuvenated or looking like photocopies of the trendiest movie stars. At first I found Dr Antell's offers perplexing. However, twins do not demand to look years younger or compare themselves to Brad Pitt. They compare themselves to their co-twin and wish to look again like twins. Twinship is a core feature of their identity and they feel at a loss identifying and being identified with the singletons, which they never were.

Another emerging phenomena is even more perplexing. Obstetricians involved in fertility treatments, excited by their reproductive powers in producing twins, have begun to emerge from the darkness of their laboratories to appear on TV shows and write autobiographies, mixing scientific explanations with personal memoirs and "philosophical" meditations. One male physician looks out from the cover of his book, immaculately groomed, self-assured, exuding an aura of competence and trustworthiness while proudly holding up twins, conveying the idea that the whole reproductive process has been safely handed over to his expert hands.[29] Another fertility specialist maintains [author's own translation] that he is "actually chasing a dream, to be as close as possible to the mysteries of creation, to be present in the moment when life starts." He sees himself as an omnipotent hero, able to redress the unfair balance of nature and to defeat intrinsically malignant sterility, and observes, "In a way we become God. Our potency is similar to that of the Creator." The surgical act, substitutive of good old intercourse, becomes a magical-religious ritual: "An operation is a great mass. The sheets to cover the patient are laid down, the servants install the objects for the surgical cult." In a crescendo of reproductive frenzy he adds, "I became a mature ovocyte hunter, a follicle toreador."[30] Fertility specialists play god and are taken over by a delirium of omnipotence, believing that the role of creation lays in their hands.

Twins themselves are now making their voices heard. A world-famous festival of twinship takes place annually during the first weekend of August in Twinsburg, Ohio, where about 2,500 to 3,000 sets of twins gather from all parts of the world, ranging in age from babes in arms to people in their nineties.

The participants take the most radical conventions of twinship to an extreme by trying as far as possible to be look-alikes. With their same flamboyant clothing, weird hairstyles, outrageous gadgets, and extreme postural stereotypes, these twins look like an alien crowd preying on intense collective euphoria. Save for the overburdened parents, twins seem to elicit an epidemic of folly, idealization, and excitement in our developed world. But we are not alone in reacting to twins in such extreme ways.

Chapter 2

Voodoo Twins

Whenever African twins are mentioned in books or the media, Togo and Benin are invariably mentioned for their celebration of twins. Twins even figure on the official currency of these countries in the form of two identical wooden statuettes linked by a chain. This glorification of twins is something that I had hardly ever witnessed in trips to other areas of Africa. It intrigued me so much that when in 2000 the opportunity arose to spend two months in West Africa, splitting my time between Togo and Benin, I accepted willingly.

The main reason for my stay in these nations was somehow indirectly connected with Vodun, more commonly called Voodoo. I had to work in several health centers instructing local doctors, nursing staff, and paramedics on the diagnosis and treatment of a specific medical topic: epilepsy. Epilepsy is the most common of brain disorders characterized by a variety of symptoms, ranging from simple, momentary suspensions of our stream of consciousness (so-called absences) to dramatic, generalized, uncontrollable seizures. For reasons of simplicity, unless otherwise specified, I will use the word epilepsy throughout to denote generalized attacks.

Twins have a special place in Voodoo.[1] Voodoo is a cult originated during prehistoric times in West Africa in the area now corresponding to the nations of Togo and Benin. From there, through the tragic events of the Diaspora, Voodoo spread to many parts of the new world, including Brazil, Haiti, Cuba, Jamaica, and various areas of the United States, such as districts of New Orleans, Miami, Los Angeles, and New York. Altogether there may be some 50 million adepts to the cult, 30 million of whom are in West Africa.[2]

Voodoo is an animist belief. The term animism derives form the Latin words *Anima or Animus,* meaning Soul or Mind, and was introduced by

Edward Burnett Tylor, one of the founders of modern anthropology in 1871 to refer to the belief that all of nature is alive and possesses a soul.[3] Currently animism takes on different meanings in different areas of the world, but generally it considers humans to be neither separate from the world nor distinct from other parts of nature, including plants, animals, and planets, which all embody supernatural forces.

The word Voodoo means god or spirit in a particular West African dialect. The adepts of Voodoo believe in a supreme, transcendent, omnipotent creator called Mawu, who had a female co-twin, Lissa, and, with her, he gave birth to other twins, who fathered the human race. Mawu then detached himself from humans and lost interest in them, but he created other divinities or spirits, variously named Vodoun or Orisha, who are Mawu's intermediaries with mankind, running the world and taking care of all the major forces and aspects of daily life. These spirits have completely human features and can be happy and kind but also mean and cross; they can assist, but also avenge when they are not paid due respect. The spirits determine human life, and whatever happens is ascribed to their will. The ideas of chance, personal responsibility, and free will are largely alien to Voodoo.

Twins are revered for various reasons. Twins symbolize our original ancestors who gave origin to the human race. Though not properly spirits, twins can impinge on the destiny of men, have the faculty of being in touch with the supreme god, and, due to their dual nature, represent the contradictory forces of life, such as good and evil, happiness and sadness, health and illness. Additionally, twins are not the norm in the human race, but belong to the category of "the different" that Voodooists venerate just as they venerate anything strange and out of the ordinary as a prodigy of nature.

The correct diagnosis and treatment of epilepsy, my reason for staying in these countries, are of special relevance in Togo and Benin, where so-called possession is an integral part of Voodoo rites. Possession is the means through which men communicate with the spirits and is viewed as a temporary embodiment, in which the possessed is taken over for a limited time by a spirit who speaks through him or her. While in communication with the spirit, the possessed are said to be in a state of mind generically called a trance, a word derived from the Latin *transire*, meaning "to pass."[4] People in a trance show their altered state by falling to the ground, shaking with convulsions, rolling their eyes backward, foaming at the mouth, and shivering. All these symptoms are shared with generalized epileptic seizures and with the so-called aura, an altered state of perception often preceding an epileptic attack. Epileptics often have to put up with severe social stigma. Voodooists are among the very few who attach a positive, sacred meaning to the attacks. However, many Voodooists are now well aware that epilepsy needs to be adequately controlled by appropriate treatment and diagnosed properly, as epileptic seizures can be a symptom of other diseases such as brain tumors.

My visit to the cradle of Voodoo began just outside *Lomè*, the capital of Togo. From there I was to make my way up to the far north of the country, cross over into Benin, and head down south before crossing back into Togo. On my way I was going to stop at a number of health centers. I was given an escort for the journey, a colossal, but gentle middle-aged man with an impossible name, conveniently nicknamed Amen. We immediately clicked.

Before heading out on the first assignment, Amen wanted to show me the main tourist attraction of the capital, the Afanya Market, also known as the "Fetish Market," where several stands displayed the most horrific items, from severed horse heads to desiccated bats and monkeys. It was explained to me that the fetishes from this region are considered particularly powerful, for they are consecrated to Voodoo gods and thus contain divine powers.[5] I must have looked finicky, to put it mildly, because Amen asked, "Why? Aren't you interested in Voodoo? People come here from all over Africa to buy every ingredient for their rites and their *gris-gris* and *jus-jus* (the names for amulets). Tourists all come here. So what are you interested in?"

I said, "Twins."

Amen laughed. "I have heard of people interested in lions, local beauties, Voodoo rites, but never ever twins!" Visitors to Togo and Benin are scarce, falling roughly into two main categories: African Americans looking for their roots and Europeans fascinated by the occult. At first Amen took my eccentric interest as yet another European fad, but soon he became an outstanding guide and my best ally.

Everyday after work Amen picked me up in his broken-down car and took me to look for twins to interview. Along the way we had to stop a few times because Amen had a colossal appetite and was mad about fish. He had to eat what he called *ma balaine*, my whale. After he was full, he smiled, patted his big belly and said, "Now that I have re-fueled, we can look for more twins."

Amen stopped at every house on the road to ask about twins. People were always delighted when they heard the word. Even in the remotest rural communities everyone knew where to find twins. "So and so just delivered twins." "If you drive six kilometers, then turn left, leave the car, and walk along the path at the end to the second house, you will find twins." "The twins should be there in that house, but you will have to wait a while, as they go to school in the afternoon."

Twins were plentiful and were treated like celebrities. Often a small crowd escorted us to the twins' house. They were invariably dressed the same. Boys frequently wore long priest-like tunics, and girls, lacy gowns. Mixed pairs on the contrary were gendered to the extreme, as if ready for marriage: boys looked like little grooms and girls, like little brides. All other children, save twins, just wore rags.

I explained to the mothers that I was a doctor who worked with pregnant women and I added that in my country all women found twin pregnancies difficult and young twins particularly tiresome. Mothers generally lit up and poured out all sorts of details, telling me about their pregnancy, the delivery, birth order of the twins, breastfeeding, and the twins' temperament. They recounted sleepless nights and local traditions linked with twins. The twins' names were habitually almost identical, such as Amen and Amin. However, longer, fixed names followed. These denoted the day of the week on which the delivery had taken place, the birth order, the presentation at birth, and whether one or both were born enveloped by the membranes or with the umbilical cords around their necks. In countries where women still frequently die during childbirth, delivery is a landmark and one that all mothers remember in great detail. It is estimated that the lifetime risk of maternal death is 1 in 16 in sub-Saharan Africa.[6] A twin delivery is a life-and-death struggle destined to be forever engraved, in utmost detail, not only in the memory of their mothers, but also in the long names of the survivors.

While I spoke to the mothers, the fathers were summoned. Most came running and looked very proud. I was asked questions too: Where did I come from? Why was I interested in twins? Was I a mother of twins? Whenever I said that I was a doctor, a crowd gathered around me out of nowhere. Everyone had questions and wanted consultations, especially to obtain medicines. I tried to listen to everyone. Many cases were serious, ranging from severe malaria to gangrenes, and I suggested they go to the main hospital in the capital. Less serious cases were invited to come to the center during the following days for a visit, though most would not come, preferring to leave their fate in the hands of their all-powerful spirits. Everybody, however, seemed grateful to have received attention, as asking about health was perceived as a sign of consideration and of caring, and in the end whole villages walked back with us to the car.

Besides these countless daily visits to twins, at each stop Amen arranged for special events off the usual scanty tourist track. The first event, organized after I had been in the country for a week or so, was a visit to one of the many kings of Togo, who was also a high priest of Voodoo. As in other parts of Africa, kings and chiefs still rule over various regions.[7] Kings and chiefs are the bearers of tradition, the keepers of magic, giving a kind of cultural identity to the population of often ruinous states. Officially most have only token duties, such as acting as lay magistrates in disputes arising in their district or representing their particular ethnic group within the central government. In fact their welfare is tightly intertwined with governmental forces and ruling classes ransacking the country. Kings own much of the land, and their subjects have to pay tribute to them. They live in mansions or even palaces, with plenty of wives, servants, and sometimes even slaves.

The few kings who are also high priests of Voodoo are particularly powerful. In both Togo and Benin they rank among the most influential and richest men in the whole country. They enjoy a special social status, exerting a strong political influence over the government. Yet even kings have modernized. They own expensive cars, television sets, and cell phones; they navigate on the net; and they are fairly up-to-date with world news.

The king we visited lived in a huge mansion. Many black Mercedes cars were parked outside his garage. The king kept me waiting for a while. In the meantime one of his many servants, wearing a uniform and white gloves, brought me a range of soft drinks as well as plenty of peanuts, one of the country's main products. When the king finally appeared, I was impressed. A tall, sturdy middle-aged man, he exuded a mixture of power, patriarchal authority, and condescending cordiality. He wore a huge, frilly, white hat, a heavily embroidered white tunic, and a white pleated skirt, white being the color of Voodooists symbolizing spiritual purity as well as divine ecstasy. Only the king's feet were not up to the rest: he wore brown Birkenstocks.

The king sized me up at once. Clearly I was not his type. "You are too skinny," he said. "I'll show you my wives." His three official wives were summoned. They were of varying ages and all were obese. The king explained, "I love meat." Then he said, "I know you are interested in twins. I'll show you the twins." He clapped his hands and summoned one of his attendants, saying, "Bring the twins."

I was expecting to see children, but the attendant came back with a small, rudimentary wooden altar with puppet-like identical statuettes meant to represent twins and sticking out of four holes. The king solemnly explained, "They represent twins, I mean dead twins. Twins are different from the rest of us. Twins have telepathic powers. They can communicate with each other at a distance without saying a word, even when one is dead and the other is not. They can see the future and perceive all sorts of events happening even in far-off places. Twins help me a lot. They even tell me about the stock exchange in Paris and New York." He added on a rather sinister note, "However, twins are better dead, when their souls are freed from their bodies. Then they really can wander everywhere." He pointed at the small altar again. "You see, these effigies embody dead twins, the best of all."

I was going to ask whose twins these had been, but possibly the king also had divinatory powers. Sensing my impending question, he stood up, called his driver, who was polishing a huge black Mercedes, and told me, "Now I will show you something." We both got into the Mercedes, and he asked the driver to take us for a ride through his property, which comprised six villages, three palaces, countless fruit plantations, and thousand acres of fertile land. As soon as the Mercedes left the garden, people began to gather on both sides of the road. The king opened his window and waved absent-mindedly to his bowing subjects. After a while, he told me, "You see, if you want to have and keep power, you have to act as I do. Royally. Never give them any importance. Make them feel dependent and valueless. Subordinate them. Flaunt your superiority, display your wealth. You will rule." When we got back to his mansion, the king had one last lesson to teach me. "If you want power, you must put on weight! Skinny people like you are associated with poverty and the poor cannot rule," and then he asked one of his servants to take me to Amen's decrepit car.

About a week later I was working farther north when Amen organized another event. So far we had twin-hunted, as he called it, in more or less isolated communities. This time we were going to visit a proper village and meet its chiefs. Very much like the kings, the so-called *cheferie*, a cohort of elderly males headed by a chief, has returned to many parts of Africa, where it has decision-making powers of varying kinds and degrees.[8] The power of these chiefs is generally limited to their villages, within which they enjoy a particular standing, although the material benefits deriving from their position are modest compared to those of the kings. Most are just slightly wealthier than the generally penniless members of their community.

The village we visited lay near the shores of the sea and was surrounded by beautiful trees.

A huge effigy of a particular god, called Legba, was positioned at the entrance. Legba, "the guardian," is one of the main deities of Voodoo, which is generally placed at crossroads and near the entrance to villages, which he is meant to safeguard from evil influences. I had seen many Legbas, but this one, at least two meters high, seated on a throne, with big horns and a huge erect phallus, was truly impressive, and I took some time to have a good look at it. I understood why Legba impressed early missionaries, who mistook him for the devil and banned Voodoo as a satanic cult.

As we entered the village, three notables, all middle-aged men, were waiting for us in the biggest house. I was asked questions. Where did I come from? Then came the usual: why was I interested in twins? The atmosphere was formal and stiff, and as the conversation dragged on I began to think they had all forgotten about my interest in meeting twins, when suddenly another notable came in. I was told that he was the head of the village. I noticed immediately the two wooden effigies of twins sticking out from his waistband. Having seen pictures of people from Nigeria, Togo, and Benin carrying similar wooden statuettes as mementos of their dead twins, I realized immediately that he himself must have been a triplet! Those two effigies were of his dead twins. See figure 2.1.

Twins, when dead, become sacred, and, as with other godly entities, great care has to be taken not to irritate them. They have to be constantly remembered by the surviving twins as it is feared that, if they are excluded from the lives of the living, they might suffer from envy and take revenge. In addition dead co-twins exert a strong pull on their survivors to join them in the world of the dead. To avert this outcome, survivors obliterate death by feeding, washing, putting to bed, and carrying around their effigies as if the twins were still alive.

Upon seeing the notable with the statuettes, I could not contain my enthusiasm, exclaiming "You were born a triplet!" The atmosphere eased at once, as the chief explained that he was in fact the first born and the biggest of the triplets. One of his twin brothers had died within a few days,

Figure 2.1 Girl carrying an effigy of her dead co-twin on a waistband. She is not allowed to mourn normally and can never part from the effigy, which stays with her throughout her life. Moreover, everybody can see that she had a co-twin and keep reminding her of his or her death.

but the other had lived for nearly a year before succumbing to diarrhea. He offered to take me around the village while explaining me about twins.

We walked some distance until we reached a big sacred tree that stood in the middle of a garden. The placentas of twins born in the village had to be buried in the shade of these trees, because the placenta being an essential component of the twins and almost like a prenatal twin of theirs, it was also considered sacred. The notable then wanted to show me a special cavern that foreigners generally were not allowed to approach. He made an exception for me, as I was there to help people from Togo, and on top of that I liked twins. When we looked in the entrance to the cave, it was dark and full of pots. Its walls exuded blood, some exsiccated, some fresh. Clearly many sacrifices had taken place in the cave. The man explained that the vases contained the souls of all twins born in the village. When twins were born, a postmenopausal woman brought a vase to the cave, where it remained forever protecting the entire community. Postmenopausal women, who could no longer carry twins in their womb, were given the task of transporting the vases, symbolizing both the twins and the container-womb, as a compensation for their lost fertility. Women with fertility problems also made offers to the pots because twins were thought to be both rainmakers and fertility enhancers. I was at a loss. I asked for some clarification but all I got as an answer was, "These are the supernatural ways."

As we were driving back nearly in the dark, Amen said, "Alessandra, offer me a whale, and I will tell you a secret." Soon we were sitting at a table in a small restaurant. Amen ate his whale, patted his belly, and then said, "You know, triplets are not like twins. One may be left to its own fate at birth." Remembering the dignitary who had told me of the death of one of his twin brothers soon after birth, I asked why. Amen pointed to my breasts and said, "How many breasts do you have? Only two. So."

I never saw any triplets during my entire stay.

Four days later we reached another little town, where I had to work in a small center. The center was in an appalling condition—no basic instruments, no medicines, no mosquito nets, no water, just a rotting building with a few rusty, filthy beds and no staff to be instructed. I felt powerless and disheartened.

Luckily Amen sensed my misery and quickly organized another special event. The main decisions in most big villages and small towns are made by an assembly of the elders. The senior males of the community gather in a special place to discuss problems. Their verdict is law. No woman is allowed to participate. Twins and their mothers are the only exception, for not only are twins sacred but their mothers are considered special for conceiving and hosting them in their wombs. Somehow Amen had managed permission for me to attend.

We entered the place of assembly, which was nothing more than a disintegrating tent barely sheltering a number of rotten benches from the sun and rain. The notables were already seated in the front row, in clothing that denoted their status. They wore long tunics and ornate hats, flashed golden rings, and carried wooden or ivory carved batons. All looked very old and traditional but displayed the odd touch of modernity: eyeglasses, sunglasses, shaky dentures, plastic sandals or flip-flops.

I was instructed to sit on a kind of podium facing them, and they all bowed their heads to me as a sign of respect. It turned out that nothing was on the agenda for that day except me: I was the topic to be discussed. Everybody wanted to hear modern views about twins. I started out by giving a simplified lesson on biology and obstetrics, explaining the difference between identical and non identical twins and some facts about their conception, placentas, and pregnancies. My audience seemed captivated until the end, when an old man, introducing himself as the village chief, restored some propriety by observing, "Everything you say is very clear. We believe it to be true, and you clarified matters for us. But we also want to stick to our traditions and cultural heritage. Twins are heavenly spirits, and they will always be spirits for us."

Then the chief gestured to a young assistant, who had been standing near the entrance, glancing in from time to time, and who now ushered in two young twins, probably aged four or five, wearing long white tunics. The elders bowed their heads, and the chief spoke again, "You see, twins are admitted to our assemblies. They enlighten us. The spirits speak through them." When I asked how this took place, his cryptic answer was, "The ways of the spirits are innumerable. It can be how their tunics stir, how their eyes blink, if they move in harmony or not. We, the elders, know how to interpret the signs." Then the chief gestured again to his assistant, who brought in four women wearing their best costumes. They were made to sit in the second row, whereupon the chief announced, "These are all mothers of twins. They are special, too. They can be admitted to the assembly in particular circumstances, but the spirits do not speak through them." By this time the entire village had flocked around the outside of the building, curious to meet me, and the elders were unable to contain them. All introduced themselves to me, mothers showed me their children, young men asked me about Europe, women inspected my clothing and touched my hair and my skin. The atmosphere was very relaxed, and the young assistant suggested playing some traditional music for me. In a moment all sorts of musical instruments appeared. The music was captivating, and people started dancing, but it was soon midday and Amen asked for his whale. I said we had to go and the entire village followed us until we got into the car.

A few days later in the northern part of Togo we reached the Tamberna, an isolated community that even during colonial times was little affected by contact with the rest of the country. Amen repeatedly asked me to visit a Voodoo healer who lived among them and was renowned all over the country for his expertise in treating people with herbs. He said I had to see the Tamberna, as their remote region was one of the highlights of Togo.

Though our stop had not been planned, I was only too pleased to be able to make the visit.

One of the central components of Voodoo is healing.[9] Angry spirits—coupled with poor sanitary conditions and rampant diseases—inflict illness on people. Voodooists, however, can also practice sorcery and black magic in an attempt to obtain wealth, love, revenge, and cause harm. Healers are able to use Voodoo to repair the harm—real or imaginary—that other Voodoo rites involving black magic have created. Healers do not practice black magic and have gained a profound knowledge of herbs through both experience and oral transmission across the generations. The function of a skilful healer goes beyond dispensing herbal remedies. He must be a true psychotherapist with deep understanding of the psychology of the people who seek his help. Healers are particularly competent in treating the so-called African sickness, the pervasive terror of sorcery and black magic. Many Africans believe that these are solely responsible for sickness and death, since natural causes are not contemplated.

The Tamberna stick very much to their traditions and generally do not welcome foreign visitors. They inhabit a long valley, where they live in beautiful, fortress-like dwellings with conical roofs handmade out of mud and straw. The only way to get to the Tamberna is on foot.

In order to reach our special healer and his family, we had to walk some distance along the valley, which was unbelievably beautiful, full of gently sloping hills covered by lush grass and huge trees. All dwellings were built under trees, which were considered sacred. Fetishes were strewn every-where around the dwellings and along the narrow path that joined the various compounds. Fetishes have various functions, but principally they serve as powerful magnets, attracting or "charming" the many evil forces lurking throughout the world and thereby sparing other living targets, especially human beings.

The healer, an old man, lived in a huge fortress. It turned out Amen had not told me the whole truth. He himself wanted to be cured before any-thing else, because he suffered from occasional asthmatic attacks. When he then introduced me as a doctor to the healer, I felt an immediate current of empathy between us. The healer actually went a step further than empa-thy, falling instantly in love with me. The Tamberna generally being rather scrawny, I would be his type. At any rate, as soon as he saw me, he ran inside his fortress and reappeared minutes later wearing his best clothes. He also held a skinny chicken by its legs, which he then gave me as a token of admiration. Based on the value of a chicken in those parts, the gift could be compared to receiving a Tiffany ring! He also asked Amen to take a picture of me with him.

Only then did he proceed to listen to Amen. He cut some herbs, burnt them, and ordered Amen to inhale the aromatic smoke. He then gave Amen another heap of fresh herbs, telling him to do the same at home. Evidently he was in a hurry, having heard from Amen about my interest in twins.

As soon as the healer was done with Amen, he quickly organized a guided tour to show me all the twins nearby. The Tamberna barely wear any clothes at all, but when I was taken to visit three pairs of male twins, they all were dressed in trousers and matching T-shirts. The fact that these twins were practically the only ones wearing any clothes at all again attested to their special status.

After walking for hours, we came to the end of the valley where the last set of twins lived in a remote compound. They were five years old and were naked. They both held onto the same oblong terracotta object with rounded angles and two cavities at each end. The twins never parted with it, walked about as if joined to it, and had to eat their meals out of the two cavities. They also had to carry the object at all times and were not allowed to be apart for any reason until reaching the age of seven, when the object was broken into two, letting each twin to go his or her own way. Until the age of seven, twins were thought to stay alive only if they shared a concrete link, so any premature severing of that link would be dangerous. As twins got older the link became internalized, and they could part without risking certain death. This custom is now nearly extinct, and other pairs of Tamberna twins were free to run around separately, although heaps of these objects are still being sold in the big markets in Benin.

After leaving the Tamberna, with my precious chicken still in the trunk, we stopped in a small town close to the historic royal palace of the former kingdom of Dahomey. I was to work there in another so-called hospital, in actual fact yet another crumbling, empty building with no windowpanes, a constantly wet and muddy floor, no instruments, only one rusty bed with no mattress, and, most notably, no staff. Just a cleaning lady appeared from time to time and swept away lazily at any tiny random spots. The doctor in charge put in an appearance only once and seemed totally uninterested in my task, except to say simply that he would send me some patients. Again I felt useless and miserable.

Some patients finally did come, whose ailments had nothing to do with neurology. Most were hopeless cases, mainly terminal AIDS sufferers who had been through all sorts of stomach-churning healing practices, such as drinking a daily jug of animal blood to cure their own infected blood. I was their last hope, and I could administer only painkilling and sedative treatment.

One day, however, I was approached by a man with adolescent twin daughters. Rumors travel fast in Benin, and having heard of my presence in the region, he had come from far away to talk to me. He suspected the girls of being dissimilar due to epilepsy, one being probably affected and the other not. As he explained, "Lena only falls to the ground during ceremonies. Lina is different; she can fall at any time. In the village they think she is special, but I am afraid she may be epileptic. Her delivery was very complicated. She was the second born, and when she finally came out her head was all misshapen. She had convulsions from the start." A diagnosis of epilepsy could have been made easily by sight, even without any instrumentation, but the father begged, "Please come and see for yourself. Come to the ceremony. Otherwise nobody will believe me. If Lina is epileptic, I want her to be treated." I had heard rumors of a full-fledged Voodoo ritual dance to take place soon, and when the father asked, I was reluctant to attend because Voodoo ceremonies are notoriously rowdy. But when he begged me just to come and watch, promising not to take part in it himself and to stand by me as long as I needed, I agreed.

Ceremonies and ritual dances with accompanying sacrifices are a central part of the Voodoo religion. They provide the means by which human beings connect with divine forces. Voodooists do not believe in rigid dualities, such as life and death or heaven and earth. Communication and exchanges with the gods take place all the time, and possession is essential for that communication. The possessed are thought to be temporarily occupied by a god, who speaks through them. Sacrifice is also fundamental to this exchange, for the gods give only if they take. The spirits are believed to become weaker over time and to depend on humans for nourishment. Sacrifices "rejuvenate" the spirits by feeding them and transferring life force to them. Each god has his or her own preference, be it a fragrance, oxen, or maize, but animal sacrifices are particularly widespread.

While Lena and Lina's father was talking to me, drums could already be heard in the distance. The father took me not far from the town to a big open space full of trees covered with lianas. People had already started gathering. Not all were participants. Several people, especially women and children, stood in the background. The area of the ceremony was marked out by half-naked men who were beating their drums in a deafening, repetitive rhythm. Drums are considered sacred instruments, which serve the purpose of calling up the particular deity for which the ceremony is staged.

The participants in the ceremony, both men and women, had gathered at the center of the arena. Many carried chickens and goats. The throats of the animals were slit open, drenching people, the ground, and several fetishes with thick blood. Two oxen were also brought in and slaughtered. The blood gushing out of their severed carotid arteries was collected in plastic containers and poured over a kind of altar. Alcohol was also poured over the altar and then passed around. Everybody became quite drunk. They sweated profusely as they danced around invoking the spirits by hopping and flapping their arms like birds. The motions were meant to chase off witches, who are thought to take the guise of birds, and any witchcraft lurking around. As the dancing became ever more frantic and obscene, I sensed danger. Some dancers made sexual advances to me, but whenever I tried to leave, someone would grab me by the arm, and the advances became even more obscene. I stood petrified, trying to make myself as inconspicuous as possible. I wished Amen had been with me, but he had trusted me to the father of the twins.

Suddenly the father pushed Lena and Lina into the arena. I had warned him: no alcohol especially for Lina, but the twins were given drinks and started to hop and shout like all the others. People were beginning to fall to the ground, indicating their possession by the spirits. Lena was the first twin to fall. She started foaming at the mouth and wriggling, making motions that were unmistakably the movements of intercourse. She reminded me of the hysterics described by Freud,[10] which we no longer see in developed countries, where most people have read or at least been exposed to his works. Consequently, the pathological manifestations of so-called Histrionic Personality Disorder have evolved into more subtle behavioral and psychological symptoms. People suffering from such a condition feel uncomfortable if they are not the center of attention, display inappropriate sexually seductive or provocative behavior, are prey to rapidly shifting and shallow emotions, and are theatrical and suggestible. Mimicking sexual intercourse is no longer contemplated as a feature of the disorder.[11]

Soon, Lina too fell. Contrary to her sister, her shaking had the distinctive character of a true epileptic seizure. All her muscles stiffened for a few seconds, then her limbs and head shook and trembled violently, her eyes turned up, she bit her tongue, and she lost bowel control. As quickly as it came, her seizure stopped, and she remained semi unconscious and disoriented on the ground. I had been worried for Lina from the start, but her father, who was drunk, was adamant that she had to stay. He no longer reasoned as a father but as a Voodooist. I now got very angry, and Lina was finally taken aside where I could tend to her. By then, however, word had spread that Lena and Lina were twins. Drunken, possessed people began to gather menacingly around me. They grabbed Lina away and started carrying both twins above the crowd to try to attract a deity. As Lina had uninterrupted seizures, they were met with general applause, being interpreted by the drunken crowd as a sign that a god had completely seized her. I shouted at her father to stop, as Lina was risking her life. When, finally, Lina was handed back to me, she had yet further seizures. I had vials of Diazepan and gave her intravenous injections one after the other until luckily the seizures ceased.

The following day I set up treatment for her at a dispensary in a nearby town, telling her father to bring her there for frequent checks. I also told him firmly that participating in any rites or drinking alcohol and taking drugs could prove fatal for her. Although this is just a guess, I fear that her father's faith in Voodoo was stronger than my warnings.

After the ceremony I still had two more days to spend in the empty hospital. Amen was complaining nonstop and bickering about Benin. I felt disheartened and was happy to leave.

When we reached our next destination, I was pleasantly surprised as the small dispensary where I had to work was clean, well-kept, and run efficiently by local staff.

My stay was pleasurable. In the early morning I gave a speech on epilepsy, focusing on diagnosis, treatment, differential diagnosis, and underlying causes, and we spent the rest of the day visiting cases, which the doctors, nurses, and paramedics had arranged to come from all over the region to attend in anticipation of my stay. All seemed very keen to learn.

I was busy until late afternoon, when Amen picked me up, and we went to have dinner in Cotonou, the economic capital of Benin. Besides a good dinner, the main attraction there was the renowned Dankopta market. It was huge, with innumerable stalls.

Objects for twins were everywhere—the little altars with effigies of twins used for divination, the vases supposed to contain the souls of twins, the statuettes representing dead twins. The oblong object that Tamberna twins must hold together until the age of seven was also everywhere, with a variation for opposite-sex twins, in which the cavities to be filled with food were placed on opposite sides, indicating that sexes were complementary, but not equal.

I have hardly ever been on a shopping-spree, but I must confess I went on a big one at Dankopta market. I bought all sorts of items for twins.

In the rear stalls of the market, because of my interest in twins, I was often asked, "Are you looking for black magic?" Twins might be part of it. Twins stood for closeness, companionship, and union, but if irritated, their bond could turn into a malignant alliance bringing death, misfortune, hatred, and disease. When I enquired further about the dark side of twinship, however, all became tight lipped, and Amen pretended to be deaf, saying only, "Some stones are better left unturned." All along I had been shown only the sunny side of twins and I was to know no more.

My stay was nearing its end, but before returning home I planned to spend a few days visiting the Mono River, as Voodoo was thought to have originated along its shores. Amen was happy to come with me. The Mono River runs along the border between Togo and Benin and separates the two countries before flowing into the ocean close to a small town named Gran Popò. We traveled it in a rickety motorboat with a young man, named Teo, as our guide. The banks of the river were dotted with Voodoo "temples," small white rectangular buildings with symbols of Voodoo painted on their walls.

By now I recognized several of those symbols. Among the many familiar spirits was Sakapata, who brought plague, represented as a man holding an axe. Oshumarè, an androgynous spirit, was represented as a mold painted in two different colors, red for male and blue for female. Dan, a god represented as a snake eating its tail, to symbolize continuity, the vital force, and the ever-changing relationship between earth and the spirits. Teo told me that he wanted to take me right up the river to a kind of island, which he said was interesting and beautiful. Amen relaxed and spent most of his time lazing and sunbathing in the boat, often commenting that this was life.

When we finally reached the island after a three day navigation, it was a secluded paradise with small sandy beaches and palm trees. Fishermen's nets and chicken were to be seen everywhere. Two identical twins, both fishermen, lived there with their parents. The twins were both called Shango, after the god of thunder who holds terrifying life-and-death powers and is always thirsty for blood.

The two Shangos enjoyed a high status as chief priests of Voodoo. Given the secluded nature of their island, secret ceremonies involving black magic probably took place on it, as suggested by the fact that the priests were extremely tight-lipped and Amen said fearfully, "We should leave. This is no place for you."

The priests smiled condescendingly at my interest in twins, implying that I was naive. Despite being monosyllabic, having received a long training in Voodoo, their language was sophisticated. They said that the fact of being twins had played an important part in their social position. "As you know, we are different from all other human beings. We are sacred." I asked why they were chosen to become priests and were given the name of a god, but they refused to answer, saying, "We cannot tell you why. You are not one of us. And anyway these are secret and private matters." They took me to see two altars crammed with dark effigies drenched in dry blood and with a vaguely human shape and cowry shells as eyes, epitomizing the powerful souls of dead twins, and explained, "We often have to make sacrifices to them. All sorts of sacrifices. Twins are moody and like to play tricks. We have to placate them." The two Shangos would say no more and were eager for us to go, then their mother, who had noticed my camera, asked me to take a picture of the whole family. The twins posed smiling, with their legs crossed, like two Hollywood stars.

Our return to Gran Popò was plain sailing, but the visit to the twin priests made me look at the Mono River in a fresh way. The landscape, which had seemed simply sunny and beautiful before, now seemed to hide shady secrets beneath its purity and idyllic appearance. I did not have the time or perhaps the wish to find out about black magic and twins, and the fair color of my skin would have probably been an impenetrable barrier.

I began to think about twins in the developed world. Despite all the many and profound differences, there were some parallels with Voodoo twins.

Twins were venerated in Togo and Benin and idealized by society back home.

In Central Park, twins and their parents were treated like public personalities, and heads turned to stare at them. In Togo and Benin, twins were public figures too, and all knew where they lived, who their parents were, and if they were likely to be at home or not.

Twins were important enough to appear on the currency of their countries as wooden statuettes linked by a chain. Some twins, such as the two Shangos, were well-known celebrities for being high priests of Voodoo. They lived on a beautiful and secluded island, did not give interviews, were protective of their privacy, and posed for photographs crossing their legs like Hollywood stars. However, the two Shangos were fishermen and did not have huge bank accounts.

In Togo and Benin, just as in developed countries, having twins was considered a special event, and mothers of twins enjoyed a special status.

The special link uniting twins was recognized on either side of the world. In developed countries, however, psychologists outlined catastrophic scenarios unless the twins were "individualized" and kept apart. Not even death parted twins in Togo and Benin, as they always had to carry around the effigy of their dead co-twin as a constant reminder.

Lulled by my boat, I thought about the fact that double sized prams, plastic surgeons, behavioral geneticists, and omnipotent obstetricians were all consistently absent from the lives of twins living along these beautiful shores. Furthermore, making offers to twins or touching their mothers' bellies were the only fertility treatments that most West African women could afford, despite the fact that in these regions women were solely valued for their capacity to reproduce.

Chapter 3

Stone Idols

Early in 2001 I was asked to act as a consultant for an orphanage in a particular region of the Cameroon. My task was to assess the neurological-psychiatric condition of the children who were going to be given out for adoption. The need for this kind of assessment is increasingly expressed by agencies acting as intermediaries between potential parents and adoptees. Some parents may be willing to take on desperate cases, but none want to be ignorant about the kind of future that may lie ahead for their children and for themselves.

The Cameroon is rich in natural resources ranging from oil to mineral reserves, an abundance of fertile land, cattle, and fish, so many of its products are exported. And yet aided by the police, and often with the connivance of non-African powers, the rich are insatiable, and the poor live in abominable conditions.[1] Tropical diseases are rampant, and recently AIDS has become a plague. Life expectancy is barely over age 50, and nearly 45 percent of the population is below the reproductive age of 13.[2]

The orphanage where I went to work held 200 children, lodged in several well-kept buildings, all surrounding a central park area. Part of the park was used as a football field, the national craze. The children, ranging in age from birth to 13, were all tidy, neatly clothed, and well looked after by the numerous local staff. Some had been abandoned at birth, but the majority had lost their parents and relatives to AIDS.

Many other orphans, mainly preadolescent boys and girls, could be seen out in the streets. All were scavenging for food. Boys formed into mini-gangs, which would turn them into dangerous truants in just a few years' time. Girls would soon fall prey to the country's huge prostitution racket.

This facility could not accommodate any more children, and so it offered children for adoption, it favored young ones because the request for adoption generally decreases with children's age. Most children awaiting international adoption live in appalling institutions, barely meeting their physical and emotional needs. Adoptive parents comprehensibly worry about the long-term effects of such traumatic early experiences. Furthermore, they prefer to take on young children, especially infants, who are more easily regarded as natural children. Parents understandably feel that they can shower their affection more readily on an infant, impart a family imprint, and pass on their educational principles.

During my stay, I worked long hours visiting children and filing reports.

After a few days, I was struck by the lack of twins. When I inquired about it with the head of the orphanage, a pleasant local woman in her fifties, named Katherine, she explained that twins were never given away or abandoned, because they were considered gods in this area. Twins had a higher status than in Voodoo, as they were not just a link with the supreme god but were themselves gods who had to be served by the whole community in return for their protection.[3] Giving them away for adoption was equivalent to sacrilege and bound to bring ill luck to all.

I found myself thinking that twins were lucky in this area. They were cared for by the entire neighborhood and did not have to face any of the traumatic lacerations that even the best of all adoptions can involve.

I got to know some twins firsthand one night when I was suddenly awakened by loud sounds of unfamiliar musical instruments. The pounding, which came from a nearby village outside the orphanage, continued throughout the night. In the morning Katherine told me that drums, horns, and bells always announced the birth of twins in the villages, just as bells ringing at Christmas celebrate the nativity. She suggested going out to find the twins the following afternoon.

Next day we had no difficulty locating them when we saw a procession heading toward a village. People walked in a row carrying small bags of salt and bottles of a reddish palm oil, all specific offerings for twins. By now nobody knew the significance of such gifts, which had become a tradition: twins, as little gods, had to be propitiated and appeased in this way. Yet twins were not wholly benign gods. Besides being placated with special offerings, they had to have all their whims and wishes met in order to avoid any potential wrath. As I was told, "Never irritate a twin."

The hut in which the twins were born was unmistakable; an arcade of foliage had been erected at some distance from its entrance, forming a sheltered porch. Two trees, called "peace trees," had been planted next to the hut. Like most other huts, it was made of red mud, and had small windows closed behind shutters protecting the interior from the blazing heat of the sun. Inside it was very dark, and the space was filled with people who had come to pay homage to the twins. When Katherine introduced me, everyone rejoiced by standing up, smiling, and hugging me. My presence was said to be a good omen, but I was not told why. I was offered a chair that was falling apart. Several men and women were sitting in a circle around a circular basket containing two tiny twin boys dressed exactly alike in dark blue baby frocks. The basket had been elevated on a table, as if on an altar, and propped up with a cushion and some straw so that the twins could be seen by everybody and revered like idols. Two big calabashes, each with a hole containing a twig—other insignia for twins—were placed at the feet of the "altar."

I could not figure out who were the parents. Everyone was staring at the twins, silently worshipping them. Nobody was touching, holding, stroking, or cooing at them. Suddenly both twins let out feeble cries. A very young woman, possibly no more than 15, stood up, bared her breasts, and approached them. Clearly she was the mother. She picked the twins up and put them at her breasts. The twins began to suck. The mother never looked at them, but she sat on a chair looking like an ancient fertility deity, distant and proud. Everyone bowed to the mother, as mothers of twins were revered, too. The mother's lack of tenderness and interest in the twins was disquieting, but I put it down to inexperience and perhaps fatigue. When the meal was over, the twins were immediately replaced on the altar, and their mother never once looked over at them.

When it was time to go, an old woman accompanied us to the door. The twins would not be allowed to be taken out beyond the arcade of leaves until they were two weeks old. Till then their tenure on earth was deemed to be too flimsy to risk exposing them to the light of day and to the community at large. The wideness and complexity of the world might frighten them, forcing them to retreat into the realm of the invisible.

A few days later Katherine asked me a favor, which I granted. The rumor having spread that I was in the area, a particularly powerful king had requested to speak with me. He owned the land on which the orphanage was built, and just as in Togo and Benin, large areas of the Cameroon are owned and dominated by powerful kings and chiefs. Kings may be either human or divine in origin, and those kings thought of as having a divine origin, generally inherited through their fathers, are especially powerful. My king was one of those.

To reach the king, I was given a driver, a guide, and a rusty old jeep. The king lived high up on a mountain in a secluded, maze-like palace adorned with beautiful old wooden masks. He had 125 wives, all of whom lived in captivity inside his fortress. During his rare visits to his huge landed properties the king picked up any woman at whim, put a bracelet around her wrist, and that was that. The "chosen" could no longer escape and had to spend the rest of her life in confinement. In this way the king had fathered some 400 children.

When I arrived, I was allowed into the king's presence. Looking old and depressed, but exuding authority, he wore a long embroidered tunic and sat on a stone throne holding a royal cane. I was made to sit on a small-scale throne next to him. He seemed to ignore me, saying only, "I am busy." Five ancient men, his dignitaries, were assembled on a bench facing the king, while a fearful young male secretary knelt in front of the king, holding a big note-book and a pen. The king started dictating a long tirade in an incomprehensible *patois*. From time to time he stopped, where upon his dignitaries immediately stood up, bowed, and baaed just like sheep in an act of extreme submission.

I waited patiently. Finally the king said, "Now I am ready." I followed him into another room full of carpets and beautiful masks. The king, it turned out, wanted to restore his youthful potency, and for a while he thought he had found the remedy by making me wife number 126! While I was carefully palpating his enlarged liver, he exclaimed "I have an erection!" At first I thought "Mysteries of human sexuality. I never heard of the liver provoking arousal." The king gave me no time for further thoughts, and, while proposing marriage, he asked me to have intercourse on a carpet right there and then, before he lost his unsteady erection.

Potency is vital for divine kings in the Cameroon, because it is thought to be linked with the fertility and prosperity of their kingdom, including the fertility of the crops, and especially female fertility.[4] For unknown reasons female fertility is low in some regions of the Cameroon, such as where this king lived. Infertility is accompanied by ruthless social ostracism. A childless woman can be repudiated, and in any case another spouse immediately takes her place.

Furthermore, she is pitied, despised, and avoided by the entire community as if she were a leper. As soon as a king's virility starts declining, he is generally killed, mostly by being forced to drink poison. Only a few kings are simply dethroned in favor of a young heir. When a king starts noticing the first signs of white hair, he begins to fear his wives who spy on his virility. One of his children is chosen by a special assembly to replace him, but the king is not allowed to know who his replacement is, which accounts for much palace intrigue. As a result, kings become suspicious of their children too, and paranoid doubts pervade all their lives. My king retreated into a separate area of his palace and no longer saw his wives and children. Only his faithful dignitaries were admitted to his presence, as they too are often killed along with their king, as the new heir wants to have his own faithful followers.

Knowing all this made me regard the king with compassion. However, I became increasingly afraid for my own safety as I was utterly isolated and sure that nobody would have come to my rescue. I managed to calm the king down by administering him some drops of benzodiazepines and convincing him that I was not a good remedy for his problems. He needed a specialist visit, and could be better helped by pharmacological therapy, such as Viagra, which would not be difficult to find in the capital.

When the arduous visit was over, the king said to me, "You like twins. I know all that goes on in my kingdom. I have twin sons, just two of them. They live in my quarters. Women are not admitted here nor are other children. The twins have no contact with them. I will allow you to take some pictures of me with the twins."

Twins did not reign in the Cameroon. Given their special godly nature, they were not allowed to rule over earthly matters. The king was not afraid of them like the rest of his children.

The four-year-old twins were brought into his presence by one of the old dignitaries. His secretary picked them up and sat them on the king's knee. The twins were immobile and expressionless, looking like stone idols. I took some pictures, and then they were led away, walking back stiffly from where they had come without a sound, a protest, or a glance backward.

I found the whole event quite sad. While I felt sorry for the king, I felt especially so for the twins, who had to pay a high price for their special status within the palace, including isolation from their mother, from their peers, from other women, and possibly from less unfeeling men working on the properties of their royal father. Any affection was denied to them, which showed in their stony behavior: their hearts seemed hardened and petrified. Emotional deprivation had left its mark.

When I told Katherine my impressions, she was reluctant to discuss the pitfalls of the country. Having to live in it, she was forced to accept many compromises. As she said to me, "You either decide to go on without too much questioning or have to become a martyr." Yet Katherine was grateful for my visit to the king, and in order to lift my spirits, she said, "My assistants have informed me that in a few days a gathering of twins, a so-called festival, will take place in a village nearby. It will be very different from what you have seen today, with mothers singing and twins having great fun."

Some days later Katherine and I went to a nearby village, which looked utterly dismal, to attend the celebration. We entered a two-story building, where a plump woman asked us to sit on a bench. She was busy preparing beverages and food. Her husband joined us, saying, "Please remain silent. The twins and their mothers are already downstairs. I will tell you when you can be introduced to them. It has to be done carefully. Twins can easily get scared." We remained quiet, and the silence was pervasive. Having been told that there were at least 20 pairs of twins, I found myself wondering if the twins were actually there. Such total quietness seemed impossible for 40 children. Had it not been for the grubbiness of the place, we could have been waiting in a temple for a solemn ceremony.

Finally the hostess and her husband came back, saying, "All is ready. You can come downstairs." They drew open a ragged curtain that separated the room from the lower floor and led us down steep, rickety wooden stairs. The lower story, a big room with walls made of red mud and a sandy floor, was completely dark. As I got used to the darkness, I saw 20 pairs of young twins ranging in age from two to ten sitting huddled together on two benches. Each pair was dressed alike. The mothers sat in front of them on another bench, holding musical instruments. Our hostess opened two windows and introduced me to the mothers. The atmosphere immediately warmed up. All the mothers smiled at me and began to sing and dance, shaking musical instruments that were double baskets full of pebbles whose sound reminded me of *maracas*. Occasionally they blew strange horns and beat twin drums. Clearly the mothers were having great fun.

The contrast with the twins, however, was marked. They remained utterly still throughout. Their mothers never looked at them. I tried repeatedly to smile at them, but only the youngest pair, twin boys, roughly two years old, responded to my smile. They came over immediately and sat on my knee, beaming, then touched my face and stared at me. I thought, "These are not yet past hope. They are still searching for human contact. The others have lost all feeling."

As the ceremony progressed, my impression was confirmed. After the dance was over, a ritual was performed of smearing a red dot on the forehead of all participants. Then some salt was poured directly on the floor and mixed with red palm oil. Each mother took a pinch of the mixture and gave it randomly to the twins to eat. None protested. Even the lively two-year-olds sitting on my knee accepted the disgusting blend without a grimace. They were probably used to it. I was told that this was a cultural ritual for twins, but its meaning and background were lost on me.

When the ceremony was over, food was served to everyone.

The twins sitting on my knee made a mess of the meal, and of my trousers too, while all the other twins just nibbled silently and tidily at the food. Their behavior contrasted sharply with that of their mothers, who drank beer and stuffed themselves with food, grabbing it with their hands. When they were full, they shoveled all the leftovers into plastic bags, saying, "No more cooking for two days!"

The mothers started talking pleasantly to me as we were moved outside the building into a big open space filled with all sorts of litter. People gathered around the mothers, who held the limelight. After I was introduced to the entire village, for a while I held the limelight, too. Everybody bowed to the twins, who were all together in a group, but that was that. I gave the twins plenty of lollipops, which they took, but none of them even smiled, unlike all the other children in the country who seemed to go off their head whenever I gave them sweets. When the festival had ended and we had to go back, all the mothers hugged me warmly before starting to make their way back home, followed by an orderly procession of stiff, voiceless, vacant-eyed twins.

A few days later Katherine asked me another favor. Cameroon is dominated not only by kings and chiefs but also by a large class of wealthy people. Many are of royal descent or are connected by a web of power to all sorts of rulers. The rich ones deal with various kinds of commerce, ranging from oil to an array of imports and exports involving deals with developed countries. They also own land and cattle. A large amount of the wealth of the country is in their hands, and they are insatiable. The disparity between their lives and that of the majority, the very poor, is unimaginable.

Katherine depended for survival on a rich family in the area, which was about to celebrate a memorial service for the founder of the family fortune, who had died recently. During the memorial service his successor would be appointed from among his innumerable children. Sinister palace plots had been raging since his death, but nobody knew who had been designated as heir in the will. The successor was going to inherit most of the family riches, besides having to take over some 300 widows from his father, but certainly none of the other heirs were going to starve. The memorial service was also an occasion for making further alliances with other wealthy people, including kings and chiefs. In order to be successful, it had to be memorable and display a huge wealth and immense power. Katherine invited me to attend because, being a white woman and a doctor, I would add to the display of power. I felt like an ornate piece of jewelry, but besides wanting to help Katherine, I was curious.

A huge man wearing a black striped suit and a gold ring on each finger, who had requested my presence and was one of the possible heirs, picked me up from the orphanage in a black Rolls-Royce driven by a chauffeur who was also a bodyguard.

Soon we were in a line of luxurious cars driving up to the top of a mountain where we came upon palaces that seemed to have sprung from the wildest of fantasies: Greek columns mixed with Roman mosaics, medieval turrets, basilica domes, modernist facades, and neoclassic staircases. The rich chose to live at an altitude where malaria did not strike. The palace where the ceremony took place surrounded an esplanade in which a stand had been erected, sheltered by a velvet tent embroidered with gold and precious stones, and was filled with ornate golden thrones. The powerful among the all-powerful were going to be seated there.

I was introduced to several sons and daughters of the deceased. Bodyguards were everywhere. The guests, men and women, were tall and extremely obese, and exuded power, wealth, and greed. They wore exceedingly expensive clothing, masses of jewelry, extravagant hats, shiny shoes, and various insignia of power, such as ornate sticks and even crowns. Though ivory has been officially banned in order to stop the slaughter of elephants, ivory was everywhere. I counted 97 bracelets on one woman. Because her fat arms could carry only a few of them, she had attached all the others to a gold chain, which she carried around as a sign of power. Gucci bags, Vuitton scarves, and all sorts of other designer items were also on display. One woman clutched ten Hermes handbags, and another wore three pairs of Christian Dior sunglasses.

The abundance of food was outrageous. One of the daughters of the deceased asked me, "We have all kinds of meat—elephants, hippos, gazelles, you name it. Would you like to taste some truly rare titbits? We have something *really* special." Dreading hearing something awful, I stopped her short by saying that I was a vegetarian.

Everyone gobbled down enormous quantities of food, using their hands and biting at the meat as if participating in a cannibalistic feast. Women and men alike drank huge amounts of every possible sort of alcoholic beverage. The women looked very tough. I was struck by the fact that only one child was present, who must have been eight or nine and was a potential candidate. The boy behaved like a spoiled brat, constantly asking for something and complaining. In order to silence him, his mother made sure that he drank plenty of beer. Soon he was completely drunk. When after two hours the meal was over, the floor was covered with leftovers and spilt wine. The sight and smell of heaps of food rapidly rotting in the tropical sun were nauseating.

The drunken crowd now gathered around a gigantic statue to be unveiled. One of the kings belched loudly and unveiled the gold-plated statue of the late businessman. The very powerful then went and sat on their golden thrones. I noticed among them a few women, one of whom was proudly and defiantly holding a submachine gun. The ceremony proper was about to start, with music and dances to be performed before the final announcement of the designated heir. The populace from neighboring villages had been invited to take part in this phase of the show, which was meant to remind them all in whose hands lay the power and the guns.

Some dignitaries, two kings and three businessmen, started paying me exaggerated compliments, commenting on each part of my body and elaborating on each comment with vulgar sexual innuendos. I did not like any of it and sensed danger. These people were drunk and intoxicated with their power. They had lost any inhibitory control, and anything could happen, with nobody daring to put a stop to them. In an effort to protect myself, I mixed in with the crowd from the villages.

The drums began to beat, signaling the start of a masquerade. Several secret societies were then going to dance. So-called secret societies abound all over the world, serving everything from mystical-religious to patriotic to criminal purposes. The members of these social organizations conceal certain of their activities from outsiders. In Africa most secret societies originated from the so-called rites of passage, a term popularized by the French ethnographer Arno van Gennep, for a ritual that marks a change in a person's social or sexual status.[5] Typically, these ceremonies accompany events such as childbirth, puberty, marriage, menopause, or death, and they are still practiced. During and after colonization, many of the secret societies became political instruments in favor of or against the ruling regime. Presently their purpose is further complicated by the presence of professional killers among them, who carry out individual or collective murders to ensure profits for some chiefs and terrify the population.[6] Masks, once ritual instruments only, are now used by these criminal societies to conceal the perpetrators of the crimes.

The secret societies that I witnessed parading in front of the wealthy, the kings, and the populace were clearly criminal in their intent. To make their purpose more evident, many of their "members" viciously hit and whipped randomly the crowd of laypeople with whiplashes, guns, and cudgels while shouting "remember" or "don't you dare" or "go to your place." The crowd was packed tight and people standing in the front rows found it difficult to avoid the blows. In the end many were bleeding profusely. I felt scared, and my first impulse was to leave then and there, but since I had been told that twins were going to be part of the ceremony, I decided to hide behind a tree and to wait.

After the masked dancers left, four men appeared carrying a small altar on their shoulders. A pair of young twin boys sat on it, looking scared stiff. At their appearance, the crowd roared and people began touching them as godly shrines. The twins became even more rigid, they looked paralyzed with terror, but did not cry. "Yet more stone idols," I thought. The twins were past everything, even past moving or crying. By now I had had enough and did not care to wait for the name of the heir to be announced. I left unobtrusively and walked back down the road until I saw a truck driver who worked for Katherine and asked him for a ride back to the orphanage.

Twins, being treated like idols, suffered from extreme emotional deprivation. They were put on an altar, they were physically looked after, well-fed, and cleaned, but otherwise nobody treated them as human beings.

Twins were isolated from the rest of the world, different from other people, and not part of any group or community. They received no affection, warmth, companionship, understanding, physical or mental stimulation, and mutual sharing from others, all of which are essential components for promoting healthy mental growth. They simply lived in a world apart. Twins were at the service of the community from the very start. Everybody, including their parents, paid attention to them only if they behaved as expected, as distant stony effigies of gods.

Wanting of anything else, twins complied by hiding their emotions, inhibiting spontaneous action and communication. Positive impulses such as joy, affection, relaxation, and playfulness were totally stunted. Emotional and behavioral withdrawal interrupted even their mutual relationship from which many twins derive enormous support.

The studies of maternal absence conducted in hospitals or other situations by Rene Spitz[7] and John Bowlby[8] highlighted, among other disturbances, indifference, lack of any feeling for others, coldness, passivity, and isolation, as symptoms pointing to severe maternal deprivation and separation. All the twins I had seen showed those signs.

A few days after the memorial, I began to wonder about Muslims. A big Muslim community lived in the area, but so far I had had no contact with them. I asked Katherine whether Muslims had been contaminated by local creeds and also considered twins sacred. Katherine said "No. Muslims treat them just like other children. Obviously twin boys receive better treatment than twin girls." The Muslims who lived in the area belonged to a large ethnic group characterized by tall stature, a lean build, fairly light skin, and graceful facial features. Katherine explained to me that all the Muslim women were subjected to the most horrible genital mutilations before puberty. The cutting of their vaginas, which was repeated every time their men left home, in order to assure continued faithfulness, transformed intercourse and delivery into a torture. Due to various complications associated with their genital mutilations, many women died.

When Katherine offered to take me to see some Muslim families with twins, I accepted.

The Muslims lived in separate quarters, hardly ever mixing with the rest of the people. Women were nowhere to be seen, but men who knew of my visit behaved charmingly. They were waiting for me in the streets and accompanied me to see their families. The houses, in which their women lived in virtual confinement, were well built and spotlessly clean, with freshly painted walls, tiled floors, and teak wooden doors. All the women were immaculately and elegantly clothed. The younger women, however, were severely anorexic and had a frightened, vacant look on their faces. Their skeletal bodies were covered with strata of flowery fabric. After greeting me, they leaned shyly against the wall, as if trying to disappear into it. I got the impression that these young women wanted to wipe off their suffering bodies and disappear from life.

In contrast, the few elderly women appeared to be fleshy, and their expression, if reserved, was relaxed. That these postmenopausal women were past the agonies of intercourse and childbearing was reflected not only in their expression but also in their attitude and approach to food. They offered me tea and sweet cakes and ate with me, whereas the younger women veiled their mouths when they saw us munching food and did not touch any of it.

According to the Diagnostic and Statistical Manual of Mental Disorders of the American Psychiatric Association, "The essential features of Anorexia Nervosa are that the individual refuses to maintain a minimally normal body weight, is intensely afraid of gaining weight, and exhibits significant disturbance in the perception of the shape or size of his or her body."[9] The self-esteem of individuals with anorexia nervosa is dependent on their body shape and weight. Other associated features are depressed mood, social withdrawal, and overly restrained initiative and emotional expression. All these features applied to these poor young women. Anorexic females can suffer from so-called amenorrhea, or loss of their periods, however, they can still get pregnant. Twin pregnancies entail huge bodily transformations. By six months a woman's abdomen looks enormous, as if she had already reached term. Even after the delivery, they continue to look pregnant for months. Some never regain their former silhouettes, their abdomen and breasts become slack and continue to be full of stretch marks, and their thighs and bottom can remain enlarged.

In a survey on contributing factors to maternal depression in twin pregnancies conducted several years ago in 1992 in my country, 80 percent of women mentioned their altered physical shape as an aggravating issue. On the other hand, women living in developed countries have various options ranging from gym classes to massage and plastic surgery to undo the ravages of a twin pregnancy. Obviously, none of these options were available to the poor anorexic mothers, as their sole choice was to increase fasting. The huge bodily transformation of any twin pregnancy must have felt doubly loathsome for these anorexic mothers.

Besides the sufferings due to pregnancy and the accompanying change in body shape, a twin delivery must have felt like an unbearable laceration for their already slashed genitals.

Twins, albeit involuntarily, caused enormously increased mental turmoil and physical agonies in their mothers' slashed genitals. One could not expect the mothers of twins to react warmly or spontaneously love their twin infants who had produced incredible lacerations and huge bodily changes. Their mothers seemed too pained even to look at them, and their grandmothers were too eager to be past pain. Muslim twins, like all other twins in the area, were also subject to a grim fate and were petrified by emotional deprivation.

In the ten families with twins I visited, no one paid attention to them. Twins were well-fed, clean, and properly clothed, but everybody kept their distance from them. Nobody, including their siblings, spoke, smiled, looked at, cuddled, or played with them. Twins were marginalized within their homes, and signs of emotional deprivation could be detected in the vacant look on their expressionless faces and the terrified way they behaved.

After the visit to the Muslims I no longer enquired about twins.

As my stay was nearing its end, adoptive parents came to the orphanage. The institution was linked with several European agencies and the adoptive parents were European. I made myself available for discussing questions about adoption with them. Most young children cried when introduced to their adoptive parents, frightened at the thought of leaving the security of the orphanage, the warmth of their caregivers, and the mutual support of their peers. The white skin of their new parents also scared them. I explained to foster-parents that initially I had met with the same reactions, and stressed how normal these reactions were. The children in the institution were not emotionally petrified.

In contrast, all the twins I had seen in the region, though kept within their community, were past crying and protesting. It was better to be an orphan than an idol in this part of the country.

Chapter 4

The Big Shock

The idealization of twins in Voodoo and in the Cameroon contrasts sharply with scientific facts.

Despite all medical progress in developed countries, twin gestations continue to be at risk both for the mother and for the twins.[1] Maternal mortality is high. Under the best circumstances and in the most modern facility, the risk of maternal death is 3 times higher in a twin pregnancy than in a singleton one.[2] Maternal complications are also elevated: high blood pressure increases 2.5–3 times, maternal diabetes 2.4 times, infections 3 times; severe anemia 8 times; and severe hemorrhaging 2.5 times before and 4 times after delivery.[3] These problems, if not properly treated, can have dire consequences. During a twin pregnancy, women are subjected to more frequent checkups, sometimes even daily ones, and frequently have to be hospitalized.

Twin deliveries, too, are potentially at risk. Twins births are usually a well-planned event, attended by a host of specialists, including two or more obstetricians, a few midwives, an anesthesiologist, two perinatalogists, and several pediatric nurses. They have a five-fold chance of ending up as caesareans.[4] Many go into premature labor and the fetuses are often in breach or other difficult presentations.

Twins are even more affected than their mothers both before and after birth. Prenatal mortality is especially high as compared to singletons, or 3–10 times more common.[5] These already grim figures skyrocket when twin gestations are not diagnosed promptly with ultrasounds, thus permitting various forms of intervention. Special units for twin pregnancies are an increasing reality in major European hospitals.

Complications vary according to the sort of twins involved. Women expecting twins generally submit to an early scan to ascertain the type of placenta and thus indirectly the kind of twins. The subsequent management of the pregnancy will vary according to this early assessment.

Dizygotic twins, also referred to as fraternal or nonidentical twins, are the least affected by prenatal complications and death. Genetically speaking dizygotic twins are like ordinary siblings, sharing only 50 percent of their genes. They can be of the same or opposite sex, and their appearance displays varying degrees of similarity or dissimilarity. Dizygotic twins always have separate placentas and inhabit distinct amniotic sacs. Twins ensuing from fertility treatments belong almost exclusively to this category.

Monozygotic twins, also referred to as identical or true twins, derive from the fertilization of one egg by a single sperm. The fertilized cell or cells, called zygote, then split into two or more embryos sharing the same genetic endowment. This division can take place at various stages of development during the first 15 days after fertilization. Early separation, affecting roughly 29 percent of all monozygotic twins, results in separate placentas and distinct amniotic sacs, the same as all dizygotic twins. Later divisions result in increasing degrees of sharing: the same placenta and different sacs occur in approximately 70 percent of all monozygotic twins, the same placenta and a shared sac occur in 1 percent of all monozygotic twins, and conjoined or Siamese twins occur roughly in 1 of every 1000 monozygotic twin pregnancies.[6]

Increased sharing brings with it increased potential risks both for the twins and for the mother. The highest prenatal mortality rate is in those very rare monozygotic twins who share the same placenta and amniotic sac, called mono-chorionic, mono-amniotic twins. As many as 50 percent of these will not reach birth alive. Mutual entanglement of the umbilical cords, with resulting asphyxia, is largely the cause of this high mortality rate.[7]

Twins sharing the same placenta but inhabiting different amniotic sacs, called mono-chorionic, di-amniotic twins, can also undergo specific, potentially lethal complications. Roughly 15 percent of these will suffer from a particular condition called "twin-to-twin-transfusion-syndrome."[8] Although the exact dynamics of this condition are still unclear, vascular connections within the shared placenta seem to lead to an imbalance between the two twins. As a consequence, the so-called donor twin shows a severe lack of amniotic fluid, and is anemic, dehydrated, and growth retarded. The recipient twin, on the contrary, has an excess of amniotic fluid and a plethora of blood, with subsequent hypertension and swelling of all organs. The mortality rate among twins affected by this syndrome is very high, or 90 percent at early onset and 30 percent after 20 weeks of gestation. Each year in the United States about 2200 fetuses die from this condition.[9]

All told, twins are at greater risk of stillbirth than singletons, or 3–13 times more so. Postnatal mortality is also elevated in twins, being 6–7 times more likely in the neonatal period.[10] Perinatal mortality rates are 2–3 times higher for monozygotic than for dizygotic twins. Twins are more frequently born premature (39.2 percent versus 4.5 percent of singletons born before 37 weeks of amenorrhea) or extremely premature (11 percent versus 3.1 percent of singletons born before 32 weeks of amenorrhea).[11] Four times as many twins are born growth retarded, ten times as many are born with a weigh of less than 1500 g, and twice as many are born with malformations affecting all systems, especially the cardiovascular, gastrointestinal, and central nervous systems.[12] Chromosomal abnormalities may also be particularly elevated and often discordant, even in monozygotic twins. Mortality in the perinatal period is consequently greater for twins than for singletons, or 22.8 percent versus 2.9 percent.[13]

As a result of all these problems and complications, 4–5 times as many twins as singletons will have to spend a long time, sometimes even months, in a neonatal intensive care unit, where they are constantly monitored with sophisticated equipment but also face an elevated risk of long term *sequelae*.[14] Twins have a 1.7 higher risk of suffering severe handicaps and a 5–10 times higher risk of cerebral palsy compared to singletons.[15] Mortality continues to be higher throughout the first year, or 33 percent versus 6.1 percent.[16]

Several of these risks are explained carefully to all perspective parents during their first visit to the special unit for twin pregnancies where I work, which is equipped with the latest technologies and the most up-to-date personnel. But parents generally tend to brush off and deny any grim piece of information. Whenever complications actually arise, they seem totally taken aback. This denial can in a sense be functional. As one mother whose twins had died late in pregnancy told me tearfully, "One cannot live thinking all the time that we are going to die. We know that sooner or later this is going to happen, but we have to carry on with life. The same applies to deciding to have a child. From conception onward we can protect our children only up to a very limited extent. Twins are exposed to many risks. I knew this, but I put it in the back of my mind. I wanted to enjoy my pregnancy. I know this is irrational. When something went wrong, I sensed it immediately. I came here in a rush, but I still had hope." Mothers tend to regard pregnancy as only life-giving and completely death-free. They are shocked when told by me that the hearts of even tiny embryos have ceased to beat.

Besides denial, a host of fantasies about the genesis of twins continues unabated, contrasting shockingly with available scientific information. Only those parents who have undergone fertility treatments of any kind, given their lengthy and detailed consultations with gynecologists, fertility specialists, and geneticists beforehand, are extremely well-informed.

In the maternity hospital where I work, after detecting twins with ultrasounds, mothers are referred to the twin unit for another scan aimed at establishing early in pregnancy the type of placenta, amniotic sac, and umbilical cord the twins have, which information is of great importance in guiding the medical conduct of the pregnancy. It always strikes me that the most difficult explanations are those regarding the placenta. This essential prenatal organ elicits strong disgust and is generally ignored. Both women and men, aided by the new technologies, tend to view pregnancy as a kind of aseptic, immaculate event and do not want to be reminded of our "animal" nature. Placentas evoke images of domestic animals delivering litters. As one mother commented, "I don't want to know about the placenta. When my cat delivered its kitten, it was such a mess. It made me sick, especially when she started licking the placenta and all that blood."

The importance of the placenta is well recognized in many other places in the world. When twins are born in many nations in the developing world, the placenta, its membranes, and the umbilical cord are generally examined carefully. Artifacts from Papua, for instance, show that people can make an accurate distinction between twin pregnancies with a single placenta or a double one. Furthermore, they associate a single placenta with "identical" twins.

Elsewhere this organ is not something to be looked at in disgust and gotten rid of, but is frequently buried in an apt "placental site." It can be under the floor of a communal kitchen or under a small shrine. Before proceeding to the "funeral," mothers may take a bite out of it and give a taste to the twins, implicitly recognizing its nutritive and growth-promoting powers during pregnancy. People living in poor circumstances who do not have access to sophisticated notions or equipments can nevertheless be very good observers.

Workers who have recently emigrated from various parts of the world, ranging from South America to the Far East, sometimes ask to have the placenta back after delivery to give it a proper burial. At first doctors were taken aback by this request, which contrasted sharply with the disgust of the national population. Currently doctors and nurses are no longer surprised to be asked about the placenta, and small placental containers are part of the equipment in the delivery room. Generally placentas go down the incinerator. This is not so, however, for placentas of twins, which are examined carefully by a pathologist to ascertain whether the ultrasonographic diagnosis of a single placenta was correct, thus proving beyond doubt if the twins are monozygotic or not. This assessment is important for various reasons. Primarily twins and their parents want to know if twins are monozygotic or not without having to undergo costly DNA analyses later on. This knowledge is psychologically important for twins, as a relevant component of their identity is based on the degree of relation with each other. Knowing the degree of relatedness can also prove essential for medical reasons: should a twin need an organ transplant at some stage, a monozygotic twin would be the ideal donor, as having the same DNA he or she would not suffer from rejection problems or need to take antirejection drugs.

Other mistaken beliefs abound even among highly educated parents, who are not immune from misconceptions that contrast sharply with scientific knowledge. A client of mine, I'll call him Mr A, a successful architect in his early fifties, had recently married one of his students, an attractive, vivacious young woman, and immediately he wanted a child. Ms A agreed and, as she said, got pregnant at "the first shot." Mr A was elated. A young wife and a "first shot" impregnation gave his ego a boost. While his wife was giving her medical history, he flirted with everyone and went so far as to tell me, "Beware! I am a dangerous man. I am sure I could impregnate a woman just by looking at her." When the ultrasound scan revealed twins, his elation was out of control. He started hugging his wife, me, and my assistant while exclaiming repeatedly, "I am a super-stud!" "I exude testosterone!" No scientific explanation was able to dispel his irritating, cocky attitude, which continued throughout his wife's pregnancy.

Like Mr A, many fathers of twins boast of their virility, equating twins with sexual potency, although being a twin actually has nothing to do with enhanced sexual potency.

In a certain remote area of Central Africa, when their wives deliver twins these superfathers have to lie naked under the glaring rays of the midday sun while a long line of other males wait to touch their "superb" testicles in the hope of acquiring the same "supernatural" powers through a sort of magical transmission.[17]

Mothers of twins can also feel superfertile and brag about their fecundity, with equally little reason, but unlike men, they only occasionally confuse it with sexiness or super-femininity. Supermoms may be touched on their huge bellies and breasts and be treated as protective deities or lucky charms in the struggle against infertility. Barren women from as far away as Ecuador and Sri Lanka will lend the supermom their underwear for a while, which they then wear themselves in the hope that the excess fecundity will be passed on to them. The effigies of mothers who bore twins may also become shrines to be stroked, given offerings, and prayed to. Immigrant women in developed countries, however, are soon informed, by the hospital or by word of mouth, of the existence of fertility treatments. Out of superstition they may continue to touch the bellies of women expecting twins, but at the same time they flock to the unit specializing in infertility. As one caught in the act commented, "I try both, just in case. One never knows."

A recurring fear is that twins might be the result of unfaithfulness, two infants meaning different partners and cuckolding. Fathers who hold this misconception look suspiciously at their companions and frequently comment, "But we have no twins in the family." Some go so far as to mention DNA analysis. Another patient of mine, I'll call him Mr B, an extremely rich, middle-aged man, came to the twin unit with his stunningly beautiful and much younger "trophy wife." When twins were revealed by the scan, he was enraged. No scientific explanation could free him from the corrosive doubt that his gorgeous wife had betrayed him. Each scan turned into a fight, and throughout the pregnancy he kept mumbling, "We shall see at birth." When twin boys were finally delivered, they were dizygotic and unfortunately very much unlike. One looked just like him and had a fairly Mediterranean phenotype. The other with red hair and huge blue eyes resembled nobody in the family. Yet another huge fight ensued as soon as his young wife woke up from the anesthetic. Ms B had delivered the twins by caesarean, and her husband began shouting while she still hovered between consciousness and oblivion. A team of lawyers appeared, and DNA analyses were agreed to in order to settle the suspicion once and for all. The results indicated unequivocally that Mr B was the father of both twins. He suddenly remembered that one of his grandmothers had had red hair, just like his newborn twin son, but the marriage was over. A few months later Ms B dropped in to say hello to us. Having received a huge settlement and been given custody of the twins, she was fairly nonchalant about the whole matter. As she said, smiling her gorgeous smile, "Perhaps this is what I wanted all along. My husband was obsessed with fixed ideas about unfaithfulness. Now I am free, I am rich, and I have two children."

While it is true that dizygotic twins can run in the family, there is no statistical evidence that reveals a fully hereditary pattern, only a predisposition. The same goes for monozygotic twins, who appear to be the result of a nonpredictable, random event. In fact we still know very little about the origins of monozygotic twins.[18]

While some societies are fairly lax and casual about sexual matters, others most definitely are not, and women whose twins are taken as a proof of infidelity can run into even more serious problems than DNA analysis. I met Ishara, a stunningly beautiful Sri Lankan woman, at the twin unit. She had been married off to Mr Chinnan, a considerably older and ugly rich man. Although the tradition is rapidly dwindling, most marriages in Sri Lanka are still arranged by the family, but not without previously consulting horoscopes to find out if the candidates are astrologically compatible. When we broke the news of twins to Ishara, she looked fearful, and her husband kicked up a row. For a number of Sri Lankans, unless twins run in the family, they are inevitably the living proof of infidelity, placing a heavy social stigma on the alleged adultery. Despite my repeated explanations, Mr Chinnan continued throughout her pregnancy to look suspiciously at his wife and to treat her grumpily. When she delivered healthy and beautiful monozygotic twin girls, she was delighted, but her husband continued to sulk. At this stage I put it all down to an unpleasant temperament.

A few months later, Ishara phoned me in tears, begging me to visit her. Her twin girls were delightful, but Ishara looked distressed as she poured her heart out to me. Everyone treated her like an outcast. Her husband still questioned the paternity of the twins and constantly tormented her with his doubts. His mother and all sorts of other relatives had joined in, and Mr Chinnan was threatening to repudiate her. Her alleged unfaithfulness was rendered all the more credible by her beauty and the age difference between her and her husband. She asked me to explain again to her husband that monozygotic twins do not run in families, then added shyly, "Could you also please leave one of your drawings explaining different twins to me?" I realized that I had not given her one of the simple drawings that generally accompany my explanations showing that dizygotic twins come from two eggs and two sperms, and monozygotic ones from one egg and one sperm, thus ruling out the possibility of intercourse having taken place with two different men. Contrary to many parents, Ishara had been too shy to ask. After she called in her husband, I took out a piece of paper and made my usual drawing. Mr Chinnan still did not seem totally convinced and just mumbled, "If you say so, Doctor." Occasionally Ishara still sends me a card saying that our encounter has changed her life. As a result, I never forget to give my drawings to parents.

When I told Lalani, another young Sri Lankan woman at the hospital, that she was going to have twins, she said, "I am lucky to have twins in the family. On both sides, too. From my mother and my father." Next time she came to the twin unit, she brought with her a huge white album with all the photos of her lavish wedding and showed it to me. Both sets of twins held the limelight, and Lalani had cleverly made sure that the twins were included in all the photographs of her marriage. By doing so, she proved wise, for now that she was expecting twins, the photographic evidence of lots of twins in the family preserved her reputation.

Besides pregnancy, delivery too is often charged with fanciful ideas, which have nothing to do with reality and scientific facts.

Currently in the developed world an idyllic idea of natural birth tends to be in vogue. Women are encouraged to go back to nature and to deliver squatting, hanging from a rope taking the place of a branch of a tree, or in a Jacuzzi pool as a surrogate for the imagined crystal clear waters of a river or lake. The popularity of a birth-attendant, called doula, is also another craze.[19] The word doula is derived from the Greek, and refers to a woman serving another woman. In an ancient Greek household, the doula probably helped the lady of the house through childbirth. The term was taken up again by Dana Raphael, an anthropologist working in the Philippines, to refer to experienced mothers who supported first-time mothers after birth.[20] The doula is currently associated with providing kindness and comfort to women, especially during labor, but also throughout and after her pregnancy. The assistance of a doula is supposed to enhance bonding, and early bonding in turn is considered a guarantee for the future mental well-being of the child.

Ms C, a young woman in her mid-twenties and another patient of mine, came to the hospital as she was expecting monozygotic twin boys. Ms C was a strong believer in the imprinting of early experiences on the fetus and the newborn, and her philosophy of life was suffused with a mixture of Zen, holistic medicine, and New Age. Long before term, she hired a doula, a middle-aged woman who always wore far eastern jewelry and clothing, such as Indian skirts mixed with kimono-like tops, huge pendant earrings, and tons of amber and turquoise necklaces. While I examined Ms C using ultrasound, the doula sat next to her massaging her breasts with Ayurvedic oils and chanting strange sing-songs. All went well during pregnancy, and when term came, since both twins were turned in the cephalic position, an induced delivery was planned. Ms C's doula remonstrated heavily, saying that delivery had to be utterly spontaneous as, "Women deliver spontaneously and without a moan in the African bush or in the Amazons, then go back to their village and are back at work the day after. Here all is medicalized, why should her delivery be planned and induced?" My colleagues were rather annoyed, but explained that twins were tricky as once the first twin was expelled, the second being suddenly confronted with a huge space could turn round. Furthermore, twins reach term three weeks earlier than singletons and besides obstetricians, pediatricians and several nurses have to be present in case they need special care. Ms C made a fuss, but when my colleagues suggested signing release papers and delivering at home with her doula, the doula herself urged her to follow medical advice. When the big day came Ms C arrived with her doula and they were both made to wait in a comfortable room. The doula started massaging Ms C's belly and kept chanting, and also lit plenty of exotic incense and candles in order to imprint the first olfactory and visual experiences on the twins. A few minutes later, however, Ms C was visited by the obstetrician in charge, who said, "The twins have both turned round and the heartbeat of the second twin has decelerated. We have to perform a caesarean quickly." Ms C forgot her resolution to imprint the twins with sweet sing-songs, fine odors, and dim candle light, and began to swear like a trooper. Nobody paid attention to her loud remonstrations and the twins were duly born through an emergency caesarean. Ms C was later to recollect the whole experience as very shocking, and when her twins turned out to be pretty riotous, she often mentioned their "unnatural" delivery without the assistance of the doula as a possible reason for their unruly behavior.

The "back to nature" idyllic view of "natural" delivery in the bush is of women delivering spontaneously, alone, without a moan, and ready to go back to work full of energy. Women living in low-income countries, however, are no braver or more energetic or less sensitive to pain. Most are terrified, as they are well aware that delivery is risky up to the point of being lethal. In most cases they would simply be shamed if they did let out a cry or take some rest. Local doulas, when present, are far from being motherly and kind, often inflicting horrible lacerations and causing infections in an attempt to help the mother. Furthermore, birth attendants can be envious and cruel spies who report to the entire village if the mother behaves shamefully by moaning and complaining about the pain.

As soon as immigrant women enter the delivery room, they are the first to ask for an epidural or for a caesarean. They may not speak a word of Italian but can still say, "No pain!" Nor do they seem willing to deliver in "natural" positions, such as squatting, being immersed in water, or hanging onto a rope. All that they carry into the delivery room are some superstitions from their culture. Chinese women, for instance, do not want there to be in the room even a dot of red, which means blood and hence the danger of massive lethal hemorrhaging. This is not hysteria but the result of poor health care at home. If they hemorrhaged during labor in their villages, nobody stopped them from dying.

Besides the enormous stress associated with twin pregnancies, educated parents living in developed countries have to deal with the ever-growing pressure of sloppy psychology, which affects immigrant mothers only marginally.

Immigrant mothers come from places where they fight for survival. Psychology has little or no interest for them. Most consider it a decadent fad.

But psychology and psychotherapy are pervasive in our world. It has taught us no longer to regard young children as unfeeling creatures that can be handed over to anyone. Women tend to take great care of the few precious children they produce. Yet if anything goes wrong with their development, all the blame tends to be put on mothers, who have been accused of causing everything from autism to dyslexia and schizophrenia. As the psychologist and sociologist Elisabeth Batinder pointed out commenting on the work of the psychoanalyst and pediatrician Donald Winnicott, the "ordinary devoted mother is defined first of all by her capacity to be preoccupied by her child to the exclusion of any other interest."[21] Furthermore, ordinary devoted mothers should find pleasure in their devotion and, "Enjoy being annoyed when the baby's cries and yells prevent acceptance of the milk that you long to be generous with. Enjoy all sorts of womanly feelings that you cannot even begin to explain to a man…Enjoy all this particularly because any pleasure you can derive from the messy business of infant care happens to be vitally important from the baby's point of view."[22]

Twins' simultaneous cries are indeed difficult to enjoy. Nurturing simultaneously two infants at the same stage of development is quite unlike tending to one. Parental attention and care are not easily shared between two babies. In the animal world larger broods are generally born developmentally more advanced and more independent, so that they mature faster, and do not require the same quality of interactions as the human child does. Full independence is acquired very late in our species. The human infant is totally dependent on parental care for survival. It is also a social creature, requiring increasing attention and distinctive emotional interchanges. Parents of twins simply cannot meet the same requirements of both infants simultaneously.

Currently psychology has extended its interest to the evolving capacities of the fetus. Prenatal psychologists have focused sensibly on those preparatory functions, such as audition, that make it possible for the fetus to meet the complex requirements of its postnatal environment. Newborns turn preferentially toward their mother's voice, for instance, since they have already been exposed to it during the latter stages of pregnancy, an ability that favors mutual recognition and mutual attachment. Unfortunately, however, out-of-control elements have entered this field.[23] Maternal emotions, especially maternal anxiety during pregnancy, are a favored target of the extremist wing of prenatal psychologists. "Negative" emotions are deemed to be harmful to the fetus, leaving a permanent imprint on it. According to this view, mothers should live in a kind of nirvana so as not to traumatize their unborn. Because twin pregnancies, given their physical burdens and risks, are highly anxiety provoking, mothers are made to feel guilty and even more anxious by being unable to suppress their often uncontrollable emotions.

Prenatal psychologists often take data from other disciplines, ranging from molecular biology to obstetrics, and interpret them out of context to try and prove that fetuses already function not only as neonates but as much older children. Fetal twins are especially important for prenatal psychologists. Intrapair stimulation, which is indeed unique to them, is taken to mean that twins are already engaged in a complex network of social and emotional relations. Their unique bond is imagined to have started within the uterus almost from the moment of conception.

Other twin data have been taken up by prenatal psychologists to boost the emotional relevance of our prenatal past. Ultrasounds have revealed that several pregnancies start as twin ones, but do not end with the birth of live twins. The extent of the phenomenon has not been evaluated. An early scan may show two gestational sacs, each containing a fetus or an embryo, while another scan a few weeks later reveals no heartbeats or just one heartbeat and a shrinking dead "twin." This phenomenon usually takes place within the first ten weeks of pregnancy and has been given the uncanny name of the "vanishing twin syndrome."[24] Some prenatal psychologists take the vanishing twin syndrome to an extreme by declaring that we are all twins at heart, mourning our blighted co-twin and looking throughout life for a replacement. Groups of mourners to grieve the loss of their vanished twins are now proliferating.

Once I was invited to be the main speaker at a huge conference on prenatal psychology in a foreign country where the gap between the wealthy and the poor is immense. I spoke to the group about the prenatal behaviour of twin fetuses, arguing that their first reactions to mutual stimulation are indirect proof of the functioning of tactile sensitivity in all fetuses. I explained furthermore that fetal motions cannot to be equated to wakefulness and to any kind of "consciousness," but are more akin to sleep. After my purely behavioral, neurological approach, the first question asked was, "Why are you interested in twins?" This query was met with an uproar from the public: "Clearly you must have been a twin! Your twin vanished!" I was urged to ask my mother whether my placenta or any first-trimester bleeding during my pregnancy showed traces of a blighted twin. Finally I was encouraged to join a therapy group to mourn my twin and purge my guilt for surviving it or to undertake "primal therapy" to revive the event. This experience left me shocked. I found the equation of previable fetuses incapable of living independently from their mothers' bodies with newborns or older children both immoral and irresponsible.

Several years later, in 2003, I was approached, along with eminent colleagues, by one of the most sophisticated trade enterprises in the world, a Japanese firm producing merchandise for extremely wealthy babies and young children. The purpose of contacting me was to put together a team of medical, design, and technological specialists to devise products aimed at increasing the "happiness" of children. I was to be the "expert" on fetal life and twins. I pointed out that my role would be difficult, as I did not know how to foster the happiness of fetuses, much less of fetal twins, but the Japanese were resolute in wanting me to join. They added, given a general aversion to twins among women in Japan, the budget allotted to them had to be small, but because fertility treatments often resulted in twins, they saw a potential market opening up.

The whole project sounded nonsensical to me, but this same unreasonableness somehow intrigued me, so I agreed to take part. I was given a first-class ticket to Japan and hosted in a five-star hotel.

I loved being in Japan, my stay was memorable for the exquisite kindness of my hosts, but I could not think of any useful products to foster the well-being of twin fetuses. My only suggestion was to produce a special CD filled with soothing music, inasmuch as music, especially if relaxing, has never caused any harm to anyone. Once it became clear that fetuses are only reachable through their mothers' bodies, the subject shifted to mothers. Prenatal products had to be targeted to erasing maternal anxiety, which was generally deemed to be damaging to the fetuses. "Prenatal" beds and bathtubs for massaging and lulling pregnant mothers were discussed. I felt that a bit of Zen would not hurt the few extremely wealthy mothers who could afford to buy the special equipment.

The team then began considering ways of making the "trauma of birth" less disturbing. A special cradle was discussed, reminiscent of the womb in texture and shape. Its texture was to be soft and stretchable so as to accommodate twins. A small engine was designed to keep the temperature of the cradle comfortable and constant, to rock it gently, and from time to time to simulate mild uterine contractions. A special cover that let in only a dim orange light was carefully designed. Recordings of the maternal voice and heartbeat, in an unstoppable crescendo of predictable sounds, were diffused within the microhabitat of this "macrowomb." The final touch was the addition of a removable partition, reminiscent of the membranes separating most twins inside the womb. By this point I was absolutely speechless. The underlying assumption behind the expensive gear was that infants do not live in a social world, and twin infants long to go back to an idyllic womb, whereas in fact their intrauterine life is generally a nightmare for all.

But apart from me nobody else seemed disturbed. As the head of the firm said, "This has been great fun. I have learned a lot. I am a bachelor and never inquired about twins."

Once the prenatal aspects had been covered, I had a lot of free time on my hands.

Before going to Japan, I had read several articles and books on a particular Japanese custom, the so-called *Mizuko Kuyo,* literally the "water-child ceremony," which refers specifically to aborted or stillborn children.[25] This memorial rite is based on the assumption that all beings, sentient or nonsentient, possess some sort of spirit or soul. The *mizuko,* having suffered a premature, unnatural death through abortion or stillbirth, can become revengeful and cause all kinds of trouble unless mollified through special ceremonies that allow it to reach a final stage of "Buddhahood." Such a stage, according to the underlying belief, is the prerequisite for eternal serenity or for proper reincarnation, giving the *mizuko* a chance to be reborn and join society again. Though many other religious cults, especially Shinto, Tao, and all their derivations, are practiced in Japan, Buddhism has acquired nearly exclusive rights to handle matters associated with the dead.

Mizukos, being watery creatures not fully formed, are buried in special cemeteries, which I asked to visit. They were not easy to find. The cemeteries were usually hidden from view in beautiful but secluded settings, often at the foot of a mountain and sheltered by gorgeous bamboo woods. *Mizukos* were generally represented by small Buddhist monk-like statuettes, all looking the same, bald and wearing the foot-length robes of Buddhist monks. The statuettes per se are actually called *Jzo* after the god who protects children; however, for reasons of clarity I will continue to refer to them as *mizukos.* They could be set in a row, piled up to form a kind of miniature mountain, set sparsely within a beautifully designed garden, or hidden away in a cave. *Mizukos* often wore a bib, usually a red one. Some were fully clothed, and their parents brought them all sorts of goods, ranging from small toys to flowers, knitted garments, and cups. The resulting atmosphere was generally one of lightness, conveying the peculiar impression that the cemetery and the nursery, two of the sites that we are most keen to keep well apart in developed countries, were here united as one. In the mind of the Japanese, the cemetery is the place that links this world with the "other" world. When aborted children are remembered, levity and even playfulness are deemed appropriate as, in this case, the cemetery is the link with the other world in which children, aborted or not, are thought to reside.

The first cemetery I visited dated back to the nineteenth century. After crossing a thick wood, I saw hundreds of dark statues of children among thick ferns. The statues were big, about the size of a four-year-old, and each had its own individuality, which spoke to the child. Some were smiling, others angry; some were pretty, others ugly; and some were boys, others girls. Twins were plentiful, I counted 15 pairs of twins out of a 100 statues, a figure that is well above the average rate of twin births. Dizygotic twins are low in Asiatics, occurring roughly in 1 out of 300 births, and monozygotic ones in 1 out of 250 births. Twins were represented in all their variety, including conjoined or Siamese twins. All these children had seen the light of day, and their parents had a good look at them before deciding their fate. The cemetery belonged to an era when infanticide was widely practiced in many areas of the world, and twins were clearly disposed of. Gifts, bibs, and flowers were no longer brought to these *mizukos,* their parents long since dead. Properly speaking, the term infanticide refers to homicides of children who have not yet had their first birthdays, the term filicide pertains to the killing of children older than one year of age, and neonaticide is confined to children who are murdered on their first day of life. However, for reasons of simplicity, I will use the term infanticide throughout to indicate all these forms of homicide. The abundance of twins among them testified to the fact that twins were not welcome in ancient Japan. Their mothers were regarded as animal-like, as twins were associated with animal litters, and the twins spoiled their mothers' bodies and imposed financial hardships on the family.

Most other cemeteries were contemporary and, save for personal touches added by the parents, all the statuettes were small, gray, and identical. Twins could not be distinguished from singletons, except occasionally by their wearing identical hats, shoes, or bibs. Upon seeing all those statuettes, I found myself thinking about the view of the fetus offered by ultrasound, where all fetuses, including twins, look the same and appear in tones of gray. Since 1945, abortion can be practiced legally in Japan, and the law permits it for all sorts of reasons under the heading of "economic hardship." Early abortion is in fact the most widespread form of contraception, and most physicians do not report it. The low dosage oral pill, Intra Uterine Devices (IUD), and female condoms were approved only recently in Japan, in 1999, and medical prescription is required for these. Viagra was also approved the same year! When looking at all those identical *mizukos,* I found myself thinking that inasmuch as twins certainly strain family finances to the limit,—and, as infants, twins are indeed difficult to enjoy—, many more twins than I could detect were possibly among them.

In the end, the special gear for twins was not manufactured by the Japanese firm, as twins were not considered a worthy investment. However, the head of the company assured me during a lavish dinner before I left, "We will keep the project in mind. Things may be rapidly changing, and twins may become a new vogue."

Chapter 5

Keepers and Outcasts

The birth of twins has always been perceived as an extraordinary event outside the bounds of nature. Since the dawn of mankind people have tried to restore the ordinary course of events by reverting to the norm of singletons, often by adopting drastic or even bloody measures, but nothing quite erased the unease. Twins simply did not fit in and could not be accommodated. Inevitably their birth gave rise to all sorts of peculiar queries and explanations.

Astrologers ruminated for centuries about twins. Earthly twins, born under identical stars, threatened by their very existence to undermine astrological science itself. In theory, twins should have displayed the same disposition. Yet frequently they were unlike in temperament and constitution. Being born under the same astrological alignments should also have produced the same destiny. But twins generally met with dissimilar fates.

The Roman rhetorician Cicero, skeptical as he was in all matters of philosophy and superstition, criticized bitterly in his *De Divinatione* (On Divination), the use of foretelling the destiny of men through reading signs of the zodiac and the liver of dead animals. He wondered how it came about that there was only one Homer if several men were born every instant, and then added the regular dispute about twins.[1]

Favorinus, a highly regarded Roman skeptical philosopher and rhetorician, objected that the position of the stars is not the same for twins at the time of conception and of birth, thus the difference in their fates may be explained by these slight, but essential, discrepancies.[2] The dilemma was never quite resolved, and the debate raged for centuries until finally astrology was largely replaced by more exact branches of science.

Twins' distinct destinies also endangered deterministic notions that our fate was determined once and for all, as the Greeks were inclined to think. Twins with their divergent fortunes served the cause of nascent Christianity, with its emphasis on free will, in two contrasting ways. On one hand, the different destinies and natures of twins substantiated the principle of those advocating complete free will. Our actions could be tamed, and the responsibility for our conduct was ours alone. Before God, each twin was alone and treated as a singleton, solely accountable for his or her behavior. On the other hand, St Augustine cited twins as an example of how humans could not save themselves on their own but required baptism to have the free will to sin or not.[3] According to St Augustine, when twins were born, if one was quickly baptized and the attendants to the delivery, busy saving the first twin, did not have the time to baptize the other, he or she was damned. Unless both were purified, one twin could be evil and the other saintly, one could be raised to heaven and the other plunged into the flames of hell. St Augustine's assertions provided no evidence; however, his unsubstantiated views prevailed for centuries, setting baptism as a precondition for salvation. Due to the elevated perinatal mortality in his times, many innocent infants expired before receiving the sacrament, and all were considered doomed. Since the flames of hell were too strong a punishment for unbaptized newborns, it was finally decided that they were to languish in Limbo hoping to be released by God's mercy.

The dispute about free will versus determinism is still at the basis of different religions. Twins, however, are no longer quoted as an argument in favor of one or the other. The birth of twins also raised more material, earthly issues.

Until fairly recently the eldest child of any sufficiently wealthy family generally inherited everything. The inheritance could not be shared; it had to be handed down intact through the generations. Younger children were generally sent to swell the ranks of the convent or army. Once more, twins stirred up a problem. They could not be made to fit in with the laws of inheritance, which did not allow for a binary condition. Though twins are generally born only minutes apart, clearly one twin had to be considered younger and consequently excluded from the family legacy, thereby reestablishing the norm.

The biblical twins Esau and Jacob are just one of numerous examples. When Rebecca was pregnant "the children struggled together within her" and Rebecca, scared by the tumult, questioned God, who told her that she was expecting twins and that, contrary to traditions, the second born "younger" Jacob was going to be the "chosen one." Birth order being the deciding factor in those days, all inheritance had to be passed on to Esau.[4] At birth, however, Esau "came out red, all over like an hairy garment."

Only through cunningness did Jacob win out against his furry brother. Esau's repugnant appearance made Rebecca a fan of Jacob, and she disguised him by making him wear a hairy goatskin. Jacob was then brought in front of Isaac, his blind father, who, by touching the goatskin, mistook him for Esau and thus gave him the fatherly blessing entitling him to become the heir.[5]

Matters of inheritance are still of relevance in some populations today. Coming out first may be taken to imply a greater readiness to be born and thus being the elder, as in the case of Esau. The contrary can also be true. The second to come out, implanted higher in the womb, may be regarded as having entered it first and hence considered the elder. Others believe the heavier twin to be the elder, who has had more time to eat. Consequently, sheep or cows or a piece of land are allotted unequally between the twins.

The question of who is the elder is still frequently asked even by highly cultivated parents, though no longer with the same monetary consequences. Birth order is always remembered by the family. Even the twins themselves generally attach great importance to birth order. Most perceive primogeniture as a sign of cleverness and intelligence. One comment frequently heard is, "I was the first to come out. I am quicker and smarter. You are tardy and slow" or "I am the dominant one. I came out first. You just have to follow." Birth order can thus have psychological repercussions by sometimes making the second-born feel less bright and less favored by nature.

Although nowadays questions about both metaphysics and inheritance have lost much of their importance, in many other ways twins continue to be "too much," or as they say "two much," and problematic. Most modern-day parents attempt to recreate a dyadic situation by more or less subtly erasing or leaving one twin behind, while vehemently denying it. An element of preferential treatment is almost invariably found in the handling of twins. Yet the idea of the impartial handling of our children is part and parcel of our idealized notion of parenthood, and contrary to all evidence, twins themselves fly the flag of parental fairness and correctness by generally declaring that they are treated "exactly the same." Most western parents know in detail the prenatal history of their twins, being not only informed about the various conditions affecting the twins but also allowed to see their image. This visual aspect has a strong impact on parents and is invariably imbued with meaning by them. Unfairness can start in the womb.

Nature itself is the first and foremost creator of inequities. Twins can be discordant with respect to potential risks and be affected in different ways. The intrauterine environment of twins can vary greatly: one twin can have a bigger placenta, less amniotic fluid, or an umbilical cord with just two vessels instead of three. All these inequalities reverberate on the less fortunate twin, sometimes stunting its growth, restricting its capacity for movement to the point of producing various deformations, or reducing the blood flow to its brain or heart with consequent damage to the precious tissues of those vital organs. Paradoxically, so-called identical or monozygotic twins are more liable to suffer from intrauterine inequalities.[6]

Several years ago, in 1989, I conducted a pre-and postnatal study of 30 pairs of twins, in which I observed their behavior in utero with ultrasounds and, besides medical parameters, recorded parental reactions to these images. I was then present at the delivery, studied the twins and their parents in the hospital, and continued to visit the families during the first three years of the twins' lives. A more or less marked preference for one twin was invariably present, although often it was totally unconscious and vehemently denied. When one twin, for instance, was bigger than the other, it was nicknamed "the truck driver," "Schwarzenegger," "voracious," "cannibal," or "the fat lady." When one moved slightly more, it was called "pain in the neck," "restless," or "bubbly."[7]

Such epithets and their attached meaning could be erased from the parents' memory at birth, but they continued to exert an influence on the lives of many twins well past the moment of birth.

Adrian and Anthony, a pair of monozygotic twins I followed during my research, began to show a marked growth discordance when Ms D, their mother, was 20 weeks pregnant. Adrian was big and Anthony was small. Adrian floated in an enormous amount of amniotic fluid, whereas Anthony could hardly move in a tiny amount of fluid. Twin-to-twin transfusion syndrome was promptly diagnosed. Ms D had to undergo several amniocenteses in order to redress the imbalance. For her, Adrian and Anthony already seemed to fit perfectly the image of the insatiable vampire and its bloodless victim, one belonging to the realm of evil darkness, the other to that of virtuous surrender. She nicknamed Adrian the "vampire" and Anthony "the victim." Ms D was impervious to any scientific explanation for the inbalance. As a follower of the radical wing of prenatal psychology, which endows fetuses with consciousness and intentionality, including a premeditated desire to cause harm, Ms D felt the condition was deliberately created by the "vampire." Luckily the twins made it to birth, but at delivery another dramatic visual element emerged. Adrian was bloated and purplish red, while Anthony was emaciated and pale. When Ms D saw the twins, she screamed at Adrian, "Look what you have done! You really are a vampire!" Although Anthony soon caught up with Adrian, the latter continued to be viewed by his mother as a predator of his saintly co-twin.

When other twins in my study suffered from similarly marked discrepancies, almost invariably the parents ascribed vicious features to one and innocent qualities to the other. Such twins were nicknamed Dr Jekyll and Mr Hyde, Dracula and the victim, or the angel and the devil. In those rare cases of twins who shared the same undivided amniotic sac, which places them at a unique risk of strangulation by each other's umbilical cord, the "strangler" too was regarded as a ruthless assassin from before its birth.

Twins, in effect, were unanimously credited with opposite and contrasting tendencies, which could ultimately be traced back to the universal division between good and bad, evil and saintly, dark and light, and black and white.

Although at birth many of these prenatal biases softened, the variety of possible reasons for continuing to "choose" one twin over the other was astounding, ranging from appearance to gender, temperament, and health.

Such favoritism can be viewed as an attempt to revert to the customary dyadic condition, which further testifies to the relative unsuitability of our species to multiple pregnancies. Interestingly, one category popular with parents were fairly dopey, lethargic twins, possibly because mothers, overwhelmed by their demands, gravitated toward the less trying twin. Fathers seemed more flexible in their preferences. When they came home after work, many just picked up the first twin to come to hand.

In the course of the study, 19 twins were found to be consistently and blatantly rejected and their co-twins were constantly favored. In the remaining 11 pairs, mild favoritism, though much less obvious, was invariably detected.

Favoritism, however, is not necessarily disastrous.

Ms E, a young woman who participated in my study, was thrilled when told that she was expecting monozygotic twin girls. She soon added "Now I will not need to have any other children." She said that she came from a large family, and added, "Large families can be very complicated. My mother was a real wizard in making us fight. One of my sisters was always her favorite, but the rest of us were up and down. One day you were in her good books and the next you were not. These two will be very similar, no issues of favoritism!" When visited at home after the birth of the twins, however, her attitude had changed a bit. She said, "Total fairness is impossible. I realize that I love them both but in different ways. Licia is cuddly and affectionate, and she appeals to my motherliness. Louise is more alert and seems to be a born explorer. She gazes at me and smiles, but does not like being cuddled much. She captures my interest, I am thrilled by her discoveries. She figures out how everything works. I can't wait to hear what she has to say. Obviously they are different individuals, who, as such, elicit different emotions. I imagine this is absolutely normal. I have ups and downs too, but my ups and downs are different from my mother's mood swings. When one is screaming or having a temper tantrum in the middle of the road, well I think I hate her. If one splatters all her food on the floor and the other pretends to clean it up, well I think I love her best. But these are fleeting sentiments. I presume all mothers have them." Needless to say the twins grew up very well, and, as their sensitive and outspoken mother had predicted, Licia continued to need physical proximity and demonstrations of affection, while Louise became very verbal and independent, albeit far from insensitive. Licia and Louise reminded me of a small research project I did abroad.

Africa is dotted with women carrying one twin in front and the other in back. Whenever possible, I never fail to ask a mother the same question: does she take turns with the twins, or is one invariably placed behind? With only a few exceptions, the answer is always: the same one is in front and the other in back. I have come to view the twin carried in back as the "shadow" of the other. The shadow is brought to the front almost solely to be breastfed, and rarely is it cleaned. When mothers are asked how they first decided which twin to carry in front and which in back, the answers vary greatly, from, "He seemed more alert, so I carried him in front" to "She was lighter and easier to carry in back" or "I chose randomly, as they were so alike." Decisions are generally made at birth. When asked for a rationale for this radical choice, mothers frequently say that the twins soon get used to their position and do not want to be changed.

Favoritism among twins was a striking feature in Mali, where I went in 1992 to work with the staff of the maternity ward in a hospital. Mali, a former French colony, is a very poor, arid sub-Saharan nation whose meager resources are derived almost solely from the waters of the River Niger, which flows across the country.

Yet Mali also attracts some tourism, from the small villages of the Dogon to the town of Timbuctu. Bamako, the capital, though chaotic and poor, has known "glamorous" times. From the late 1970s its nights, known as "*les nuits de Bamako*," were famous for attracting the best music and dance in all the continent. The inhabitants of Bamako are used to foreigners, and its women are vivacious, outspoken, and not in the least shy.

Twins are plentiful in Bamako, where they are considered "good luck," and their mothers often bring them to a big market, called "*le marchè des jumeaux*" (the twins market), where twins receive all sorts of offers ranging from food to money from strangers and passersby (see figure 5.1). On a visit to the market I decided to carry out an experiment, so I went around the place asking mothers of twins if they wanted to participate. All accepted willingly, and I gathered together a group of 18 mothers of "identical" twins, basing my judgment on the children's appearance, because performing costly DNA analysis was not possible there. The twins ranged

Figure 5.1 This proud mother walks through the twins market in Bamako, Mali, holding her young twins. Everybody pays homage to them and the crowd parts as she goes by. Possibly preparing for the parade, the mother has put on good clothing. Compared to other children in the crowd, the twins also are dressed well and the same.

in age from two to twelve months. Because women in Bamako take pride in wearing bright clothes, huge earrings, elaborate turbans, and colorful make up, we made an extravagant and colorful group when we walked together with so many twins in tow to an open space next to the market, where I could watch the spontaneous interactions between mothers and their twins.

Mothers talked, sang, looked at, and played only with the twins they carried in front. The "shadows" enjoyed minimal face-to-face social interaction but, by being in constant close contact with their mothers' body, were lulled by the maternal motions. Even their faces were pressed against their mother's body, rendering their view of the outside world problematic. After a while, I asked mothers to switch the twins around. Both children and mothers seemed disturbed by the change. The twins normally carried in front started to fret and turned their heads in all directions, as if trying to regain a wider look at the world. The twins normally carried in back withdrew from visual contact and stretched their arms toward their mother's body. In a moment all the twins were crying! Laughing, mothers quickly put the twins back in their original positions. The twins clearly had adapted to one type of contact.

Though I was curious about the fates of the twins, I could not plan to return in six years' time to see how the twins had developed cognitively and emotionally by school age. Even if I had, the same mothers might have moved abroad or elsewhere in the country. None had a permanent address. So I went around Bamako asking for six-year-old twins. People were very cooperative. Soon I was wandering the town followed like the pied piper by an increasingly large crowd of young twins. Finding their 20 mothers was more arduous, for by the age of six, children in general are left pretty much to wander alone in the streets. In the end, however, by scouring the maze of lanes in Bamako, I managed to locate all the mothers. We arranged to meet a few days later in the garden behind the hospital.

Once everyone was organized, I studied the spontaneous behavior of the twins. They fell roughly into two groups: one more outgoing, verbal, and interested in the surroundings; the other more withdrawn, disinterested, and prone to seeking self-comfort. The withdrawn twins frequently rocked themselves by swinging their bodies and huddled together indiscriminately, as if in search of some kind of animal warmth. When I asked all the twins to come near, those from the outgoing group were not hesitant about approaching me. They also showed an immediate and straightforward interest in the unusual color of my skin, which they touched, stroked, and pinched, comparing it to their own. Most of the reserved twins came timidly and reluctantly toward me. The visual element seemed less relevant to them. Mostly they just smelled my skin—two even licked it—and then withdrew. The discordant odor of my skin, not its color, was what seemed off-putting to these twins. When mothers were then asked to tell me where their twins had been carried as infants, in front or in back, the "lookers" turned out to have been carried at the front and the "smellers" at the back.

The women loved my little experiment so much that they started dancing and singing and asked me join in with them. We had great fun and danced through the night, singing, laughing and sharing jokes.

All that dancing gave me another idea for research, looking for twins in the nightlife of Bamako. By now I had plenty of guides to take me through many nightspots downtown. We managed to find several pairs of adult twins, some of whom could be classified as "dancers" and others as "singers." I wanted to find out whether the dancers were those once lulled on their mothers' backs, while the singers were those who had enjoyed verbal and social contact with their mothers. My final "experiment" was a failure, however, as only two mothers could be located and neither of them remembered who had been carried where. As one said, "I had so many children after the twins, I cannot even remember their names."

Yet another African experience involving the choice of one twin over the other occurred two years later in 1994, when I was in Kenya. A lay organization was building a school and a dispensary for the populations living on a remote northern region close to Lake Turkana and had asked me to supervise for the dispensary.[8]

Due to its striking color, Lake Turkana is also called the "Jade Sea." Extinct volcanoes and black beaches give the landscape a lunar look, a magical, otherworldly appearance. The view was stunning, but this was an illusory paradise. Lake Turkana is infested with crocodiles, its waters are salty, the land all around is desert, the heat is intolerable, and the sun unrelenting. Subsistence in the region is extremely hard.

The main ethnic group in the area lived on stock, was nomadic, and prided itself on its warriors. Other nomadic groups crossed this hostile environment, but clashes with the belligerent inhabitants of the Turkana region were so frequent that the other nomads left quickly, heading toward better destinations. Another group, smaller and nearly extinct, lived on the southern shores of the lake in a village made of straw huts and positioned on a volcanic hill gently sloping towards the bank of the Jade Sea. They were mainly fishermen and non nomadic. The only edible fish in Lake Turkana being tilapias, they ate tilapias for breakfast, lunch, and dinner.

The school and dispensary were built at some distance from the village and the lake, and all the children were boarders. I was lodged there, but was often asked to go and visit some patients belonging to the nomadic or fishermen population on a jeep accompanied by Thomas, a guide who acted as an interpreter.

At the time of my visit, Kenya was in a state of chaos. The president and his entire entourage had ransacked the country, accumulating immense wealth and leaving the rest of the population to scrape out a living. Urbanization had increased, transforming Nairobi, the capital, into a huge and dangerous shanty town. The Turkana region itself was a kind of no-man's-land, neglected by everyone.

All the children in the region would have liked to attend school, but most families chose to send only their boys. As somebody told me, "Girls have to stay at home and cook for us." When I asked as usual about twins, I was told that there were twins in the region, but nobody seemed to know of any twin at the school. One day, however, I was approached at the school by a very pretty ten-year-old girl, who smiled at me and said, "I am a twin." When I asked where her co-twin was, she replied, "I have a twin sister, but she is in the village where the fishermen live. Nobody knows about her here at the school. She doesn't look like me. My parents wanted her to stay there to look after them."

A few days later I visited the parents of the girls. The other twin, contrary to her sister, was unattractive, with big protruding teeth, a hooked nose, a sharp chin, and skinny bent legs. She was clearly deformed by rickets and severely undernourished. The girl looked at me with sad eyes and acted like a shy, battered animal. I told her parents that I was prepared to pay for her schooling. I felt that discriminating a twin by favoring her co-twin was going to be particularly harsh on her. The parents seemed perplexed, they spoke for a while in their dialect, then suddenly the mother came out with "She has no market value," the only phrase that was duly translated to me by Thomas since it summarized the crux of the matter. Now I was perplexed. The parents managed to explain to me through the interpreter that spending money on that twin would be a bad investment for me. I still did not understand why the fishermen treated their daughters as if they were on the stock exchange, but the difficulties of communication were such that I simply indicated that I did not mind paying. The parents may have thought that I was a bit dotty but accepted my offer. The "ugly twin" beamed, and two days later she was at school.

While in the region, I noticed another exceptionally beautiful young girl named Dana, who belonged to the nomadic population. Tall, lean, and graceful, with a magnificent smile, this eight-year-old was a stunner. She was also very seductive, clearly indicating that she knew how to get her way with men. So far I was only aware that the locals witnessed practically from birth scenes of seduction and intercourse. Every single man was courting her, but Dana became really attached to me. She followed me around, hugged me often, and in the evenings she came to see me in the dispensary, where we shared the usual fish, a tilapia. As I always have ballpoints and notebooks with me, I decided to teach her the letters of the alphabet. She was delighted and quick to learn. Soon we were on to numbers. Her dream was to go to school, and I decided to sponsor her education as well. When her parents were summoned by Thomas I made my offer. They looked grave and started a lengthy, incomprehensible discussion. Finally Thomas told me what the problem was, explaining, "Her market value is too high." The parents would not allow the girl to receive an education because they did not want to lose a fortune. As Thomas went on, "When she marries, she will be paid a lot of cattle and camels, too." Yet the parents had a proposition to make. Dana had a twin brother, Mulji, who could be sent to school instead of her, because he had no "market value" anyway. I had been unaware of the existence of the twin, but countered that I was only willing to pay if the girl could go to school along with her twin brother. The parents stood up and went out. Dana was in tears. But on the following day the parents changed their mind and accepted my offer. A few days later I took the twins to school in a jeep. Dana was thrilled. A month after returning from Kenya I received a letter from the teacher, with whom I had left the money to pay for the twins' education. She told me that the parents had taken Dana out of school, as she was too valuable. Mulji had stayed on.

Pretty girls were highly valued by the nomadic group, because as soon as they reached puberty, they were exchanged for cattle and married off to some elder. Only old men, who had time to acquire property, could afford to buy and keep wives. But young men have robust sexual appetites. In order to satisfy them without their having to pay for a wife or run the danger of an unwanted out-of-wedlock pregnancy, each young warrior was given a prepubescent girl "to play with." This was particularly tragic for the so-called "Lolitas of Turkana," who were renowned all over Kenya for their beauty. These young girls generally became deeply attached to their warrior boyfriends. Being exposed to sex or sexual foreplay, even when very young, was possibly the strongest, if not the only, form of attention and affection they would ever receive. Puberty and marriage broke this special bond with their boyfriends, as well as any tenuous links with their own families. From then on they belonged to the clan of their old husbands and shared their lives with relatives by marriage, often including especially nasty elder wives.

Unfortunately, there was nothing I could do about Dana from abroad, since I had been told she had moved somewhere else.

By now Dana is certainly married to an old man, lives in an extended "family," and has several children. She has probably lost all her beauty and has no future ahead of her. Often I feel guilty about her, wondering if it would not have been better to leave her alone. A glimpse of a better life can open up expectations that are best left untouched, as they can cause too much pain. My most tormenting remorse, however, is the way I was blinded by my cultural biases. I should have acted in a politically incorrect way and bought the girl. That would have enabled me to place her in the custody of a trustworthy institution. Only through this kind of monetary transaction could I have given her the real chance for freedom she deserved. Yet I was deaf to what her parents clearly had been asking all along.

Favoritism can take on other radical forms in extremely harsh environments and cultures, as I found in 2004 when I spent two months in the Amazonian region of Venezuela, visiting the indigenous groups spread along small tributaries of the River Orinoco. Carlos, a colleague and a general practitioner expert in tropical medicine, and I had been commissioned by a group of missionaries to carry out a survey on the health conditions of the tribes and to create a health program for them. The area we were to visit was remote. Access to the region was possible only by small planes that were literally falling apart, with cracks in the ceiling and windows, and the doors locked with a piece of string. After two hair-raising flights to reach the only "town" in the area, a mass of collapsing barracks, we had to travel by a small, rusty, slow motorboat. Needless to say, there were no hotels or guest houses. We had to sleep in hammocks, trying to fend off swarms of tiny ferocious mosquitoes nicknamed "meat eaters" or "men eaters." The river was nevertheless outstandingly beautiful, surrounded by impenetrable forests and small *tapunos*, dark volcanic rocks shaped like extinct volcanoes, which gave the landscape a dawn-of-creation quality.

The *Indios* living in the area had contact with civilization mainly through missionaries, anthropologists, and unscrupulous traders trying to rob them of their land and its riches, ranging from minerals to precious wood. Their special knowledge of medicinal herbs also attracted several pharmaceutical groups, aiming to gather information and plants for free, eventually even pushing them out of their territory.

Contact with outsiders had often been far from beneficial. Among other things, measles and flu had decimated the population. The *Indios,* having once been hunter-gatherers inhabiting the forest and living off its many resources, had in recent times largely abandoned the forest, from were they were being driven out, and built their dwellings along the banks of the river, where they lived mainly off fishing. Though they battled to continue their traditions, a lot of customs were changing, especially among the young who wore T-shits, short trousers, and skirts, and often tried to leave their villages to reach one of the missions in the area.

After 20 days we reached the most remote village along one of the tributaries of the river, where the *Indios* were living in isolation and had become particularly wary of foreigners. Our guide, an *Indios* nicknamed Che, who had left his village with his family to migrate to "town," was acquainted with the villagers and knew how to get us accepted by the population. He had brought along lots of gifts on our shaky little boat, especially red cloth and plenty of red yarn. The *Indios* had a strong penchant for red, which no anthropologist had been able to convincingly explain. The men went naked except for a piece of yarn that they fastened round their waist, across their buttocks, and on the tip of their penis. Women often went naked, too, but some wore grass skirts.

Upon arrival we first paid homage to the shaman, who was in charge of the village. The word shaman derives from "saman," which in the Tunguse and Mandchou dialects spoken by various ethnic groups inhabiting Siberia and Northeastern Asia means "an excited, troubled person taken over by the spirits," but also "he or she who knows." Shamanistic practices originated in those regions in the Neolithic period, and have since spread to vast areas all over the world.[9]

Shamanism, like animism, is based on a belief that the visible world is permeated by invisible forces and spirits. Otherwise it is difficult to define, as it can take on many variations according to the geographical and cultural characteristics of the different populations where it is practiced. In general, Shamanism is not a proper religion, but is rather a set of traditional beliefs and practices that require special knowledge, training, and skills. It can be practiced only by those who have shown multifarious signs of being "elected," by receiving the calling announced by various "supernatural" signs, such as visions, peculiar dreams, physical symptoms including epileptic fits, which in the developed world would be thought of as belonging to the realm of neurology and psychiatry. Once the calling has manifested itself in an individual, he cannot reject it and must overcome hard initiatory practices, such as fasting, meditating, abstaining temporarily from intercourse, enforced isolation, and "learning to dream" with the tuition of an older shaman. This long training sets the shaman apart from ordinary individuals and gives him his special authority.

Shamans are ascribed the ability to diagnose and cure human afflictions by entering into direct contact with or gaining control over the spirits. But their powers go beyond simple healing practices to an ability to forecast the future, control the weather, interpret dreams, and travel to different realms, generally with the aid of hallucinogenic drugs. By virtue of these faculties, Shamans perform multiple roles within their societies. By acting as intermediaries between men and spirits, they have spiritual powers. Due to their healing capacities, they have the lay function of medicine men. Shamans also have sociopolitical powers, acting as chiefs of communities and performing a fundamental role within their societies. Women, too, can be shamans, but this was not so with the *Indios* we were visiting.

The shaman who met us was a lean, muscular, middle-aged man, with beautiful but distant eyes. His nose was transfixed by a long stick, and he wore only a red loin cloth. He had a complicated name, which I could not pronounce properly, because it required deep, guttural inhalations, so from then on I just called him "Shaman." After we gave him our gifts, he did not thank us, and continued to observe us silently. As it was already dark and a torrential rain was falling, the *Indios* retreated inside their crowded, circular dwelling, made of various fibers from the forest. Despite the downpour, we set up our hammocks in the open air. Shaman seemed impressed.

Over the following days we took a sanitary census of the population. We sat in the middle of the open space surrounded by the circular dwelling and I examined the women and children, while Carlos examined the men. Sanitary conditions were appalling, ranging from infections, to tuberculosis and goiter. Most ailments could easily have been cured, and we made a list of necessary medications and various tools. While I tended to the women, most of them very young and very pregnant, over the next days, Shaman would come and sit nearby. Although the women were diffident at first, soon they became quite friendly. Shaman continued to observe silently. On the sixth day, however, he let out a guttural, "Sandra," and began to explain his own ailments in a mixture of Spanish and sign language. I tended to him with some Paracetamol to cure his splitting headache, a pomade to relive his conjunctivitis, and another ointment to lessen his urge to scratch the bites of the innumerable insects. He seemed satisfied. From then on he became friendly, talkative, and each day asked for more treatment.

One day Shaman told us that the *Indios* were gathering from all the neighboring villages in order to participate in a celebration that night. At the time I was examining a pregnant young girl called Helena, and I realized that she was expecting twins. When I said *"Morochos,"* the name for twins, the girl looked frightened and Shaman disgusted. I asked him, "You don't like twins, do you?" He shook his head and growled out a strong, "No." The *Indios*, had a reputation for disposing of one twin, the last born, at birth.

By the time it was almost dark, an enormous crowd had gathered inside the circular enclosure. Everyone started sniffing hallucinogenic drugs. At first everybody danced, but soon they all began falling to the ground and looked completely spaced out. I was concerned about Helena, who, although seemed close to delivery, had earlier refused an internal examination. In the middle of the dancing, her waters broke. I called Shaman and asked him to let me have a private space inside the dwelling. He let me enter and, still inhaling drugs, stood next to me. The delivery was straightforward. Both twins were cephalic and were born only minutes apart, and they were males. Helena had not let out a single cry, although her expression revealed severe pain. When the second twin came out, I dreaded witnessing something horrible, his disposal. Shaman only mumbled, then took the twin and gave it to me, saying, "You can have him. A gift for you." I called Carlos for help and we set up a plan to bring the twin with us to the nearest mission. Luckily we had some powdered milk and a few bottles and baby wipes. The twin was lovely, with big black eyes and a gentle nature. His dark eyes reminded me of my eldest son, so I gave him the Spanish equivalent of his name, Felipe. I carried Felipe around with me all day, just like the local women, wrapped up with a piece of cloth fastened around my neck and hanging slightly below my breasts. During the night, Felipe slept with me in the hammock. Nobody else, save Carlos, wanted to look after him. His mother Helena cared tenderly for his identical twin brother but completely ignored him. For her he was dead. Helena was well capable of maternal love, but her love did not include two infants. Those were the rules of her group and she gave in to them without any remorse.

In the meantime, Shaman had grown increasingly fond of me. He often called me by my name and followed me around wherever I went. Once he even followed me to the "toilet." I had gone into the forest and was pulling up my panties when I noticed Shaman squatting nearby. I screamed. Shaman merely smiled and went back to the village, letting me finish zipping up my trousers alone. He never did it again. His glance had been inquisitive, not lecherous, showing only he wanted to find out whether white female witch doctors functioned like ordinary women. Having found out, his curiosity was satisfied.

That evening Shaman asked me for some more pills for what was apparently another splitting headache. I told him he was inhaling too many drugs. He nodded but then shrugged with a smile, indicating he was not going to change his habits.

Two weeks later when we were about to leave, to everyone's surprise Shaman jumped on board the boat, making it clear that he wanted to come with us. All he said was, "Sandra, Ok?" And when I agreed, he smiled. Helena had come with the other women to see us off, and they all waved at me, but she never once glanced at Felipe.

On the trip back to the mission the nights were particularly difficult. I was sleeping with Felipe, doing my best to take care of him, but Shaman always set up his hammock next to mine and periodically throughout the night woke up and began to sing an incomprehensible litany of his dreams. Sigmund Freud considered dreams to be the "royal road to the unconscious,"[10] and many of us have come to regard dreams as an important tool to reach into and understand our own unconscious thoughts. Contrary to us, Shaman thought of dreams as the "royal road" to another world, that of his spirits and demons as well as of the future. Sharing his incomprehensible dreams with me was an act of great trust. I just could not say, "Shaman, please shut up!"

When we all finally reached the mission, I told its head I had a twin with me. They took Felipe in, while seeming surprised that he had been allowed to live. Felipe was going to have a very different life from his twin brother who had remained in the village. He was going to have an education, learn a job and another language, and as the head of the mission said, "May be one day he will become a doctor too." Parting with him was sad, as I had grown fond of him, but I also felt relieved that he was now in good hands.

Parting from Shaman was difficult too. When we reached the airstrip, which was near the mission, he wanted to come to Europe with me, and saying no to him was heartbreaking. Shaman would not give up. Being an intelligent man, he finally came out with, "*Jo, morocho!*" ("I am a twin!"). That claim just had to convince me to allow him to board the rickety old plane back to Caracas, the capital, just as I had taken Felipe on board the boat. I smiled at his lie and said, "Not true, Shaman, you don't like *morochos.*" I gave him a pair of red shoes and a red shirt that he had been eying all along, but I still miss both Shaman and Felipe.

Chapter 6

Forced Adoption and the Sex Trade

Until the 1970s, twins were often adopted separately by different families, making many scientists happy and keeping them busy indeed. Behavioral geneticists are always on the lookout for monozygotic twins reared apart. These twins, who share the same genes but have been brought up in different environments, are considered a precious tool for teasing out genetic and environmental components. Currently, however, twins are invariably assigned for adoption together, in recognition that they are linked by a special bond and give each other needed mutual support. Their psychological well-being predominates over less cogent scientific matters.

Adoption, as defined by the Oxford Dictionary, means "to take somebody else's child into one's family and become its legal parents." In the developed world the adoptees generally come from poorer nations or from marginalized and desperate strata of the native population. Children born to unwed, low-class, teenage mothers, who waited too long to have an abortion, are typical candidates for autochthonous adoption. When these children are twins, the chances that they will be given away for adoption more than double. In low-income countries, where formal adoption with its legal implications is rarely practiced, more elusive, less official, and sometimes even less permanent ways of handling one or both twins are widespread. Even in Europe, however, matters of adoption can sometimes take on dubious tones.

For quite a while, I dealt with one of the many immigrant groups in my country, considered to be utter outcasts and totally marginalized. Nigerian prostitutes are plentiful all over Europe, where a kind of abominable new slave trade has opened up. Only a few years ago Nigerian prostitutes were mature, often married, women, who chose voluntarily to enter the trafficking in order to help their families back home and to afford education for their children. Currently the age of the girls involved in the trafficking is getting younger and younger; some of them have barely reached puberty.[1] These unfortunate young women are recruited in their villages by an intermediary, usually a mature woman, with the promise of a better future and work, especially in the textiles trade. Most families know that this is just a cover up but sell their daughters anyway as they need the money. In order to deter the girls from coming back home, rebelling, or reporting the trade and its players to the authorities, they are usually subjected beforehand to Voodoo rituals with the idea of terrifying them. Generally the performer obtains bodily stuff from the victim, such as hair, nails, and organic fluids, such as underwear stained with menstrual blood, and threatens to carry out black magic on them causing, via transfer, the death of the victim or of members of her family. Voodoo is powerful in the area and rarely unsuccessful. Very few would dare challenge its rituals especially when "black magic" is involved. If Voodoo fails there are always more conventional means of preventing the girls from trying to change their fate, such as beating them up brutally and disfiguring them.

After completing the transaction and the rituals, the recruiter pays for an airline ticket. Once the girls reach the destination, they are handed over to an older woman, a so-called "*Madame*," also a Nigerian. A few days later they are forced to hit the streets. Needless to say, their lives are a nightmare. Catapulted into a foreign country, shocked by the cultural transition, unable to speak the language, isolated and disoriented, the girls have to satisfy their clients by "working" without respite. Their dreams are shattered, and so is their trust in their families. They face the additional dangers of AIDS, inasmuch as many clients consider them too cheap and shoddy to wear condoms.

Many of these poor Nigerian girls turned up pregnant at the twins' unit of my hospital. Nigeria's main ethnic group is particularly famous, among those interested in the biology of twinning, for having the highest twinning rate in the whole world. Approximately one in every 11 natives is a twin.[2] Theoretically these should be mostly dizygotic twins, the rate of monozygotic twins or one for 250 live births, is thought to be the same worldwide. Yet, this is not what I have seen. Over the course of two years, 30 Nigerian prostitutes delivered twins at my hospital, of whom 11 pairs were monozygotic. Because monozygotic twins are frequent in other parts of Africa and of the world, such as Papua, a more accurate assessment is needed to better understand what lies at the basis of this type of twinning.

Following my initial contact with them, during which I monitored their pregnancies, I got in touch with a lay association involved in rescuing them from the streets, as well as protecting them from their exploiters and offering them the chance of a less debasing job. I worked twice a week for two years with the association giving psychological and psychiatric support to the girls who were already living there and also to those who were still out in the streets and needed help to leave the streets.

A tall, pretty girl, whom I shall call Lurleen, was in her late teens and expecting twins when I met her at the hospital. Contrary to many of her "colleagues," who soon learned the hard way what was expected of them, such as acting vulgar or obscene and getting fat or even obese to better suit their clients' needs, Lurleen had remained sweet, dignified, and slim. I followed her pregnancy closely, and she became very fond of me, showing her affection in shy glances, warm smiles, and whispered "thank yous" while gently hugging me each time she left. I was present at the delivery of her gorgeous twin boys. Lurleen held my hand all the time and never let out a moan or a cry, but at the same time she looked terribly distressed and from time to time wept silently. When she first saw her boys, she smiled, and for a moment I caught a glimpse of happiness in her lovely face. But when I was about to leave, she looked at me in despair and said in a whisper, "Please come and see me. Will you? Please come soon," then added urgently "Will you bring your camera with you? I want a picture of the boys." The rumor had spread that I was engaged in research that included filming and photographing of twins. I put her requests down to her desire to stay in touch with me and to have a souvenir of the twins.

By that time, a powerful religious association had taken over from the lay organization and was now in charge of the protection and "salvation" of Nigerian prostitutes and I no longer worked with them, as Lurleen knew, but I promised to visit her in the shelter run by the new group. The religious association required a declaration of faith from its operators, which I could not give, but principally I did not share its punitive attitude toward the girls, who were offered no other future than a cloistered life.

When I phoned Lurleen at the shelter, someone very suspicious and rude answered the phone. However, I managed to get through to Lurleen, and we made an appointment. When I went to see her, a mistrustful social worker opened the door. At first she wanted literally to push me out. I told her that I was doing a follow-up on the twins who had recently been born at the clinic and asked her to contact the hospital if she wanted to check my credentials. Reluctantly she let me in. In order to further dispel her suspicions, I acted professionally by carrying out a lengthy medical check on both Lurleen and the twins. When finally the social worker lost interest in us and left the room to join some other young women who were also living in the home, Lurleen immediately begged me, "Please take some pictures of me with the twins." I quickly took out my camera and did so. Tearful, she whispered, "I have no choice or any other alternative. I am forced by them. In a few days my boys will be given out for adoption. The photos will be all that is left of them."

She could not stop crying. She was devastated. A jobless ex-prostitute was considered unworthy for motherhood. Her tragedy was further accentuated by the fact that maternity is everything for most African women—and not only for them. Marriage is often the other essential status, but maternity ranks higher. A childless marriage is considered to be valueless and a curse. Most societies value women especially for their maternal role, and childless women have hardly any status. Mothers of twins are doubly valued and enjoy special status in Nigeria, just as they do in the neighboring countries of Togo and Benin. Thus, for Lurleen to have her boys taken away not only was heartbreaking in itself but also meant losing whatever value and identity she had. My photos were both a precious souvenir and a proof of her worth.

The whole episode left me shaken. I made inquiries at the association, asking whether forced adoption was the rule for Nigerian prostitutes having twins. I knew that Nigerian prostitutes were often prevented from keeping their children by their *"Madames,"* as children would interfere with their profession. However, I had some faith that this would not happen once the prostitutes had been taken in by a religious organization. It turned out that those with only one child stood a chance of keeping it, because African children are possibly the least sought after by prospective adoptive parents, most of whom are white. A mixture of reasons underlie this preference. Many parents want to adopt children who may look like their natural children. Many others worry about marginalization and exploitation, especially at adolescence. An undeclared fear of "otherness" can play its part. But not so with twins, who are considered by everyone to be a kind of trophy, irrespective of their racial origin. Twins being so much in demand, Nigerian prostitutes who delivered twins were forced to give them up. Lurleen paid for our collective fascination with twins. After that day, despite repeated attempts to contact her, I was denied access to her and never saw Lurleen again.

A mixture of superstition, monetary considerations, and acquisition of a status symbol lay at the basis of the adoption of other twins from another marginalized group with whom I dealt in my country, the gypsies, or more properly the Rom. I worked for four years visiting three gypsy settlements in Milan on a weekly basis, focusing principally on medical problems related to women and children. The check-ups took place in the shacks and caravans where the gypsies lived.

Gypsies is a general term covering various subgroups, which have different names and can differ profoundly despite having remarkable similarities. The origins of gypsies have been debated at length. They themselves fostered some legends, wanting to create a halo of mystery around their own roots. The term gypsies, shortened from egypsies, means "from Egypt," and for quite a while that was thought to be their land of origin. Careful linguistic analyses have since proved that the gypsies originally came from northwestern India, where they belonged to the cast of the *pariah,* the outcasts. For unknown reasons, around the turn of the first millennium they left India, crossed Iran, Armenia, and Caucasus, and from there spread throughout Europe. More recently they also spread to the Americas and to Africa. The first written records about them date back to the fourteenth century.[3]

Gypsies were always nomadic, moving in small groups. Their nomadism was "parasitic" in the sense that they did not live off permanent, fixed resources of their own but off various activities such as predicting the future, mendacity, metal forging, small commerce, and horse trading. Generally speaking, they solicited their clients, not the other way round. These characteristics explain their need to spread in small groups, as the hosting populations easily reached "saturation." Their spreading in small groups along many different routes also explains the differences to be found among them. Additionally these "children of the wind," as they are sometimes called for their sudden comings and goings, created an aura of strangeness, which together with their "parasitism" irritated and troubled the local populations. Due to these factors, gypsies have always been persecuted and marginalized. Possibly more than any other group, they have been considered over the centuries "the other" and "different." Along with Jews, the gypsies were the main target of Nazi "ethnic cleansing," and it is estimated that between 500000 and 1500000 of them were exterminated during the Holocaust, although, given their marginalized situation, accurate figures are hard to find.[4] To this day their presence frequently elicits extremely harsh reactions in the population of any country in which they reside.

The sites the gypsies are granted often reveal this general hostility. In Milan their two main settlements were located next to a huge municipal waste dump and opposite the biggest cemetery in town, although gypsies are notoriously afraid of the dead, whom they consider to be malevolent entities. Other people often threw their garbage onto the gypsy sites, set them on fire, and threatened them in all sorts of ways. When I visited them, I also became an object of hostility. Cars regularly tried to run me over when I crossed the street to enter the gypsy compounds.

On the other hand, gypsies do not mix easily with the rest of society and often refuse to live by its rules. Their settlements were fairly impervious, and they regarded "others," the so-called *gadjé*, as silly and dumb. Not just approaching them but above all gaining their trust took plenty of patient work. When I began working with them, I was put to the test. All my medicines were inspected carefully, to make sure I was not bringing in poisonous substances. People ignored me and made me feel like an outcast. Women openly teased me for being a dumb *gadjé*, and called me a whore. Men tried to seduce me. Gypsies go crazy for *gadjé* women, whom they consider as having no moral standing, and take pride in having affairs with them. In addition, everyone wanted to make sure I would not call in outside forces, especially the police, who might put them in jail, and social workers, who often tried to take their children away and give them out for adoption or temporary care.

Gradually I was able to gain their trust, and in the end the queue of my patients was very long. I was also invited to weddings, baptisms, funerals, dances, and feasts. Although I no longer visit the gypsies regularly, [since their camps are now under the aegis of the same powerful association that has taken over Nigerian prostitutes], all my gypsy friends ring me up frequently to find out how I am. Whenever I see them in the street, they call me over and hug me, saying, "Anything you need, Doc, we are always here for you. Just let us know." Needless to say, I have grown fond of them.

Initially, however, our contact was far from easy. One of my early mistakes was to ask about twins. The immediate answer was, "You should not ask about them. We all remember Dr Mengele, and we shiver when a *gadjé* asks about twins." The infamous Dr Mengele, nicknamed "The Angel of Death," "working" in the Mathausen concentration camp, was enthralled by twins. He put them aside in special barracks and treated them with apparent affection and care.[5] This did not prevent him from performing the most horrific "experiments" on them, such as injecting chemicals into their eyes in the attempt to change their color, stitching twins together, castrating and sterilizing them, and removing their limbs and organs without using any anesthetic. Gypsy twins were particularly "dear" to him, as he loved their extraordinary sense of music and dance. Almost every night they were made to play music for him. One gypsy twin boy was his favorite. Dr Mengele was extremely fatherly and tender toward him, until one day, smiling and holding his hand, he accompanied the boy to the gas chamber, even blowing him a kiss before waving good-bye. A few days later their music was heard no more. Utter silence at night told the other "guests" at the camp that all the remaining gypsy twins had been exterminated.

Clearly, by asking about twins, I had been untactful to say the least. It took a long while before the gypsies could broach the subject themselves. First I was shown some opposite-sex pairs, then I was introduced to some same-sex but clearly different twins. For a long time there seemed to be no monozygotic twins at all, until finally one day I was invited to a communal baptism.

The gypsies I worked with were non-Muslim in origin and officially devout Catholics, but in fact they preserved strong animistic roots. The numerous saints of the Catholic pantheon were revered as pagan deities, to be prayed to in order to obtain special favors or to be placated in order to keep any evil at bay. Animistic roots could be detected in many other habits. Until recently, for instance, gypsies delivered their children in special barracks, which they then burnt in order to drive out all the dangerous impurities linked with childbirth. Nowadays gypsies go to hospitals to deliver. But they do not use health facilities merely for reasons of safety. By delivering in a public facility, they no longer need to provide the barrack or the burning. Cunningly, in their view, all impurities, malevolent forces, and evil consequences are left behind in the hospital with the community of the *gadjé*.

On the day of the collective baptism many gypsies gathered from all over Italy, for celebrations such as marriages, baptisms, and funerals are very important for the gypsies. During these gatherings family ties, business dealings, including dubious ones, and identification with the community are all reinforced. Coming together also makes a good excuse for traveling, thereby allowing the gypsies to reconnect with their nomadic roots, if only symbolically and temporarily. Furthermore, these are moments of explosive, collective, "pagan" joy, in which the religious meaning of the ceremony is utterly secondary.

Before the baptism the gypsies organized a feast with heaps of food and drinks, accompanied by dances and songs, which went on for hours. Then they all went off to church tipsy, in flamboyant clothes and flashy cars. This time I spotted three pairs of monozygotic twin infants, all dressed ornately and literally covered in gold. Unlike silver, gold is believed to bring good luck. Gold also signals affluence. The twins were shown to me with enormous pride by their "parents," who were also covered in gold, displaying their wealth. During the entire banquet the twins were paraded around like trophies, applauded by everyone and repeatedly toasted.

Gypsies believe that when identical twins are born their parents may die. According to their superstitious beliefs, two individuals sharing the same sex and appearance emerging from cohabitation in the same womb are thought to be the antithesis of marriage and a threat to it, as parents cannot be identical in gender, birth, and appearance. In order to avoid parental death, identical twins are given out for temporary adoption among other gypsies. A wealthy family buys the twins and keeps them for one year, then returns them to the parents when the danger is considered to be past. Generally, however, the adoption becomes permanent. The parents receive a big sum of money and are happy to leave the twins with the rich "adoptive family." On the other hand, gypsies like showing off, and those who are wealthy like to flaunt their affluence. Buying monozygotic twins is a sign of wealth, as these twins are highly costly.

At the communal baptism, I could not detect who the real parents of these twins were. They were surely there, but the twins were treated like family "jewels" by being shown off by the adoptive parents. All applauded and toasted to them, but nobody gave any indication that they were the natural parents. By now their mothers were indifferent to them, having had neither the time nor the will to form a tie of love with children who were feared of being capable of causing their death.

The festivities went on for three days and nights, but I left on the first day when the religious celebration started, and never saw the twins again. When I went back later for a regular visit to the settlement and asked who the parents were, everyone was tight lipped.

Acquiring twins through monetary transactions as a status symbol is also found in other parts of the world. In both India and Sri Lanka the rich sometimes love to flaunt twins. Since twins are twice as expensive to raise, the poor often cannot afford to keep them, so they are given away for "adoption," in exchange for money. Apparently no superstitious beliefs guide this purely financial decision.

A man, whom I shall call Mr Rabayan, a rich trader belonging to the Indian community in Milan, was married to a much younger wife. Despite repeated attempts to conceive, no children came. The couple became a constant feature at the fertility clinic. Mr Rabayan just refused to give up, and Ms Rabayan complied, as she dreaded the prospect of rejection and divorce. Infertility per se could not be officially used in a divorce claim, but judges were in fact prone to grant separation on the basis of bad marital conduct. During one of the numerous attempts at in vitro fertilization, Mr Rabayan met another Indian woman, whom I shall call Merkanti, who was pregnant, clearly not wealthy, and expecting twins. Mr Rabayan stopped her in the corridor, spoke to her in their dialect, and they exchanged cell phone numbers. From then on Mr Rabayan began to appear during Merkanti's checks in the twin unit acting as an interpreter and feigning a humanitarian interest in his fellow-country woman. Merkanti's major worries were not of a purely economic nature. She had come to Italy alone, leaving her husband and two children behind, because women often find work there more easily than men. They are employed in looking after the elderly, cleaning, and minding children. During her stay in Milan Merkanti began an adulterous affair with a Sri Lankan man, with whom she was clearly in love. We met her lover only once, because as soon as we broke the news that Merkanti was expecting twins, he vanished. The poor woman was heartbroken and terrified. Not only had she lost the love of her life, but she also dreaded the prospect of divorce back home on the ground of unfaithfulness.

Mr Rabayan immediately understood the situation and took advantage of it. He struck a deal. The twins would be his. Mr Rabayan, however, did not want to run the risk of applying for formal adoption in Italy, where nobody could guarantee that the twins would be handed over to his family. Thus he arranged for Merkanti to deliver in another country outside Europe, and to make sure that everything went smoothly, he and his wife went with her.

A few months later I was invited to a huge birthday party. The twins were dressed like little princes. Decorations were lavish, the menu exquisite, the cake as big as Buddha's temple and similar to it in shape. Plenty of Sri Lankan servants tended to the guests, and all were given expensive golden gifts as a souvenir of the event. Having twins was a sure status symbol. Ms Rabayan occasionally sends me pictures of the boys all dressed up in the latest fashions. However, I have never heard from poor Merkanti again.

Other forms of "adoption" without any monetary transition take place in different parts of the world.

When I was in the Turkana region of Northern Kenya, I was told of a young woman who had recently delivered monozygotic twin boys, and I went to see her. The woman was in her day hut, which gave her some privacy and sheltered her from the midday sun. She was incredibly beautiful, and so were her twin boys, but she also seemed to be terribly unhappy. She showed me her twins and then continued stroking them gently, completely absorbed in her own thoughts. I asked Thomas, my guide, why she looked so sad. He explained, "The twins are two weeks old. In six more weeks she will have to give one to an elderly woman, who is generally her husband's or someone else's first wife." The locals attached only a market value to girls, while boys were valued in a noneconomic way for their capacity to work. Twin boys, however, were deemed to be too much of a burden, so one was regularly handed over gratis to another woman.

This contingency did not fully explain the mother's extreme sadness, so I continued, "But she will see the boy all the time. Someone else in the same compound will take care of him and give her a hand. I suppose nothing much will change."

My interpreter seemed a bit reluctant to explore the subject but finally added, "You see, an elderly woman generally has no milk. It is of course

Figure 6.1 This beautiful woman from the Lake Turkana region of Kenya is sheltering from the heat and the sun in a special day-hut. She tenderly hugs the newborn twin girls she will be allowed to keep.

difficult to breastfeed two infants, but at least the mother has some hope. An elderly woman is just a death sentence. Plus these people are very mobile. The mother may be sold to another compound and never see that twin again." All the cruelty of this custom showed in the woman's sad face. After being with the twins for two weeks and breastfeeding them, she had grown attached to both. Now one was probably doomed, and in any event she would probably never come across him again. The Turkana region is huge, and its nomadic population moves from place to place all the time looking for pasture. Quite often the paths of nomads cross only once in a lifetime. Those were the pitiless rules of the clan, and the young mother could not oppose them. The penalty for trying to do so would be abandonment of her and her remaining twin without any possibility of survival in a harsh desert land. See figure 6.1.

Nomadic tribal groups are now the exception rather than the rule in most developing countries. The rest of the population either still lives in villages or increasingly migrates to the towns. When Hillary Clinton referred in a speech at the Democratic Convention on August 27, 1996, to the Nigerian proverb, "It takes a village to raise a child,"[6] she was not talking about the African village as such, but about the whole American nation, which had to act in ways that valued family values and thereby help all families to cope with the task of raising the nation's future, its children. She had in mind practical issues, like prohibiting the practice of forcing mothers and babies to leave the hospital in less than 48 hours and providing affordable health insurance, flexitime policies at work, and tax credits for adoptive parents. The African village seemed only like an apt metaphor for an oasis of friendliness, where everybody is ready and willing to give a hand.

Yet this is an idealized view of the culture of the village. Most children in villages in low-income countries both in and outside Africa are not looked after lovingly by the entire community of adults. Villagers are generally too busy fighting for survival. Women are perennially pregnant or else breastfeeding, which is often their only form of contraception. It would be impossible for them to look after their numerous progeny while also scraping out a living wherever they can. Mothers care only for those infants they are breastfeeding. As soon as the infants are weaned, they are dropped. Slightly older children take care of younger ones. Children are simply abandoned to themselves.[7]

In actual fact, villages worldwide are far from idyllic havens, and their "culture" is frequently one of oppression, rivalry, envy, nastiness, and more.

By and large the elders rule over the community. More often than not, elders are far from wise or interested in promoting the happiness and well-being of future generations. When it comes to the bleak destiny of many twins, chiefs and older women are frequently the main decision makers as well as the perpetrators of the crime. The village, however, offers some sense of security and belonging. Children know the place and all the people around. The environment of the village is a familiar one. Should they remain orphaned, at least this familiarity will continue. Children wandering around with no sense of belonging and completely abandoned in the streets were seldom mentioned in Africa a few years ago. Now they are increasingly apparent. Massive urbanization and the plague of AIDS have stripped them of even the flimsy shelter of the village.

I like taking pictures of twins and by now have hundreds of them. The pictures can be revealing. I once decided to count how many twins were being looked after by adults in villages worldwide. While breastfed, twins were usually held by their mothers or by their mothers and another adult woman. As soon as breastfeeding was over, however, twins were looked after by slightly older children in 78 percent of the pictures. No adults were around.

Parents who cannot cope with the expense and fatigue involved in the upbringing of their twins can take another grim route. The twins can be sold to a third party in the pedophilia trade, or the parents themselves may set up the lucrative business.[8] Although it is not just twins who enter this abominable trade, twins are often sent in this direction, both because they are especially burdensome and because "hot duos" (male and female) are in great demand.

I was once passing through Bangkok airport on my way to another far eastern destination, the so-called Golden Triangle on the border between Laos and Myanmar. Since I had to spend a few hours waiting to catch my next plane, I began walking about and looking at various goods in the duty-free shops. One window attracted my curiosity: it was full of teddy bears. I remember thinking, "How funny, teddy bears in this heat," but then I thought about the famous psychoanalyst Donald Winnicott's description of the so-called "transitional object"[9] and concluded that children were the same at all latitudes. The transitional object is something that has a special value for the suckling or young child, especially when the child is on the point of falling asleep. We can all picture Charlie Brown sucking his thumb and holding his precious blanket against his face. Besides a blanket or a napkin that is sucked, teddy bears are habitually thought of as transitional objects.

My thinking was probably clouded by jet lag, for a few minutes later I noticed a crowd of fat, middle-aged, European men all holding teddy bears and I thought, "Really strange." Then it suddenly occurred to me that these were not presents for their children back home but a cheap way of buying the favors of the local children. Out of some 40 men, I noticed 15 holding either two or four identical teddy bears, wearing the same costume, hat, and shoes. I approached a man with a big belly who seemed particularly talkative as well as clearly tipsy on beer, as he was holding an empty beer can, I asked, "Why four identical teddy bears?"

He belched and laughed, "Twins! Two for one!" I walked away.

Two months later after coming back from the Golden Triangle, I went to visit a beautiful Khmer temple in Cambodia. The usual small market lay at the foot of the temple. Among flowers and candles I noticed a large photo displaying two sets of twin girls and asked the woman running the stall if these were her children. She said, "Yes, I have four girls. Twins twice. The younger are eight and the older ten. Do you like twins?" When I said yes and started explaining my interest, the woman interrupted me. "No problem, *maam*, you can take the picture, so you will recognize them. I will write down their address in Phnom Pen. They work there. It's a nice place, clean, and cheap. A good bargain. Tell the lady there it's me who sent you." Twins were for sale right there outside the temple, and I could have had four. Never before had I been taken for a lesbian pedophiliac when asking about twins. Whenever I look today at the picture of those poor twin girls, dressed in pink frills and heavily made up, I wonder about their fate and their awful experience. Sold by their own mother, uprooted from their village, brought to a brothel in town, and probably dead from AIDS or some other sexually transmitted disease.

A few years later when coming back again from the golden triangle, I decided to spend a few days in a beautiful, un-touristy seaside resort near the Thai border. After a demanding period of work, I felt the need to relax. During my stay in the golden triangle I had not met any twins, but here twins were plentiful. In talking to one family, I asked if having twins was hard for them. The father answered with a smile, "We are lucky. Our girls are pretty. Plenty of money for all." A few minutes later the seven-year-old twin girls walked away with an elderly local man. I asked, "Is he their grandfather?" Both parents laughed, "If you want to call him that. No, their grandfathers are dead."

The horrible trade was not just for foreigners, as locals also patronized this brisk market.

In a unique document, Chou Ta-Kuan, the successor of Kublai Khan, writing about the customs of thirteenth and fourteenth-century Cambodia, wrote, "Daughters of rich parents, from seven to nine years of age (or eleven, in the case of poor people), are handed over to a Buddhist or Taoist priest for deflowering, a ceremony known as chen-t'an...at a given moment the priest enters the maiden's pavilion and deflowers her with his hand, dropping the first fruits into a vessel of wine. It is said that the father and mother, the relations and neighbors, stain their forehead with this wine, or even taste it. Some also say that the priest has intercourse with the girl; others deny it. As Chinese are not allowed to witness these proceedings, the exact truth is hard to learn."[10] The very young age of the girls having to undergo this horrible rite may have had a grim rationale in times when the average life span was barely twenty or twenty-five. Nowadays anyone willing to perform "the rite" could obtain "two for one" by paying the price of a couple of teddy bears.

The experience of twins sold to the pedophilia trade that distressed me most took place in Europe. When the twin unit had just opened in my hospital, one of our first patients was a beautiful Philippine woman in her mid-twenties, whom I shall call Ruby. Ruby had arrived in Europe two years before, worked in a restaurant, and had been having an occasional affair with a young man from the same country. When she was told the news that she was expecting twins, Ruby thought first about abortion. Her boyfriend had vanished and her wages were not high. Then she said, "I'll wait. If they are girls I will keep them, if they are boys, I won't." When she was told that selective termination based on gender was unlawful, she said, "I have found a solution. If they are boys, I will send them to live with a barren woman in my country. She will be delighted." The vaunted "adoption" sounded murky, more like a sale than a proper adoption, but at the same time many immigrants send their twins back to their country of origin, as they cannot cope with two children and work. Two weeks later, when Ruby was informed that she was expecting monozygotic twin girls, she was overjoyed. We were all surprised by her elation, because Ruby did not seem a "motherly" type, and the twins were going to represent a heavy physical and economic burden for her. The pregnancy was straightforward, and the girls, though born slightly premature, were soon discharged. Ruby agreed to participate in a follow-up study of monozygotic twins, in which I would visit her and the girls for yearly checkups.

On my first three visits I was surprised by the amount of Barbie dolls around. The twins had no other toys, and I counted 80 dolls. Ruby also looked different, heavily made up and dressed in an increasingly provocative way at each successive visit. Yet the girls were delightful, and Ruby seemed to look after them well. When the girls were five years old, I was shocked. Their faces were smeared with lipstick, they wore no underclothes, and they masturbated openly and simultaneously while moving their tongues in a studied way. Ruby, who now looked like a whore, announced that she was going to send the girls back to Manila, the capital of the Philippines, as she could no longer cope with work and having to care for them. Her younger sister and her aunt would look after them.

Four years later, as I was about to leave for an assignment in the Philippines, I thought about Ruby and decided to phone her. Ruby asked me over for a drink, as she wanted to give me the address of her sister in Manila. She showed me many photographs of the twins. The girls were beautiful, but all the photos were pure pornography, including one sadomasochistic number with the twins tied tightly to an enormous bed. I tried talking to Ruby, but she just laughed, saying, "They earn a lot of money, much more than me! You remember how pleased I was about having twin girls! I was right! They are a good investment." There was no way of reasoning with her.

When I passed through Manila, I took a taxi to go and see the twins. As it turned out, Ruby had given me a fictitious address. Probably she was afraid that I might do something to cut her "income" short.

During my travels abroad I was involved time and again in one other form of "adoption" without any sale at all. Generally I approached a mother holding newborn twins and complimented her on the children. The woman looked perplexed, then randomly handed me one twin, saying, "You can keep it. It's yours." And she meant it, just as Shaman had. The same scene was repeated throughout Africa, Asia, Papua, and South America.

Twins being sold, given away, prostituted, exploited, and torn from their mothers' arms left me very shaken. These horrible acts did not belong solely to distant cultures and underdeveloped societies but took place in the heart of Europe. Lurleen lived in Italy, the gypsies had acquired Italian citizenship, the clients of the teenager Nigerian prostitutes were Italian, and the tipsy men holding teddy bears in Bangkok were Europeans.

In a bestselling book "*Touchpoints*" the pediatrician T. Barry Brazelton portraying a typical family during a visit to their baby says, "Bonds of affection are weaving them tightly into a unit...Both parents tickle and coo the baby and do anything to elicit one of its "adorable" response...They know him now and are at the peak of their love affair with him...Parents are in love with their baby, feel awesome...and of course they are wrapped up in that baby. Everyone who has ever had a baby knows the feeling."[11]

How could one reconcile this view of family life with what I have just described? Where were the cooing men having a love affair with their children? Certainly not in the Lake Turkana region, where prepubertal lolitas were given to young warriors as sexual playthings and later exchanged for goats to be married off with some old man. These tickling and cooing men were not in Bangkok either, or in certain Italian streets filled with child prostitutes.

Of course women were often accomplices or even perpetrators in the crimes. However, as the writer Adrienne Rich claims in her book "Of Woman Born," having some link with male power is the closest that most women can come to sharing power directly. To have no link with any form of male power, however petty and corrupt, leaves women unprotected and vulnerable. Women, like other dominated people, have learnt to manipulate, seduce, and internalize a man's will in order to make it theirs. Men sometimes characterize this as power in women; but it is nothing more than the child's or courtesan's power to wheedle, and the dependent's power to disguise her feelings—even from herself—in order to obtain favors, or literally to survive. In fact only the helplessness of the child confers a narrow kind of power on women across the world. Often women may not desire such power; however, this power may compensate for their powerlessness everywhere else. As Rich says, "The power of the mother is, first of all, to give or withhold nourishment and warmth, to give or withhold survival itself."[12]

Chapter 7

Let Nature Take Its Course

"All twins are killed here." Stunned, I asked why, having thought this occurred only in the past. Father Giorgio shrugged, "They throw them in the bush and or abandon them. Twins are just a double burden. Many are too small to be worth the effort, and in some groups there are superstitious reasons, too."

In 1990 during my first assignment abroad I was expected to help organize a medical outpost in a remote region of southern Ethiopia where no medical facilities were available. Missionaries were going to build a small dispensary, and I was to instruct the local personnel in dealing with basic medical matters, such as administering essential medication and starting a program of fundamental vaccinations. Ethiopia is one of the poorest countries in the world, plagued by drought and all sorts of tropical diseases, especially in the south. Men have a mean life expectancy of 43 and women of 45. Only 4 percent of the total population lives to reach age 60, and the mortality rate of 46 percent between birth and 24 months is extremely high. Less than 30 percent of the population receives any education, less than 30 percent has access to potable water, and more than 60 percent is completely excluded from medical care. On average, there is only one doctor per 300 thousand inhabitants.[1]

Ethiopia was once an Italian colony, and some of the elders still speak Italian. Signs of this former dominion can be found everywhere in Addis Ababa, the capital, but as soon as one leaves the capital, these signs progressively fade. Ethiopia is scarcely urbanized, in that 84 percent of its population lives in rural conditions and is involved in some sort of farming. As for population, religion, and geography, however, Ethiopia is not homogeneous at all. People in the north are Coptic, an old, Christian orthodox religion. The north is poor but not desperately so: wet and dry seasons alternate, making grazing and farming possible. The same can be said of the highlands starting immediately south of Addis Ababa, where most of the inhabitants are Muslim and also live off farming and pasture.

In contrast to these regions, the lowlands of the south are a dry no-man's land. Even the flimsy semblance of an organized state vanishes completely in the south, as do any primary resources, such as roads, hospitals, schools, and especially drinking water and food. The area can go for years without rain, and tropical diseases are rampant. Most inhabitants wear little or no clothing, and with few exceptions, all are animistic. People barely manage to survive in this hostile environment.

Traveling in a small convoy of six jolting jeeps, stashed to the gunnels with all sorts of necessities, we passed through the chilly hills in the north and prepared for the first night stop. Tents were pitched, and we sat down at a table on the terrace of a rather filthy restaurant. The veranda was surrounded by gorgeous bushes of bright flowers and overlooked two stunning lakes, one of them incredibly pink-colored. The clear sky was turning red and beginning to reveal the many stars of African nights. From this breezy spot Ethiopia looked beautiful and livable.

Father Giorgio, who was to accompany me during my stay, explained how illusory this sense of serenity, beauty, and comfort was. The spectacular lakes were salty and infested with huge crocodiles. Water became an increasing emergency as one neared the south and, once there, the little water available was polluted. Men and skinny cattle all fought for it. There were no pastures and no grazing, save in a few spots infested by tze tze flies. The rest of the lowlands was just sand and unbearable heat. Thorny acacias, the only scarce trees, were no good for providing shelter against the heat, as the sun filtered through their dry, leafless twigs. It was almost impossible to get food supplies. The only river in the region offered no solution to the problem. Crocodiles abounded, causing innumerable deaths, and the murky waters contained only inedible perches, which the locals ate despite the fact that they were filled with parasites. Malaria was a constant plague. Life expectancy was below 40.

Disheartened by Father Giorgio's list of implacable diseases, I was still under the illusion that motherhood at least is connected with life and hope, and I started asking him about it in order to brighten the atmosphere. How many children did women have on average? He said, "Roughly eight. They start at puberty and end at death. I don't know the figures—nobody knows them—but many die during delivery." Trying still to retain the beauty and serenity of the moment, I asked about twins, naively assuming to be a universal object of fascination. Father Giorgio's dry, matter-of-fact reply was, "Twins are killed." Then he stood up, and we retreated to our tents for the night.

The following day while driving through an increasingly sparsely populated, dry, hot wasteland, we met a nomadic group of women. Their men were probably miles ahead. We stopped for a break. I immediately spotted a woman carrying twins. She held one twin in her arms and the other loosely strapped to her back. She was beautiful, with a tall, lean body and graceful, delicate features. I approached and complimented her on her twins. She smiled. Closer up, she looked tired, slightly sad, and shy. Her colorful clothes had been soiled by the twins. She tried to cover the stains, but one could not fail to smell the stink of feces, urine, and sweat. A cloud of flies circled around her.

A wrinkled, bent old woman looking like an evil witch suddenly hit the mother hard with a long, thick stick and shouted something incomprehensible in a shrill voice. She was clearly the leader of the group. Then she started hitting all the other women at random, to make them run, like a herdsman urging on cows. Except for the chief, they all had at least one child in their arms and several more in tow. The mother of the twins also ran, but she lagged considerably behind, impeded by the double burden she carried.

Older women, past the "impurities" of menstruation, take on important roles within many communities worldwide.[2] They can become shamans, religious priestesses, or leaders of the nomadic herd. Though I found the old chief revolting, I found myself thinking that nomadic women could barely carry one child, let alone two during their constant walkabouts. The well-being of the adults was the main concern of the group, taking priority over the life of children. Unless adults provided food and protection, all members of the group were put at risk. Abandonment or murder of weak, very young, or over burdensome children, such as twins, could become inevitable in such extreme conditions. Allowing both mother and twins to lag behind her group could mean death for them all, as the bush was no safe place to wander around alone.

Father Giorgio must have read my thoughts, for he commented, "Soon this mother will have to leave her twins behind. When twins start walking, they are too heavy to be carried but at the same time cannot walk fast enough to follow the group. The mother will be obliged to leave them behind, otherwise it will be certain death for all. The twins will be slightly more autonomous by then, and their mother may hang on to some hope. Some abandon twins near a road or a village. Occasionally we are able to rescue a few twins. We are always on the lookout for them, but too many hyenas and innumerable mortal dangers lurk around. Most of the time we just find their wretched remains." See figure 7.1.

While observing this sad scene I was reminded of "Nisa," the book by the ethnographer Marjorie Shostak that first informed me about twin infanticide, although it suggested that this practice belonged to the past.

Figure 7.1 Nomadic woman carrying twins, one on her front and one on her back. The twins are unwieldy, and she has to run in order to keep up with the pace of her group, which has already left her behind.

The book recounts the life of the nomadic bushmen inhabiting the Kalahari Desert of Botswana, a Southern African country. Nisa, an old woman, says that in her day twins were killed regardless of their gender because it would be debilitating or even impossible for a woman to produce enough milk for two children "... The day your baby is born, that day your heart is miserable ... the anger at birth and the pain ... a woman I did know gave birth to two children in one day. Two of them! First the pain of one rises inside you, than the pain of the other. That's when the woman's heart may leave her, especially if her heart is weak. Then she cries when the first one is born and cries when the second one is born. I don't know myself, but to have the anger for two children! What do you do, but die of pain?"[3]

We in fact saw only one pair of twins during our trip, two little girls who had been abandoned by a nomadic tribe near a village belonging to an ethnic group that did not harbor superstitious beliefs about twins. Nobody knew exactly how old the girls were, but they must have been six or seven. They lived in the street, scavenging from the scanty remains left lying around. They were never apart more than an inch and always held each other's hand. Probably they had managed to stay alive precisely because they were twins, joining their forces and providing each other with mutual comfort.

Their mother, before leaving them behind, had wrapped the girls in identical "clothes": an orange piece of cloth now all tatty and torn, with a hole for the head and a frayed string as a belt. Finding a piece of cloth in a place where most people went totally naked was possibly an indication of her wish to protect the girls, as was her decision to abandon them in an indifferent if not friendly village. Due to the kindness or perhaps the indifference of strangers, the twins had survived. In the end the two little girls had even met Father Giorgio, who was going to secure a decent future for them, well away from the rascals out in the streets. Others would not be so fortunate.

The belief in the "kindness of strangers" was very old indeed. The historian John Boswell, who coined the expression in his 1989 work "*The Kindness of Strangers: The Abandonment of Children in Western Europe from Late Antiquity to the Renaissance*," calculated that as many as 40 percent of all infants were abandoned in early Christian Rome. According to him, exposure, as opposed to murder at birth, did not imply wickedness, since it expressed the hope that the child might be saved by "the kindness of strangers."[4] Perhaps this was what the nomadic mother had also hoped when leaving her twins behind near a village.

When we reached our destination we started organizing a basic outpost as best as we could. Three young men who worked at the mission in Addis Ababa had traveled with us. They built a small cement shelter and put in a table, a couple of chairs, and a bed. The medicines and few medical instruments we had carried with us were locked in a cabinet. Father Giorgio miraculously managed to dig a well, with the help of the young men and a team of skinny locals. Everything looked neat and orderly.

But there was no electricity, no drinking water, let alone any possibility of sterilizing all the instruments properly or keeping the vaccines on ice. I felt disheartened.

The locals, too, seemed mistrustful.[5] They tried out every possible kind of magic, applying filthy amalgams to wounds, chanting, and making sacrifices to malevolent spirits before coming to see us. We were their last resort, and when they finally came it was generally too late. My days were spent visiting these impossible cases: terminal patients, pervasive cancers, gangrenous ulcers, and the like.

In this region, and in other parts of the world where animism is prevalent and sanitary conditions are very poor or just recently established, the locals first try magic and other forms of nonmedical healing, such as the use of herbs and potions. Magic has always been with them, while western practices are a recent acquisition, and as such these elicit a fear of the unknown. Furthermore, western practices are often linked to a ruthless colonial past, and as such are frowned upon. Once the locals start realizing that medicine works, however, they come to whatever medical facilities are available. Generally, however, both forms of "healing" continue to coexist.

By mid-morning every day, the heat was already unbearable. There was no relief from it and no shelter from the sun, whose implacable rays filtered through any available recess. I was dying for a shower, but a shower was a wild dream. Not even a drop of clean water could be wasted on such a mundane necessity. The water from the well was barely sufficient for drinking, and before drinking, we had to boil, filter, and disinfect it. If I wanted to find some respite from the heat and the dust, I had to do so at my own risk in infested waters and murky ponds polluted by two parasitical infections, schistosomiasis (once called bilharzia) and onchocercosis or river blindness, the first eventually destroying several internal organs, mainly the bladder and the liver, and the second destroying the eyes.

I was standing outside the building one day when a young woman, whom I shall call Kara, followed by three small children and an old woman, shyly approached me. She looked very pregnant. In sharp contrast with her skinny, almost skeletal arms, her ankles and feet were enormously swollen. She seemed worried about them and pointed them out to me. She had reason to be worried. I measured her blood pressure and found it enormously high. Kara was suffering from eclampsia. This condition, generally occurring in the second half of pregnancy, is characterized by an acute elevation of blood pressure and progressive kidney failure, frequently accompanied by seizures and coma. Eclampsia is the most common cause of pregnancy-related death in civilized countries. It also is one of the many complications of twin pregnancies, affecting them three times more often than singleton births.

When I patted Kara's distended abdomen, she turned out to be suffering from an excessive volume of amniotic fluid, so-called polyhydramnios. Polyhydramnios, by overstretching of the womb, can bring on premature delivery. Then I heard two heartbeats instead of one: the young woman was carrying twins and, using sign language, I managed to communicate this to her.

In Europe women are immediately hospitalized and treated when polyhydramnios and, even more so, when eclampsia set in. The mother's health is cared for by monitoring and trying to lower her blood pressure. If this continues to rise, a caesarean needs to be performed promptly. Several measures are also adopted to assure a better outcome for the twins. Steroids, for instance, are administered via the mother to accelerate lung maturation, should the delivery be premature. The twins are constantly monitored to detect any signs of suffering in one or both fetuses, in which case the twins can be delivered promptly and immediately handed over to the perinatologists. Yet even these careful measures do not guarantee a positive outcome for all involved.

In my opinion Kara's delivery was imminent and likely to occur within the next 24 hours or so, as contractions had started, and in any case could not be delayed as her blood pressure was too high to prolong pregnancy further. I wanted to try and lower her blood pressure, and, since a caesarean was out of question given the scant facilities, I also wanted to induce the delivery through an intravenous perfusion.

I was unable to communicate with Kara, who only spoke her local dialect. I called in the young men who were completing the construction of the dispensary in the hope of convincing her to stay. I explained to the men what I had in mind, but they told me, "Pregnant women just don't stay." Women preferred to deliver alone in the bush. Generally speaking, they were brought to dispensaries only when some intervening complications had already put them in a terminal state. All that the young men could manage to do was get Kara to promise that she would come back the next day.

The following day Kara was nowhere to be seen. A few days later, I met her by chance near the well. Her three children and the old woman were with her. Her abdomen was no longer distended, just incredibly flabby, and her sagging breasts were leaking. It was clear that she had already delivered the twins. I inquired about them through the men. The answer was, "They have gone away." I thought that in all likelihood the young woman had killed or exposed the twins to certain death at birth.

Many Africans, but also gypsies and numerous other ethnic groups, seldom mention death directly, as they fear that openly evoking it might bring on more death. Following a kind of "magical thinking" they believe that if death is not talked about, it will go away.

A few days later when I was walking with Father Giorgio in the bush trying to locate a sheltered place for building a small dormitory, we saw a cloud of flies circling a small heap. As we approached, the smell of putrefaction was unbearable. The rotting remains of the twins were by now almost completely decayed, however, we could see that their small mouths had been stuffed with dry grass mixed with soil in order to suffocate them. We gave them a decent burial.

Although I felt horrified for the twins, contrary to my expectations, I only felt pity toward Kara. I thought that the decision of this poor young woman to deliver in the bush may have been prompted by the fact that no other delivery had yet taken place in the dispensary. In many developing countries women know that they can die during childbirth, or that soon after giving birth they can die of infections or unstoppable hemorrhaging. The prospect of twins is even more formidable. Yet the bush was familiar to Kara, and the fear of a new place, of a foreign woman, and of strange instruments and medications had prevailed.

Probably once the delivery was over, the decision of this poor young woman to murder her twins was tainted, just as for Nisa, the old woman living in the Kalahari desert, by the fear and the pain of parturition still shaking her. Kara was clearly terrified when she came to show me her incredibly puffy legs. Furthermore, she may have decided that the demands of caring for the twins would have been too great to let them live. In many parts of the world women, who are often equated with child-producing machines and on top of all that are made to work like pack animals, know that there is a limit to their meager resources and to what they can do. Quite probably Kara had had her first child as early as at the age of 12 or at best at 15. Certainly her "reproductive career" would not stop at the twins. Possibly in a "Darwinian" manner, she had decided to follow natural selection and just concentrate her efforts on those infants who had a chance of survival, or as the economist and Darwin's contemporary Herbert Spencer would have called it, on the "fittest" to live.[6]

The three children who accompanied her when she came to the dispensary were all alive and looked relatively well. Sharing the meager resources available with two more infants would have meant subtracting vital nourishment from the other children and from herself. In such harsh conditions it may even have meant the death of another family member.

Perhaps one of the reasons that mothers preferred to deliver in the bush, even when basic medical facilities were available, was that this gave them the option to decide on the spot which children were to be selected and which were best dropped. The bush offered these unfortunate women a say and a choice, the only freedom they would ever have.

Another element was possibly of paramount importance in Kara's decision to murder her twins. In many African countries, as well as in other parts of the world, children have no status. When engaging in infanticide, one is not abandoning one's flesh but is merely discarding "a thing." As Maria Pierce described in her book "Infanticide": "When choices must be made, who is chosen to survive at any price? And who is the most expendable? Very likely, it is the newborn, who cannot yet foreknow his death, who has not yet formed a strong attachment, not yet cast a firm anchor into this world, and who, though perhaps even loved, has not yet become deeply meaningful for his parents. He may be chosen to slide back into oblivion."[7] Twins, regarded as "excessive" infants, are often the first to be chosen to "slide back into oblivion."

Ethiopia left me very shaken, but it also was a turning point in my life. I could never before have imagined finding myself sympathizing with infanticide or with deserting mothers, yet now I did. After returning home,

I felt the need to increase my engagements abroad as well as my contacts with immigrants in my own country, to understand more about maternal behavior in extreme conditions. I realized that so far I had taken many things for granted, such as the existence of unconditional maternal love and my more or less covert tendency to blame those who did not conform to this norm. Ethiopia and its unfortunate twins had started me on a long quest.

A few years after visiting Ethiopia, I was contacted by a "non profit agency" and asked to do a survey on the physical and mental health of several ethnic minorities in the Philippines. As in Ethiopia, my work was not directly related to twins, but by now each time I worked abroad I inquired about them. Contemporary literature on the Philippines did not mention twins as being a particular issue, but several immigrants told me of ancient traditions that were still alive among remote ethnic groups. One person said, "You know Philippinos love twins, they dote on them, but in the mountains it is different." Another reported, "My grandmother told me that they used to kill twins. Now things have changed, but some groups still do it."

I traveled to Luzon, the most important of the innumerable islands making up the Philippines. Manila, the nation's chaotic capital, is located in the southern part of the island. I was to work on another island in an area crossed by mountain chains.

Despite plentiful natural resources and enormous human resources in this nation of incredibly hard workers, the Philippines have been plagued by corrupt governments, typified by Imelda Marcos and her insatiable craze for shoes. Corruption has spread to other organizations holding power, such as the army and the police. Those conditions have left the population impoverished and has led to emigration.

When I arrived in the Philippines, I headed straight toward my destination in the mountains. The environment was completely different from that of Ethiopia: cold, foggy, muddy, and wet. There was no shortage of water, for rain was frequent and hard, but just like Ethiopia, poverty abounded among the natives.

People in the region did not suffer from tropical diseases but rather from serious chest conditions, especially tuberculosis, and from chronic malnutrition. The main source of food was rice, and each single grain was planted and picked with inhuman effort, one by one, by hand, the workers' bare legs and bare feet covered with leeches and mud. I calculated the average caloric intake of the locals to be less than 1,200 calories per day, a figure similar to the dietary conditions in concentration camps.

Women cultivated the rice fields because, as I was told, "It is a woman's job." They worked with their backs constantly bent, which soon resulted in chronically painful deformations. Their "clothing" was perennially wet and torn, offering no protection from the dampness and chill. These same women hardly ever got a break from the most typical of all women's job, looking after their children, especially if the children were young and still breastfed. Breastfeeding was normally stretched over two to three years as a form of contraception, and by then mothers were often pregnant again. Men generally helped with the care of children only after they were fully weaned. When still in their twenties, women looked old and worn out. In this region, life expectancy was barely over 40.

When moving about the rice fields assessing the health of the locals, I frequently asked if there were any "*Kambal*" the Philippine name for twins, in the area. The answer was inevitably, "No," or else something along these lines of, "Not in the last 80 years" or "There were some *Kambal* perhaps over that hill, but that was long ago. They must be gone to live in town." At first I was inclined to ascribe this absence to the supposedly low twinning rates of Asian women. While the frequency of monozygotic twins is supposed to be fairly constant all over the world, or roughly 1 in 250 live births, dizygotic twinning rates present wide variations in different racial groups. Asiatics are assumed to have the lowest ratio, or approximately 1 in 330 births.[8] Gradually I surrendered to statistical evidence: even by these low Asian standards, the conspicuous absence of "*Kambal*" had to be ascribed to other causes. Twins were probably disposed of in the area.

I received confirmation of my suspicions one day when I was invited to lunch by a rich woman, whom I shall call Ms Arroyo. Ms Arroyo lived in a small town at the foot of the mountains and was actively engaged in caring for the poor. Doctors still have considerable standing in low-income countries, and whenever working abroad, I often receive such invitations from the local "aristocracy," just as I did in the Cameroon.

Looking forward to some decent food, I put on my best clothes for the occasion.

Ms Arroyo's house was built out of solid cement, her kitchen was spacious, and her living room was well decorated and illuminated by many windows overlooking the valleys. Her bathrooms were lined with precious marble. She had plenty of servants and set out a big lunch for us.

The contrast with the living conditions of people in the fields could not have been starker. Rice planters inhabited windowless huts with no kitchens, no electricity, and no beds. When "nature called," they just squatted in the fields. At night when the cold was particularly bitter, they slept huddled together on the floor, trying to find shelter from the chill. Huddling together had for them the additional meaning of keeping at bay the malignant forces that they believed were unleashed at night. Though by no means untouched by modern civilization, mountain people's living conditions seemed to belong to an ancient past. Even people residing in the small towns usually led incomparably better lives.

Ms Arroyo, a sturdy, outspoken, and energetic middle-aged woman, told me of her links with the local *"Iglesia,"* an independent Philippino church that is largely taking over from the Roman Catholic religion. Save for the southern island of Mindanao, where Muslims are fighting for independence, Philippines is commonly regarded as a Catholic country. In many developing countries the Catholic religion is declining, charged with being linked with the colonial past, enmeshed with power, and distant from the spiritual needs of the locals.[9] A secessionist element is embedded in the new churches, whose distant roots are to be found in the Protestant religion. These churches pattern themselves on a literal interpretation of the Bible and the beginnings of Christianity. Hierarchy and liturgy are often nonexistent, allowing believers to relate directly with God. The emotional component is very strong. People are asked to participate directly in every function from choral singing to the unanimous sharing of the religious elements involved in the ceremonies. A high degree of syncretism with indigenous animistic traditions is not only tolerated but encouraged. Other churches, by contrast, wish to make a leap forward by molding themselves on western variations of the Christian religion, such as the Pentecostal and Adventist churches. These believers feel both advanced and pure, by breaking with traditions that they often find embarrassing, while embracing modernism from the United States. They participate in progress, even if only with their "souls."

Among Ms Arroyo's various activities in the local *Iglesia* were: providing food, shelter, clothing, basic education, and medical care for the poor in the inner-city area. As we talked, it occurred to me that she might be able to tell me something about twins, so I asked, "Do you know of any twins?" She smiled, "I will take you to see a woman who has four twins. I mean she had two and then two more."

After finishing our lunch Ms Arroyo took me just around the corner and introduced me to the woman, whom I shall call Venus, who was living in a small hut next to an *Iglesia*. Then she dashed off saying that she had to attend a Church meeting. Venus was clearly poor but dignified, and her twins were immaculately clean. When I started talking to her, and asked her about her twins and the lack of twins in the rice fields, she told me, "You see, I am robust. My twins were born robust, too. They were all quite healthy and big, plus the church and this lady helped. This is why I decided to keep them. I am no believer in the *Iglesia*, but saying a few prayers costs me nothing. Still it is hard. My husband left after the second pair of twins was born. He went off with a younger girl from another province. Twins can be too much. Imagine four. Nobody up there—pointing to the rice fields—could afford to keep twins. They dispose of them at birth."

Some time later, on another Philippine island, I visited a densely populated community of fishermen numbering about 2000 people. The fishermen were nicknamed the "gypsies of the sea." They had been marginalized as outcasts by the rest of the local population. Though officially Muslim, they were closer to pagans as testified by the many small ribbons and flags tied to their dwellings and nearby rocks in order to scare away malevolent spirits.

For these fishermen, who could not afford to buy land or pay any form of taxation, dwelling on water was their "fiscal haven." They lived in cramped huts built on rotting piles over murky stagnant waters swarming with malaria. Hygienic conditions were appalling, with cholera, hepatitis, and typhoid epidemic. Malnutrition was even more pronounced than in the mountains, with an average food intake of 900 calories per day. Their diet was extremely unbalanced. Foods other than fish, such as fresh vegetables and fruits, were only erratically available and affordable. Hence scurvy and other nutritional disorders were rampant.

During my visits to the community I was escorted by two huge, fully armed policemen and by an imposing, matron-like social worker, whom I shall call Imelda and who was acquainted with the locals and acting as a go-between. This labyrinthine environment was considered to be too dangerous for a European woman to wander around alone without a guard. I was told that I might be robbed, harassed, or kidnapped. Although the fishermen looked too weak from starvation even to attempt anything like that, initially their hostility and anger were almost tangible.

Only one pair of skinny, opposite-sex twins lived in the overcrowded community. Their mother had died at childbirth, and this had been taken to mean that the twins were malevolent spirits capable of causing death. The fishermen had been too scared to kill them fearing their revenge. The twins lived isolated from everyone and looked liked terrified skinny rabbits. I enquired with Imelda if there was any way of taking them outside the community, but she indicated that the fishermen would not have accepted this, dreading some improbable ghostly vengeful act if the twins were taken away from their kinfolks.

Apart from this one pair, the fishermen could not afford to keep twins. Women on average had seven or eight children, of whom they choose the fittest to live, and twins generally did not stand a chance. At birth they were dropped into the water. Nothing much could be done by the social worker or anyone else. Just as in Ethiopia, the crime was due to the incredible harshness of life.

Children are nevertheless valued in most areas of the Philippines and, contrary to parts of Africa, have a social status. The Catholic religion possibly helped Filipino children in the past by giving them a standing soon after birth, through baptism. Yet the women working in the rice fields up in the mountain chain could not possibly have carried two children on their bent backs. The skinny women living crammed together in the community of fishermen could not possibly have fed two infants. Again I found myself sympathizing with them.

In many low-income countries, nothing much has changed since the beginning of the twentieth century. Women do not have access to any medical care, medical facilities, contraception, insurance, or the right to extended maternity leave.

Often women living in low-income countries have no other choice than to let nature run its course, even if a caesarean could save their lives.[10] A hospital might well be in the region, but it is frequently far away and unreachable. Save in some bigger towns, ambulances and paved roads are nowhere to be found. It may take hours or even days to get to a hospital, and many hospitals may lack even basic facilities, let alone a well-organized operating theatre or a neonatal intensive care unit.

Often, all that these women can offer their shockingly small and sickly twins are ritual creeds, such as making them wear protective amulets and torn cloths to shield them from evil forces, or calling them with foul-sounding names, such as "Bag of shit" or "Heap of garbage" in the hope of making them seem unappealing, thus deterring wicked spirits from approaching them. Most women resort to traditional healers, the only alternative to modern health care. Traditional healers can be of great help by instilling a sense of security in their terrified patients. The high infant mortality rate and low life-expectancy in many developing countries, however, speak for themselves about the success rate of these healers.

Parallel to the lack of basic facilities and modern medicine, a disturbing new phenomenon is acquiring increasing proportions in most low-income countries. In 2003, after spending over a month working in few small "clinics" dotted over a beautiful island located east of Papua New Guinea, and forming part of it, I spent some time in the Sepik area. The Sepik River is one of the biggest in the world and could be considered the Congo or the Amazon of Papua. The region is renowned for its visual art, including magnificent masks, ancestral figures, shields, pottery, and bark paintings, all of which can be found in museums throughout the world. The Sepik is also famous for the seminal research conducted in the area by two towering figures in anthropology, Gregory Bateson[11] and Margaret Mead.[12] The landscape along the river is overwhelmingly beautiful. It is one of the most beautiful places I have ever seen. However, the Sepik is environmentally quite hostile: hot, unbearably humid, and filled with malaria-carrier mosquitoes. Though by no means unaffected by modernization, mainly through Christian churches and a scanty tourist trade, traditional life continues in most villages in the area, which remain quite remote.[13] Papuans inhabiting the region have a name for ferociousness and are among the very few ethnic groups in the world still openly accused in several textbooks of continuing to kill twin infants up to the present day.[14,15] This did not match my experience. I had seen many twins in the area, at least one pair in each village, and everyone seemed quite proud of their twins. In regions where twin infanticide was commonly practiced in the recent past, the age of the oldest twins, sometimes no more than six or ten years, can give a rough idea of when the habit stopped. Here in the Sepik, although nobody knew their exact age, several twins looked to me to be well over 40. See figure 7.2.

During my stay, I slept in huts, huddled in my sleeping bag and covered by my mosquito net. I traveled around by canoe during the day guided by a lovely old local man called Gideon. One day when there was a torrential rain, I had to spend the night in a village where he had not planned to stay. To my surprise, we were greeted not by the usual head of the village but by three white women who were identified as "health inspectors." The women did not introduce themselves. Two looked middle-aged, and one looked young. I said that I was a doctor and asked if they belonged to some nonprofit organization. Hostility and suspicion became almost tangible.

Figure 7.2   This lovely Papuan father is very proud of the young twins he holds tenderly in his arms. Possibly aided by the fact that matrilineal societies are common in Papua, fathers take great pleasure in bring up their children.

One told me that they belonged to a nonprofit organization but did not say which one. All three were tight-lipped and gave me no more information than that during the day they traveled from village to village administering vaccinations to the locals.

The villagers seemed particularly fearful of the health inspectors. Gideon seemed fearful too. I had brought along a few cans of beer for him, and each night I offered him one. This filled Gideon with delight. He would sit on his boat looking up at the stars and drinking his beer. That evening, however, Gideon just covered the cans with a piece of cloth, half-glancing at the women as if to indicate that they were a potential danger. They seemed to have a bad reputation in the area.

The health inspectors lived in a comfortable wooden house located at the center of the village, but they did not ask me in. I settled instead in a hut. As I was preparing to sleep in my sleeping bag, huddled inside mosquito netting, I heard one of the women call out, "Missis, could you please come down and have a look at this woman?" Carrying my medical box, I followed her inside the house. A hugely pregnant young native called Julie was stretched on the kitchen table. Julie was moaning and looked terrified. The three women asked, "Do you think she is about to deliver?" I put on a pair of disposable gloves and examined her. The delivery seemed imminent, within no more than a day or so. I measured her blood pressure, which was normal. Then I put my stethoscope on Julie's belly and was suddenly seized by doubt. I heard two distinct heart-beats and a weaker, but still clear, third one. I said, "She is going to have triplets." Then speaking to Julie in my rudimentary Pidgin, the second language to most Papuan New Guineans, I said, "*Three pella pikinini.*" Julie beamed.

Contrary to Julie's beaming smile, the health inspectors seemed shocked by my news, but they did not say a word. Having helped to deliver many twins in my country, I knew I could cope reasonably well with an emergency with triplets. A caesarean was out of the question, but I made a list of the available instruments and asked the health visitors to keep them sterilized with boiling water and a sterilizer that I gave them. I also asked them to sterilize the table and the room, a necessary measure for any delivery. Throughout all this, Julie continued to smile at me. She had clearly put her faith in my hands. When I said that I would spend the night there as a cautionary measure, the health visitors thanked me acidly, promised to call me if anything happened during the night, and pushed me away. I stressed that they should call me if anything happened during the night. They slammed the door in my face.

I was restless and could not sleep. I got up at dawn and asked immediately about Julie. All the villagers were silent. Gideon asked again. They gathered around him and whispered something in their local dialect. Julie had delivered three tiny infants during the night, but she had died, apparently of a hemorrhage, "because they meddled and cut." Her corpse had already been buried by the villagers, ordered to do so by the health inspectors, under threat of some kind of retaliation, which I could not figure out. Gideon was speechless. I was appalled.

"Where are the health inspectors?" I asked "And the triplets?" I was told that the women had left hurriedly, carrying the infants inside a cardboard box. As one villager commented, "We would have kept them here." The health visitors had taken all their personal belongings with them and headed toward a larger village that was connected by a gravel road to a town where the nearest dilapidated hospital was located. The whole trip could have taken at least three days. The women had a powerful motor boat. There was no possibility of catching up with them. By now it was no longer raining and was terribly humid and hot. I found myself thinking that the triplets would probably soon be dead of dehydration or some other ailment.

When I passed through the town on my way back, I inquired at the hospital. They told me that the triplets had never arrived but had been found dead in a box along the road. The health inspectors had vanished. I went to the local police, but the only "policeman" in the town just shrugged.

It all made me sick. The so-called health inspectors probably had meant no harm. Like many others, they had wanted to "play doctors" and get a kick or a kink out of it. They had no medical knowledge, and they had greatly underestimated local conditions. They were not acting in a modern country where even gross mismanagement can often be fixed in the nearest hospital within easy reach. They had not calculated that the triplets would find a long journey in terrible climatic conditions "too much." The villagers were wiser in saying, "We would have kept them here."

Not knowing how tiny or premature the triplets were, I could not tell whether they would have died anyway, but even if they had a chance, a three day trip in that kind of heat and humidity was sure to kill them. I didn't even know the health inspectors' names or their country of origin for a possible follow-up. I was only pretty sure that at least Julie could have been saved. I felt impotent and angry.

In low-income nations, nongovernmental organizations running parallel to the state actually stand in for the government in vital areas, such as the protection of human rights and the provision of health care. Traditionally nongovernmental organizations were few and well-known and most effective during disasters and emergencies, such as earthquakes or wars, whereas Christian churches, especially Catholic and Evangelical, were generally active on more long-term projects, such as organizing education, orphanages, and hospitals. This picture is rapidly changing. Today along with many remarkable organizations, dubious professionals, unclear groups, and ambiguous religious sects are proliferating at an alarming speed and making their way into the farthest corners of the world. This growing underworld is aided by the fact that it is acting in regions where police control and law enforcement are absent or virtually nonexistent. These countries are also "cheap," in the sense that acquiring land, building churches or lodgings, and buying forms of transportation, including small airplanes, can all be done at an infinitesimal price as compared to the country of origin of these shady characters. Additionally, to criticize this so-called humanitarianism, generosity, or spirituality is like criticizing the institution of motherhood: it is just not done.

Given the often appalling living conditions of the locals and the absolute lack of government control, anyone can get away with almost anything. Many so-called charities, religious fundamentalists, and dubious do-gooders, up to who-knows-what, far from helping the locals, have become businesses in a kind of uncontrolled Wild West. As Graham Hancock wrote in his book "*Lords of Poverty*," the achievements and performance of these purveyors of international aid "are in no way subjected to the same exacting and competitive processes of evaluation that are considered normal in business. Precisely *because* their professional field is 'humanitarianism' rather than, say, 'sales', or 'production' or 'engineering', they are rarely required to demonstrate and validate their worth in quantitative, measurable ways. Surrounding themselves with the mystifying jargon of their trade, these lords of poverty are the druids of the modern era wielding enormous power that is accountable to no one."[16] Unfortunately, Julie had ended up in the hands of such unscrupulous, incompetent "professionals," and it cost her and her triplets their lives.

Chapter 8

The Hold of Superstition

A friend of mine who knew of my interest in twins phoned me to ask, "Did you know that they loath twins in Madagascar? I read it in a magazine at the hairdresser's. There was an article about missionaries who save them, with pictures, addresses, and names. You should read it." The ethnic groups mentioned in the article were said to kill twins regularly for superstitious reasons, and a religious association run by two missionaries, a husband and wife, was glorified for rescuing twins in the area. The wife was especially praised, as she belonged to the local population but disavowed the superstitious beliefs of her ethnic group. In a picture both missionaries were shown smiling and proud as they held infant twins, surrounded by local helpers who were also holding twins, all of the babies wearing identical, fashionable clothes. A pretty garden could be seen in the background. The whole picture was reminiscent of a Swiss kindergarten, with plenty of flowers, a well-mown lawn, educational play-stations, and a solid wooden fence all around.

The missionaries were reported to be linked with a European organization of parents trying to adopt twins. I phoned the association and was told, "We are a group of parents wanting to save twins and we have formed an association." The head of the adoptive organization seemed very reluctant to talk. I asked a few questions about the official and legal status of the association. All I got was, "It's all regular and regulated," but a minute later contradicted herself adding, "All twins are duly paid."

Legal adoption has to be authorized by official associations certified by the governments of the countries of both origin and destination. Prospective adoptive parents are generally submitted to lengthy assessments before being declared fit for adoption. The child or children they are granted become in all respects their legal children. Monetary transactions are not part of the process and are considered illegal. As a result of an international agreement, those who resort to nonofficial intermediaries run the risk of incurring heavy legal sanctions.

When the conversation turned to other matters, the head of the adoptive organization, herself a parent of adopted Madagascan twins, was much more talkative. She said, "Adoptive parents all gather regularly to exchange views about their twins. Many of us have become good friends. Twins are so lovely." Everyone was apparently delighted by the attention their twins received, especially in response to hearing how the children had been saved. The head enthused, "Everybody asks us about the twins. They can't believe the story. Even passersby want to take pictures of us." She explained that the parents were currently organizing a crusade to go back to Madagascar in two or three years with their twins, explaining, "We can show those savages that the twins brought us no harm. That will teach them a lesson."

The following year, I was asked by two missionary organizations to go to Madagascar to assess the physical and mental health of the children sheltered in their orphanages, to provide guidelines for improving their general condition, and to instruct the local staff through classes and discussion groups. Due to poverty, and the increasing plague of AIDS, children were abandoned in the streets all over the country, and Madagascar was filled with such orphanages.

Madagascar, the third biggest island in the world, lies 400 kilometers off the east coast of Africa. Geographically speaking, Madagascar belongs to Africa, but its population is a unique blend of ethnic groups of varied descent, including Indian, Melanesian, and Indonesian, as well as French, because Madagascar is a former French colony. When I arrived in Antananarivo in 1996, the capital of Madagascar located in the north of the country, democracy was a dream. The president was an all-powerful tyrant, and the whole country was in the hands of a few "noble" families linked to him. Slaves were an official and conspicuous social group.[1]

In order to keep the situation under tight control, the old Roman dictum "Divide and conquer" had been applied. French, once the unifying language, had been erased from the official "school curriculum," and a range of different local dialects had reemerged, making communication among various ethnic groups nearly impossible. All means of transport, ranging from road transport to trains, had been totally neglected, further isolating most parts of the country. Small planes were in operation to many districts, but the majority of the population could not afford to fly. Fragmentation, isolation, and a lack of primary resources had plunged most of the country back into the middle ages. The average life expectancy was barely 45 years for men and 48 for women. Infant mortality was high, at 82 deaths for every thousand births.[2]

In Antananarivo I took a small plane. My first stop was in the central part of Madagascar, at an orphanage run by nuns belonging to a well-known order. The nuns spoke fluent English but little French. They could hardly communicate with the local population, and their attitude was one of superiority and haughtiness. Nobody, they felt, dealt with such desperate cases as they did. They prided themselves on holding the record for looking after the most "untouchables."

The appalling condition of the orphans was in stark contrast with the immaculate appearance of the nuns. The nuns lived in a freshly painted colonial building, while the children were packed into dark windowless rooms. The younger ones were confined to minuscule beds resembling cages. Walls and floors were smeared with blood, bedsheets were foul-smelling and heavily soiled with feces and urine. The children were undernourished and infested with lice, many of them having runny noses and infected eyes. Babies were covered by seriously infected diaper rashes, showing that nobody cleaned or took proper care of them.

I was immediately struck by the abundance of twins, 26 out of 50 children. The nuns and two local attendants were very open about the reason. Twins were regularly killed by the same ethnic groups referred to in the popular magazine article. As a result, whenever twins were rescued, they were generally moved for safety to some orphanage far from their region of birth. When I asked why twins were killed, the nuns said, "Plain superstition."

The nuns were not interested in making any changes to improve the conditions of the children. They needed to deal exclusively with untouchables and those in pain. As one told me, "We take care of those nobody wants. Our duty is to take on their agonies. We are not interested in those who are well." They therefore did nothing to foster the well-being of the children.

I could not accept this "philosophy" and its consequences. I expressed all my indignation to the nuns by saying that they were refusing to improve the living conditions of the children and even putting their health in serious danger. The children had to be untouchable and suffering just to suit their need to feel saintly. The nuns were impervious and laughed saying, "You don't understand our mission." They told me I was pathetic and ignorant. Sadly, after that I left.

My next stop, also in the central part of the country, was utterly different. It was a large institution providing everything for its orphans: excellent shelter, plenty of food, clean, warm clothing, schools, sports, recreation, and training in a range of specialist skills, which would allow the children to earn a decent living once they reached adolescence. I worked with infants and young children in a spacious, spotless, well-lit, well-equipped building, and I got on very well with the nuns presiding over the institution.

Twins abounded here too. The head of the dioceses, whom I shall call Father Bruno, an unassuming pleasant man in his fifties, explained that in Madagascar being born even 300 kilometers apart made all the difference. The country being fragmented into many ethnic groups, each had its own beliefs about and conduct toward twins. In the north of the country, where the capital was located, twins were accepted; in the center, where the dioceses was located and I was working, superstition against twins was beginning to be felt strongly.[3] One twin, generally the second to be born, was believed to possibly embody some evil spirit of the dead. In order to prove its innocence, the second twin was often submitted to a terrible trial, the so-called "test of the oxen." The poor baby was placed near the entrance to a cattle pen, then the gate was opened and the herd allowed to rush out. If the baby was trampled, its atrocious death meant that he or she was truly evil and rightly done away with.

During my stay Father Bruno took me to visit three "lone twins" whose co-twin had not passed the trial. Because the oxen tests were performed in the open, everyone in the area knew about them, and looked upon them favorably. I was stunned by the openness of the mothers in declaring their crime of slaughtering one twin and by their bold and unwavering conviction in having done the right thing. No pity showed in their faces or words, and they seemed to feel no guilt or shame. It just had to be done and society supported them. On our way back to the mission Father Bruno commented, "These customs are hard to die. We seldom manage to convince these women to let us have the doomed twin."

A few days later Father Bruno told me, "I have a special surprise for you." We called on a high-ranking priest in the main diocese of the region. The archbishop, an imposing man in his seventies, was particularly affable. He shook hands with me and said, "I know of your interest in twins. Father Bruno told me about it. Well I was born a twin. Apparently I was the evil one, but God must have been merciful to me, and I survived the 'test of the oxen.' Perhaps I was not such a bad soul after all."

Toward the end of my stay Father Bruno prepared yet another surprise, when he summoned me and said, "Now you should go and see for yourself where most of our twins come from. In a large region in the south both twins are killed at birth by the two main ethnic groups." The slaughter of the twins was so evident and so openly acknowledged by everyone that I had almost forgotten about the two "missionaries" mentioned in the article and had not even planned to visit them. Father Bruno had arranged for one of the young locals working with him, whom I shall call Christopher, to drive me to them in a jeep. Christopher was very knowledgeable about the customs of the country and spoke most dialects, so that people easily opened up to him.

In a minute I was in the jeep and we set off toward the south. The road was in appalling condition. In former times it used to be a tarmac road, which could be covered in six hours. Now it was full of big holes and mud, and it took at least 20 hours to reach our destination. In the rainy season the south was completely cut off.

Our trip, however, lasted three days, since Christopher stopped frequently along the way to show me features of Malagasy life especially linked with maternity and twins.

In the south of the country both twins were considered evil forces, who could harm the entire community if they were allowed to live. Even their mothers, however, were tainted and often excluded from their community. One morning we spotted a pretty young girl breastfeeding newborn twins along the road and Christopher stopped the car. The girl immediately covered her breasts. The girl did not cover her breast out of shyness or modesty, because many women went bare breasted in the region. She seemed to fear my looking at her breasts.

Yet when I approached the girl and complimented her on her twins, she smiled. This teenage mother, like all mothers of twins belonging to the same ethnic group, had been abandoned by her husband and was obliged to live the rest of her life on the outskirts of her village. Nobody wanted twins in the community, nor would any other man ever again dare to touch this poor girl. That the girl had harbored twins in her womb tainted her body forever, and her presence was forever to be avoided. Passersby not only ignored her but also turned their faces in the opposite direction, as if malevolent forces could be transferred to them by the look of this frail, innocent girl and her twin infants. See figure 8.1.

Fear of the "infection," of malevolent forces which could be transmitted by "contagion," was widespread in Madagascar. This sort of transmission was described by Sir James George Frazer in 1922 in his book "The Golden Bough."[4] This theory, though oversimplified, still had a relevance for me in Madagascar where, just as Frazer described, twins were thought to transmit their evil to their mothers, and these in turn had the power to infect the entire community.

When the poor girl covered up her breasts upon seeing me, she was dreading another malevolent force, the so-called evil eye. My allegedly envious eyes looking at her full breasts could make her milk disappear.

A superstitious belief in the so-called "evil eye" or "envious eye" is ancient and widespread. Such a belief possibly originated in ancient

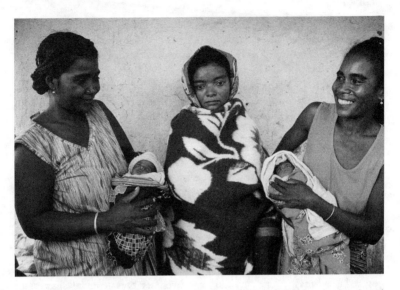

Figure 8.1 This Malagasy woman has just been left by her husband and banned from her village for delivering twins. She seems to be extremely depressed, does not look at the twins, and, despite the scorching heat, is all wrapped up in blankets as if she were a corpse enveloped in a shroud.

Sumeric times. Mention of it can be found in the Bible, the Koran, and Roman Catholic writings. To this day the belief is widespread. The phenomenon was described in detail by Alan Dundes, an anthropologist and expert in world folklore, in 1981 in his article "Wet and Dry: The Evil Eye."[5] The essence of the belief is that a person can cause harm by looking enviously at a coveted person or animal and by praising them. Dundes thought that the evil eye was based on underlying beliefs that equated water with life and dryness with death. The Sumerians, who possibly initiated the belief in the evil eye, lived on desert land, and for them dryness literally meant death. When the evil eye looked upon the envied living being, be it a baby, a milking animal, a potent man, or a nursing mother, it dried up the being's liquids, causing the child to be sick, the man to lose potency, or the woman to lose milk.

The poor girl feared that my evil, envious eyes could dry up her breasts, thus taking away all nourishment from her twins, who were going to be the sole human presence in her isolated life.

The following day, Christopher took a detour and took me to see another village, in a part of the country where women who delivered twins were expelled from society and confined to special villages far from their

Figure 8.2 A village of "outcasts." Notice twin girls holding unclothed twin boys in the first row, next to them on the left are non-identical twin girls. The two taller girls in the background are also fraternal twins. Two ex-prostitutes hold twin infants. Two transvestites can be seen on the far left. All other children belong to women who have left the prostitution racket.

community. Whereas the girl we had just seen the day earlier was kept outside the community but made to live near it and ignored by everyone, here the mothers were sent far away. Only transvestites, prostitutes, and outcasts were allowed to live with them. See figure 8.2.

The outcast village was filled with twins. I counted six pairs in a group of 40 people. Three of these pairs had been left behind by their mothers, who had returned to their original villages. This choice was not available to mothers until the twins were three or four years old and their mothers had ceased breastfeeding them. For mothers, therefore the stigma was not permanent, but a penalty of three years of confinement had to be paid before being reinstated in the community. Once back home, these women, having lost their twins, had to undergo extensive, often tormenting purification rites in order to be readmitted into their group. In particular, their vaginas had to be harshly and repeatedly "purified" with all sorts of abrasive or bristly objects, inasmuch as the twins' passing through the birth channel were thought to have "contaminated" it. Not all women, however, returned to their communities, as after three years of close contact with their twins, some loved them too much to be able to leave them behind.

As we were about to leave the outcast village, two middle-aged women, possibly ex-prostitutes, approached me. Christopher had explained that I was a doctor, and the women told me about a mother with newborn twins who had just been sent to the village three days before and was terribly sad and listless. They asked if I would see her, adding, "We will try to pull her out of her bed and bring her here." When they came back, each holding a twin infant, the mother followed slowly and apathetically. Her gaze was blank, her face grayish and expressionless. Although it was a very hot day, she was completely wrapped up in heavy blankets, and her head was covered by a scarf. On the whole she reminded me of a walking corpse. The women tried to coax her back into life by showing her the twins, but she was totally unresponsive. I asked her name, but she seemed not to take in my question.

I then made physical contact with her, stroking her face and cuddling her in my arms. She looked at me sadly but half-smiled, so I continued to hold her. I wore a small silver bracelet on my wrist, which I gave to her. I also gave her a T-shirt, some perfume, and a balm for her lips. She cried silently and smiled at the same time. In the meantime the community had gathered around her, and all seemed concerned and affectionate. Having earlier taken some pictures of the village, I now took pictures of her with the two women holding her twins. As I always do, I also promised to send them to her. She mumbled something in her dialect, which the middle-aged women translated, "She wants to have your name and address." I wrote everything down on a piece of paper, then hugged her again. When we left, I felt very sad, thinking my attempts at helping had been pathetic and utterly inadequate.

Yet four years later I received a letter from her with a photograph, asking how I was. She was happy. Her twins were growing well and she was going to stay with them in the outcast village. Could I write back to her? In the photograph she was smiling, wearing my bracelet and my T-shirt. Her twins looked chubby and well taken care of. I wrote back to her. I also wrote to Father Bruno asking if he could offer her some work at the mission, allowing her to live there and giving the twins the opportunity of attend-ing its school. Every year at Christmas I now receive a letter from her from the mission, with a new photograph. Other twins, who were confined in the same village, several of the outcasts, as well as the two middle-aged women I had met in the village, are all in the picture. Father Bruno had taken them all in.

Each time I receive a letter from her, I wonder again that my action helped this woman. Verbal communication is often inadequate with women in the developing world. They are not allowed to have a say in countless matters, and their voices are silenced. Meeting a white woman who is also a doctor can be very intimidating. The gulf between us seems unbridgeable with words. During my stays abroad I often found myself instinctively using physical contact and body language to communicate with women. Generally women respond very well to this kind of nonverbal communication. Additionally, I am helped by my age. Middle-aged women are past childbearing and regarded as past sex, so that sexual rivalry can no longer be an issue. When working abroad, I avoid any gear or attitude that could hint at sex.

Just handing out some small "feminine" present, such as a lipstick, a little perfume, soap or a nail varnish, which is the most popular of all, can work wonders. Despite my being a doctor, which is a profession associated with masculinity, these gestures establish a sisterhood. We are sharing the knowledge that all women like to adorn themselves and be alluring, even when past the age. Possibly by hugging the woman, sending the photos, and giving her my small gifts, I had made her feel less invisible, worthless, and virtually dead.

After one more day, Christopher and I finally reached our destination, the town described in the article. It was set in a dramatically beautiful location, surrounded by the waters of the Ocean on one side and by many canals on the other. Otherwise it was just another terribly filthy shanty town. Only a few decaying colonial buildings remained as a reminder of its former French rulers.

We made a visit to the hospital, although one could hardly have called it a hospital. The building was crumbling, with broken windows, muddy floors, and collapsed ceilings. Nobody was around. I wandered through filthy, empty corridors until finally meeting a woman, presumably a nurse, but her tatty overall made her look more like a third-rate cleaner. When I asked her about the maternity ward, she answered perplexed, "We never had a ward. As you can see, we have nothing here." I asked if mothers came to deliver at the hospital. She said, "Mothers come only when it's usually too late. Right now we have a caesarean, but she is dying." She took me to see the young woman, lying on a filthy bed drenched with blood. Nobody had bothered stitching her up, and she was clearly dying.

When I asked about the child, the nurse snapped, "Twins," as if that said it all. When I asked some more questions, she became evasive. It was obvious that whoever had operated on the woman had left the job unfinished when the twins came to light, superstition against twins being so strong in this place. The nurse added about the twins, "They are probably dead, too, by now." Both twins were "*fadi*," meaning taboo or bad luck, which would harm the entire community.

The concept of "*fadi*" was pervasive in the region. Unexplained phenomena stirred up a fear of the unknown and people tried to explain such phenomena with the idea of *"fadi"* equating all that was strange with evil forces capable of triggering bad fate. Twins, being outside the norm and generally coming as a surprise, evoked sheer dread of the unknown and as such were considered evil forces. Superstition condemned them to death at birth.

The nurse warned me about a terrible outbreak of cholera in town, with people dying in numbers. Realizing that I was not seeing in this hell anything to match the blissful description of the mission in the popular magazine, I asked the nurse if she knew about it. While showing me the way out, she gave me some indication of how to reach the place.

We drove across sandy beaches and beside lush canals. The place seemed nowhere to be found until finally, hidden by lots of bushes, a gate appeared with a signpost, "Housing for young children and for twins." While reading the sign, I noticed a stern, middle-aged woman spying on me. She looked quite different from the idyllic photo in the magazine, but I immediately recognized her as the wife of the missionary in charge of the orphanage. I walked over and introduced myself. She just nodded, looking tense. When I said that I was a doctor, she asked after a moment's reflection if I could examine the children. When I said yes, she asked, "Will you do it for free?" Again I said yes. Half smiling, she seemed to soften a bit. She gave the impression of being extremely calculating. The woman, whom I shall call Katia, lived in a large three-storey colonial building immaculately restored, and a new complex had been built next to it. The whole property was surrounded by a beautiful garden, and part of it was used as an open-air playground, the kindergarten I had seen in the picture of the magazine. Walking with me toward her house, Katia paid no attention to Christopher, possibly judging him to be of no use. She acknowledged that she belonged to one of the main ethnic groups who regularly killed twin infants, but she claimed, "I found the light of God. Now I rescue them."

In this region all twins were condemned to death at birth. Many, however, were actually saved, as testified to by the 23 pairs of twins in Katia's orphanage and by the 86 pairs coming from this region and whom I had seen in the other orphanages. Before any birth, women regularly went to deliver near the sea or the canals, because watery places were regarded as free from the evil forces that otherwise lurked around delivery places in order to take the life of mothers and their infants. Watery places were a reminder of the watery medium in which children floated during pregnancy. If the child was stillborn or if the woman had a miscarriage, all the remains were put in a clay container filled with water. The container was then left to sink in the river or the sea. These remains, like *Mizukos* in Japan, were called the "children of the water," because they had been in the water before and were returning to it. Water was the natural burial place for creatures who were believed still to be "watery," meaning not well-shaped or fully human. Infants, and older children too, were not considered to be fully human and thus to be dangling between the realms of water and earth. If they died, they were buried directly in the ground, as they had already touched the earth, but they were excluded from family tombs, where only the fully human could be buried.

Twins were different in that they were considered evil from birth. As such, both twins were killed or abandoned near the water where their mothers had delivered them. They might be drowned right away, left to die of dehydration near the riverbank, or put in a container, usually a basket, and launched out to sea. The ocean here was very rough and full of sharks. Missionaries who wanted to rescue twins knew the spots where mothers went to deliver, and they kept a constant eye on those places. Many twins were thus rescued, even by being snatched out of their mothers' hands. The mothers offered no resistance and immediately ran away, thinking that the evil had now been transferred, as if by contagion, to the rescuers.

As we approached Katia's house, she pointed at all the high bushes surrounding her property and said, "We have lots of problems. We have to hide from the population. These bushes are thought to be a barrier protecting the community from evil." She paused, wiping the sweat from her face, in the terrible heat and humidity, and added, "We founded an organization linked with Europe. Twins are very much in demand, and infant twins are especially popular. Everybody wants to adopt them." Then she apologized for her husband not being there, giving me the impression that he may have gone for good.

We had now reached her house, which was completely sheltered from the road. I was struck by the luxury of the place. Beautifully polished, precious teak floors, finely embellished decorations, and lacy curtains contrasted sharply with the utter poverty of the area outside the enclave. The children, too, were well kept, neatly clothed, nice smelling, and clean. I noticed a pair of twins wearing baby sweatshirts with the logo "Calvin Klein." Six young assistants aged no more than 12 or 13 tended to the children. Even the most finicky prospective European adoptive parents would have been more than satisfied and reassured by the whole atmosphere.

I started giving the children a general checkup and a neurological examination. I examined 17 children, 10 of whom were twins, and they all seemed to be well. Possibly counting on my fatigue, Katia seemed to have deliberately left the most difficult cases to the last. She first handed me a pair of six-month-old twins, who were clearly neurologically damaged. The twins were growth-retarded and markedly hypotonic, or flaccid. They were totally expressionless, with a vacant empty gaze in their eyes and seemingly unable to focus on anything or anyone. They bore on their faces a number of notable features: short eyelid fissures, narrow eyes, a short upturned nose, posteriorly rotated ears, pronounced underdevelopment of the upper jaw, and abnormal smallness and posterior deviation of the lower jaw. Medical examination revealed cardiac defects, multiple skin angiomas, and a sunken chest. The diagnosis was clear: their mother had drunk herself to death throughout pregnancy, and as a consequence the twins were suffering from fetal alcohol syndrome. As Father Bruno had warned me, everybody drank, and sex was very casual down there. The fate of the twins was set. Children with full-blown fetal alcohol syndrome hardly show normal mental ability.

When I told my diagnosis to Katia, she said, "They have been given out for adoption. Their parents will be here in a week." When I asked if the adoptive parents had been warned, she shrugged, "Twins are all the fashion. European parents go mad for them." I said that the parents ought to know what they were taking on. Some people may be prepared for a life of sacrifice while others not. Another shrug: "They would take on anything, provided they are twins." I felt outraged, but Katia seemed adamant in wanting to proceed with the adoption. She told her assistants to take the twins away. Despite my outrage, she seemed unable to stop her ravenousness and was greedy for a last opinion on a big baby girl. The girl was also a twin, but less "valuable." She was one of an opposite-sex pair, I was told, and mixed pairs were not so much in demand. Apparently only monozygotic twins were "the" big hit with Europeans. Other twins did not look like twins and did not cause parents to be stopped in the street in wonder. And when people noticed monozygotic colored twins, they went mad. As Katia explained, "We don't get much out of boy-girl pairs. Only identical twins are very valuable."

By now I understood Katia's monetary transactions to be her primary object. She rescued twins just to make a business out of them. While I was examining the child, Katia asked repeatedly and insistently, "Check her heart. Is her heart all right? How is her heart?" I got a spine-tingling feeling. By now I regarded Katia as a totally immoral person, capable of even selling the girl as an anatomical preparation for an organ transplant. Almost instinctively, I said that the girl's heart was enlarged and had murmurs and possible valve defects too. She asked furiously, "Her heart is not all right then?" I said no. I was not being completely insincere, for the girl's heart was slightly enlarged, and I could hear some murmurs, indicative of a mild heart condition. Nothing more was said, but Katia probably sensed that I understood her dealings to be shady and possibly criminal. She could hardly contain her fury, and snatched the girl from my arms nodding to her assistants. In a moment they had all gathered in another room, singing religious hymns and totally ignoring me. When I left with Christopher, Katia did not even say goodbye.

On our return to Father Bruno's mission, Christopher and I took another route crossing over to another side of the Island. We noticed plenty of twins and even triplets around. Being born even a few kilometers away made all the difference.

A few days later I told father Bruno of my disturbing experiences. His comments were, "Of course, we have no direct proof of this, but organ traffic is a strong suspicion. Twins make good candidates, as most of them are doomed. By saying that the girl's heart was failing, you probably saved her life. Although we do not know for sure, so far we have been unable to gather any concrete evidence, but thank you for telling me. We will investigate the matter further." Currently, the so-called Bellagio Task Force, a team of experts from various backgrounds, is investigating organ trafficking worldwide.[6]

Being born even a few kilometers apart could also make all the difference to twins in Laos too. In 1993 I was asked to work in Laos in two hospitals, one in Vientiane, the capital, and the other in Luang-Prabang, the magnificent former capital, in order to instruct local staff in the use of psychotropic drugs.

During this first visit to Laos, my guide-interpreter alerted me to the fact that twins were treated differently in various parts of Laos. In Vientiane and Luang-Prabang, twins were not an issue. They may have represented a physical and economic burden and a psychological strain, just like everywhere else in the world, but they were not persecuted as such. Matters changed outside these towns and especially in the area of the Golden Triangle, where, as my guide put it, "Twins are killed." I did not, however, have the time to go to the Golden Triangle on that occasion.

Several years later, in 1997, I was asked to investigate the health conditions of various ethnic groups living further north in the Golden Triangle.[7]

The hills of the so-called Golden Triangle, a rugged area shared between Laos, Myanmar, and Thailand, were inhabited by ethnic minorities, all living off the cultivation of poppy fields. These crops were transported some kilometers down the main road and then down the Yellow River to be sold. This area is one of the most bustling drug markets, hence the adjective "Golden."

I was based in the town of Kentay (a fictitious name) and I spent most of my time with the minorities living up the hills. Kentay was a small, sleepy town with practically no cars. Electricity often failed at night. Whenever I made my way back to Kentay from outlining villages, I felt a rare happiness. Built around a crystal clear lake, with sparkling air, beautiful wooden houses and small Buddhist temples, in a landscape with plains colored with every possible shade of green, and a chain of gently rolling hills completely surrounding them, Kentay was the nearest thing I can imagine to a lost Shangri-La. Its inhabitants were welcoming and kind, more than willing to answer my queries about twins.

Around Kentay, grandparents usually took care of twins, as twins were thought to have an adverse effect on the fertility of the rice-fields that were cultivated at the foot of the hills.

After having twins, women needed a long break to breastfeed, which had a negative effect on their fertility. Some women never recovered from childbirth, and many actually died at childbirth. Parents, who usually tended the fields with their children, could not do so with twins. Twins were presumed to transfer their negative influence to the crops, in a sort of contagion of the rice fields. Twins were handed over to their grandparents to be brought up by them, because grandparents, including men, were thought to be past childbearing age and so immune from the twins' negative influence. In the many households with twins I visited in the plains, twins were invariably looked after by their grandparents. See figure 8.3.

Matters changed up in the hills. It took hours to trek by foot up the hills to the first villages. A guide and an interpreter, a young woman

Figure 8.3 Twins being brought up by their grandmother, so that their negative influence does not "transfer" onto the fertility of women of childbearing age and the fruitfulness of the crops.

whom I shall call Karin and a young man who I shall refer to as Yushi, accompanied me.

Although "civilization," in the form of radios, bikes, plastic containers, shoes, and, most importantly, certain medicines, was beginning to reach even the remotest ethnic groups, women were little affected by this change. They just cultivated the poppy fields and orchards, grew millet that they ate and from which they extracted a strong alcoholic beverage, looked after their numerous children, but especially their hens and pigs, and generally had no contact with the outside. Their men, due to the precious poppy crops, maintained all of the contacts with dealers and were much more acquainted with the "modern" world and with westernized habits. All, including the children, were addicted to opium.

Although different minorities inhabited the remote corners of the mountain chains, they all shared on thing in common, a loathing of twins. On a purely statistical basis the total absence of twins wherever I went was already a cause for suspicion. Of some 800 people from whom I collected information based on their memory, not one of them was a twin or apparently had ever even seen a twin.

The true destiny of twins was finally confirmed for me by an intelligent shaman, whom I shall refer to as Sou, presiding over a densely populated village up in the hills. Sou was still fairly young and attractive, but his teeth were completely decayed and blackened. Worse than that, his lungs were burnt out by smoking opium. As he told me, "I know that my lungs are burnt beyond repair. I will never quit smoking, but, Doc, could you please help in relieving some of the pain?" I tried my best. In a token of gratitude Sou gave me a beautifully carved silver bracelet, which I wear almost every day. From then on he also became my best guide and ally in explaining the customs of the various tribes. Owing to language barriers and unusual diffidence, the women in the area were difficult to contact directly. Unlike African women, they did not mellow with physical contact or small presents. They remained aloof. They also took heavily to drugs.

Sou accompanied me together with Karin and Yushi on my visits to many neighboring villages. Most villages were fairly similar. A green gate, which was merely an archway hung with all sorts of protective amulets to look like a summery Christmas tree, was positioned in a wood outside the village and announced that we were entering the village area. Nobody was allowed to violate the space of the gate by passing through it, which would have meant unleashing into the community all the malevolent forces that the gate was supposed to keep at bay. One just had to be careful to walk around it. Other than the symbolic gate, the villages were not protected by any actual fences. Once inside the village, however, one was struck by the absence of any openings in the walls of the thatched huts, or even of the slightest cracks in them. Talismans abounded all over. The only aperture was a small door looking like a narrow hole, and covered with innumerable protective talismans that almost concealed it. At night the door was shut tight with strings, and camouflaged with leaves and moss. Malevolent spirits were thought to be ready to penetrate the household through any fissure at night, as night and darkness were their realm. For other activities that usually take place at night, villages were furnished with a special "love hut," an oblong structure with several partitions, whose entrance was also totally covered with leaves and special amulets. Those couples who wanted to make love had to retreat inside this hut. The love hut was also meant to protect lovers from having twins, who were considered malevolent entities coming from the underworld. Since evil forces could not penetrate the hut, they also could not penetrate the women. When a woman delivered twins, it meant that she had had intercourse in the open air, where evil spirits could enter her. The woman had in effect failed to adopt "contraceptive measures" against the spirits, and so the spirits had fathered twins, who were regularly disposed of at birth by strangling them in a special hut, where women went as soon as they felt the first contractions heralding parturition. Their remains were then buried in the woods far from the village, as it was feared that twins might return at night to bring misfortune on the village.

During the day, women, men, and children were everywhere in the villages. Most women went bare-breasted, and many were suckling an infant. The infant was generally breastfed using only one breast and always the same one, usually the left. This was another reason for murdering twins. One of women's two breasts was exclusively for suckling infants, while the other was exclusively for pleasure and lust. Lust and feeding could never be mixed. Twins would complicate matters, as they took up both breasts.

The split between lust and nurture mirrors the recognized split between women almost universally categorized into either "madonnas" or "whores." Up in those hills, however, the split applied mainly to women's breasts. Lustful women were appreciated, just as were fertile ones, but infants could not be contaminated with lust, nor lovers excited by the nurturing functions of the maternal body, which they considered to be a taboo.

The psychoanalyst Melanie Klein traced this kind of split into a "good" and a "bad" breast to earliest life. The infant is born into a sort of chaos of opposite and contradictory perceptions and desires, pleasant and unpleasant. Very soon the infant resorts to splitting, so as to establish order in the initial chaos. All badness and persecution are projected onto a bad object, the "bad" breast, and all goodness onto an idealized object, the "good" breast. Maturation brings about integration and fusion of the division.[8] A similar split between the two breasts and their function was indeed operative among these women in the Golden Triangle. More to the point, all evilness was split onto twins and the split between a lustful and a nurturing breast mercilessly condemned twins even further.

Despite the cruel fate met by most twins, some mothers were kind-hearted and rebellious. One day, back in Kentay, I met a pair of twin girls living with an old woman. The girls appeared to have come from the same communities I had been visiting up the hills. As often happens, their mother had delivered her twins alone. Though the girls were born alive and well, she declared them dead immediately and stole away from the community, taking them with her, on a trip that probably took days, until she found a compassionate woman to care for them. The mother never returned for the twins, thereby saving them from all the superstitions of her group.

Unlike all the superstitious groups encountered in Madagascar and the Golden Triangle, we westerners believe that we live in a fully rational world illuminated by scientific knowledge. Yet when dealing with "the mystery of life" and the nature of our own existence, we too face questions that are not completely explained by the hard facts of scientific reason. In such cases both uneducated and modern people almost invariably resort to nonrational, mystical, or religious explanations, such as believing in souls, heaven or hell, and wondering if the embryo has already full personhood from conception. This nonrational response is doubled in the case of twins, who are the exception rather then the norm for the human species. A response to personhood in the embryo actually derives from the formation of twins, as the embryo can potentially split giving rise to monozygotic twins during the first 15 days after conception. Many scientists claim that the embryo cannot be considered an individual until it has the potential to divide into two entities.

For those who do not have access to modern scientific knowledge, the origins of twins are considered to be not just different but also uncanny.

Especially in the past, the link between intercourse and pregnancy was itself unclear. The time span between intercourse and the first unmistakable signs of pregnancy—the cessation of menses, a bulging belly, and quickening—was too long to assume a connection between the two events. Intercourse could be practiced with prepubertal or barely pubertal girls, who were not yet menstruating, and the fact that they then did not get pregnant was taken as evidence of the dissociation between sex and pregnancy. Infants were believed to be conceived in many different ways, such as by eating special foods or being penetrated by spirits or snakes. Such theories still linger on in some areas of the world, from islands in the Pacific to regions of Africa, including Madagascar, where all children are thought to be the reincarnation of a deceased ancestor. Twin births, by being especially unusual and frightening, are assumed to be caused by malignant entities, including evil, vengeful spirits, with drastic consequences.

When women from high-income countries harbor absurd theories about the genesis of twins, such as marriage to a superstud or the splitting of mature fetuses into half, these myths are not a matter of life and death for mothers and their twins. Scientific explanations can dispel such myths. In contrast, theories of conception have major consequences for women living in many other areas of the world, especially for their twins. These theories can color each twin birth and turn them it into a blessing or a nightmare.

The superstitions surrounding twins cannot be dismissed as simply the product of "primitive minds," as the European mothers adopting Madagascan twins referred to them and believed. The tendency to try to attach meaning to natural phenomena and to explain them in the light of some theory is universal. The history of science is filled with often bizarre explanations, heavily tainted with superstitious and religious beliefs, which nonetheless, in a trial-and-error way, have contributed to its advancement. Those living on the periphery of the developed world can give very accurate descriptions of the phenomena linked with twin births. Many distinguish in great detail the various types of placentas and amniotic sacs in which twins are contained. These people do not lack superior minds, they simply lack the means to attach proper meaning to accurately examined facts.

The widespread superstitious loathing of twins can be explained by current scientific knowledge. Twin pregnancies, for example, are much more dangerous and taxing for both the mother and the twins. Though this difference is no longer so dramatic in the developed world, maternal mortality is still greatly increased in twin gestations and deliveries. For less fortunate populations, twins are easily associated with frequent maternal death. This may be one of the reasons why twins are deemed to be "bad luck." It may also partly explain why twins are associated with the dead and with evil forces who allegedly penetrate their mother's bodies.

Maternal complications are also much more frequent in twin gestations. In high-income countries these situations are generally treated in well-equipped maternity hospitals. In less fortunate circumstances, such complications, even if not causing death, may well affect the future health of the mother. The potential dangers range from diabetes to varicose veins. It is not hard to imagine how a woman living in the hills of the Golden Triangle might link these bodily alterations and ailments to the protracted malevolent influence of her twins. The Ethiopian woman who delivered her twins in the bush suffered from a rare complication exclusive to twin pregnancies, called acute polhydramnios, in which an enormous amount of amniotic fluid rapidly accumulates in the amniotic sacs, causing massive stretching of the uterus and abdomen, breathing difficulties, and a premature birth. The swelling suddenly recedes when the twins come out, accompanied by an unusual outpouring of fluid. An astonished village could easily interpret the sudden and dramatic swelling, accompanied by heavy breathing, as possession by evil entities. Cause-and-effect reasoning could lead them to think that the evil entities were the expelled twins.

Placental problems with consequent massive bleeding are also more frequent in twin gestations. Twins might therefore be thought to have filled the maternal body with all sorts of impurities. The almost universal taboo against menstrual blood and the association of any vaginal bleeding with impurity could similarly explain why mothers of twins are kept outside the community in Madagascar. The twins are thought to have tainted them, making their genitals so impure as to bar them from intercourse for the rest of their lives.

A twin birth is no longer a surprise in our well-equipped delivery rooms. Due to the advent of ultrasounds, most mothers know from the early stages of pregnancy that they are expecting twins. In less developed countries a twin birth is almost invariably a surprise. The second twin to come out is the surprise, and possibly a shocking one. This shock may have contributed to the perception of the second twin as having a dubious origin, requiring it to undergo some kind of trial, such as the "test of the oxen," in order to verify its humanity.

Nowadays twins generally reach term at least three weeks before singletons,[9] and many are born before then, requiring more prolonged stays in an intensive care unit. If not promptly treated, many twins die at birth. This widespread prematurity and mortality may also have led to the association of twins with the uncanny and the dead. The increased risk of infant mortality in twins also extends well beyond the first year, which may have made their mothers and the community especially callous toward them. The decreased fertility of the mother, in the sense of her being unable to bring twins to maturity, may then have been associated with her having a bad influence on the fertility and maturation of the crops.

Deformations, especially misshapen heads and limbs, are frequent in twins, mostly caused by intrauterine crowding. For largely unknown reasons, other malformations and the abnormal development or formation of parts of the body are also more frequent in twins, as are chromosomal aberrations.

Variously conjoined or so-called Siamese twins present an even more shocking problem. It is bad enough for expectant Western mothers to learn the news in the early stages of pregnancy when abortion is still an option. One can well imagine how a community living in different circumstances might react to the terrifying sight of such oddities viewed as "monsters" emerging from the mother's vagina. It is a short step from "Monsters are twins" to "Twins are monsters," and finally to "Mothers of twins have generated monsters, and are monsters too." These people may not have our knowledge and explanations, but they can and do observe things carefully.

Chapter 9

Heart of Darkness

In 1999 I was contacted by a humanitarian organization based in the region of El Chaco or El Gran Chaco, a huge area of land stretching over three countries: Paraguay, Bolivia, and Brazil. I was asked to conduct a survey into the physical condition of indigenous communities in the region, with a special emphasis on gender issues, and to put forward a plan for improving women's health. While preparing for the work, I read in an old book a passing reference to a native population that sacrificed twins for unspecified "selfish" reasons. This brief comment further increased my interest in the project.

Many of the indigenous populations, commonly called *Indios*, inhabit El Chaco. Historically the *Indios* were periodically exterminated and stripped of their land. Between 1968 and 1972 the *Indios* became the subject of another genocidal campaign. Following international investigations, the manhunt appeared to cease, and the *Indios* were given some land in the so-called Gran Chaco. Killings continued throughout the 1980s, however, and by 2002 were still being brought to the attention of the United Nations.

El Chaco is sparsely populated. Only 2.5 percent of Paraguay's population lives in an area covering 60.7 percent of the entire country. The three governments have granted the heterogeneous ethnic groups living in the region small reservations called "*campos*," where various communities of *Indios* manage to survive in utter poverty, practicing agriculture that barely covers their basic needs. Infrastructures are completely lacking, including basic health care facilities. On paper, education is guaranteed for all, but this is not so for the *Indios*. Infant mortality remains high even in urban areas, where there are 26 deaths for every 1000 births and life expectancy is 72 for men and 77 for women.[1]

Besides the *Indios*, El Chaco is populated by people of Germanic stock of varied descent. The largest component is a tight-knit community of Mennonites, who migrated from Germany, Switzerland, and Ukraine via Canada during the First World War. A second Germanic wave of more sinister origin, including many Nazi criminals, came directly from Europe at the end of World War Two. Some Nazis were still rumored to be living comfortably in the region while I was there. The most recent wave of foreigners over the last ten years are of mixed origin, and have come from all neighboring countries.

Before these successive waves of immigration, El Chaco was covered by forests and inhabited almost exclusively by the *Indios*. Now deforestation has taken place on a massive scale, and the *Indios* are reduced to small numbers. The only tiny "islands" of intact forest remaining in an ocean of heavily cultivated land are in fact those inhabited almost solely by indigenous communities.

The *Indios'* health was particularly poor, being undernourished and suffering from all sorts of chest ailments, especially TB, and parasitical diseases. Medical facilities were only available for those *Indios* who had left their *campos* and worked on the land of the foreigners. Throughout my stay I was accompanied by a local guide, whom I shall call Ramon, a gentle and intelligent man of mixed blood in his late forties. We became good friends. When we visited the first communities, we came back at night to a small guest house in the main town of the region. When a fortnight later we went to more secluded *campos*, Ramon and I slept in tents. The *Indios* lived in crumbling barracks, whose nooks and crannies hosted a bug responsible for the so-called Chagas Disease or American Trypanosomiasis, resulting in massive enlargement of many organs such as the heart, oesophagus, and intestine and eventually leading to death. Chagas disease is considered a typical illness caused by poverty and poor housing. See figure 9.1.

Ramon picked me up for my first visit to a community when it was almost dark. Driving his dilapidated car, he cleverly found his way through a labyrinth of dusty roads, all looking exactly alike, while playing on tape the same tango song, "Malena," over and over again. As he drove, Ramon explained that each *Indios* community was run by a chief, the "*casique,*" to whom one had to pay homage on first meeting. Women were also very active in the communities, especially sexually.[2] As Ramon noted, "They take all the initiative and can never seem to get enough, even when they are well into old age. It never ends." Prostitution, which was common among young girls, was not treated as a stigma. On the contrary, it was considered to indicate a pleasantly "hot" nature. When it came to marriage, ex-prostitutes, who had usually practiced in town before coming back to their villages, were much in demand. This attitude probably stemmed from former

Figure 9.1 The *indios* live in utter poverty and in appalling conditions. These twins, being held by an old woman, are skinny, undernourished, and half-naked. Like the old woman, they are all unprotected against the cold nights. This explains why infant mortality is high and chest diseases rampant.

beliefs about pregnancy, as the fetus was once thought to need the sperm of numerous and varied men in order to grow healthily to term. The *Indios* no longer believed this now, but appreciation for promiscuity still continued. Women were expected to be sexually active as soon as they started menstruating.

When we reached the community, I was struck by the abysmal poverty and appalling living conditions of the inhabitants. It was winter in this hemisphere, and El Chaco was bitterly cold at night, but I was the only one wearing warm clothes. The barracks were the *Indios* lived were crumbling and cold, everyone was coughing and had runny noses, water taken from nearby small rivers was icy, and often the only food available were tuberous roots mixed with the meat of small animals, including rats. Needless to say the *Indios* were severely undernourished.

I greeted the *casique* first, a middle-aged man whom I shall call Horacio. The *casique,* after introducing me to the rest of the group, told me that in order to stay with them, I had to be renamed by one of the women, who would then become my godmother. A middle-aged woman, whom I shall call Alina, with no teeth, long dirty nails, and a hostile expression on her face, approached me. She told me to squat down and, without any warning, poured an entire jug of cold water over my head. Laughing she said "Your name is: The Last to Come." Still laughing and ridiculing me, Alina asked Ramon, "Is she another anthropophagous?" Ramon explained to me that the *Indios* generally nicknamed anthropologists "anthropophagi" because they just exploited them and gave nothing in return. My "godmother" seemed surprised to hear that I was actually a doctor, but continued to sound unfriendly. I sensed the same hostility when I approached the other women. I was not used to this response, and it surprised me until I suddenly remembered that Ramon had told me of women remaining sexually active well into old age. In most other low-income countries, from Africa to the Far East, women are often already considered old and sexually unappealing by the age of 25, and in those areas I was never perceived as a threat. Here, however, I represented a potential sexual rival, so I had to be extremely tactful.

Later in the evening I nevertheless asked a decidedly untactful question. The *Indios* were squatting around the fire and few armadillos were wandering around like small, tame dogs when I asked "Any twins?" All the women laughed derisively. They then grasped the armadillos by the tail and obscenely pretended to insert their tails between their wide-spread knees. I was at a loss to understand, except that both twins and armadillos were touchy subjects at the least.

As I later learned from Ramon, armadillos, which are carriers of Chagas disease, also regularly have twins, which are invariably identical, the only "true" twins according to the *Indios*. Although *Indios* loved to eat the tasty armadillo meat, women of childbearing age never ate it, for fear of having twins. Their men had to spurn the meat as well, because by eating it, they might pass on to their women the risk of having twins. Contagion of Chagas disease was a realistic fear, but the *Indios* having little choice in matters of food did not bother about it. Over the next few days we visited other communities, where twins continued to be a touchy issue. Whenever I mentioned them, I was regularly told that there had been no twin births in living memory. Then everyone changed the subject and tightened their lips.

Finally we reached a little community where, after being introduced to the *casique*, whom I shall call Julio, I noticed an old woman holding two severely undernourished twin boys. Her fictitious name was Paula, and she was the *casique*'s wife. When I asked about the twins, Julio said, "Their father is my son. My wife has to look after them, as their mother ran away. She breastfed the twins for six months but then abandoned them and went back to her village." He told me the mother's name and the name of her community, but when I asked why she had left, he said nothing. Obviously he did not want to talk about it. Upon closer scrutiny, I could see that the twins were in an appalling state. They had tuberculosis, their eyes were infected, their hair was infested with parasites, and their skinny, filthy, naked bodies were covered with deep scars, which I judged to be burns. When Paula noticed my looking at the scars, she said, "They both fell on the fire." I realized at once that this was impossible, as the twins could not even sit up yet. The burns had been intentionally caused.

The rest of the day was a nightmare for me, as I could not stop thinking about the skinny twins. Knowing why twins were loathed now seemed imperative to me, and I mulled over the same question, "How on earth can I make a *casique* talk?" I realized intuitively that somehow I had to pay special tribute to the Julio, recognizing his leadership within the community, and so that evening I asked him to come with me for a ride. When he accepted, I took Ramon's dilapidated car, put "Malena" on full volume, and started driving around in the immense darkness of El Chaco. The more we wandered through the night, the more Julio relaxed and seemed to enjoy our drive. Without my asking any questions, he suddenly broached the subject of twins.

Twins were regularly disposed of by the *Indios* who buried them alive at birth, he explained. They took them to a secluded place, dug a ditch for each of them, and filled the ditch with earth, leaving only the twins' head uncovered. Since the sun is strong during the day this ensured a quick death by dehydration. This horrible death somehow released the *Indios* from guilt, as Julio said, "We do not kill them, we just leave them." Originally the *Indios* were nomadic and could not cope with twins, but now the reason for discarding them was different. Twins implied the need for especially prolonged sexual restraint. When women had twins, they had to abstain from sex for at least two years, because getting pregnant again soon after the delivery of twins was too much. Due to the frailty of twins, many of them also had to be breastfed for a longer time. Women knew only too well that in the meantime their men would not observe asceticism. By the time infant twins were weaned, most women would have been replaced by more or less official "extra" wives. This was the "selfish reason" for disposing of twins that had been mentioned in the book I read before visiting El Chaco.

As Julio told me, "Another pregnancy, no more milk. Mothers cannot cope with twins and sex. All women rebel when twins are born. They don't want to give up sex. They bury them." When I asked why his wife had decided to keep the twins, he said "She is too old to get pregnant. Even if she keeps the twins, she can have sex." I asked him why twins were not regularly handed over to older women like his wife, who could have both sex and twins. He said, "They would not want them. Twins are tiresome. Women just feel like sleeping when you have to look after twins. Paula is helped by two young girls." Julio had another reason for keeping the twins. He lived too close to a small town with a police station. Nobody should suspect the bleak destiny of the twins. Especially the police. Policemen were terrible in the area—and I suspect in other areas too—taking anything as an excuse to persecute the *Indios*, kick them off their land, and rape their women. The police virtually had a green light to exterminate entire communities.

Contrary to my expectations, I found myself thinking that these poor *Indios* women lived between two cultures. In the recent past they had inhabited the *Silva,* the forest, as nomadic hunters and gatherers. The same as in Ethiopia, nomadic life and twins were antithetical, so the *Indios* disposed of all their twins. Presumably this knowledge was still with them in their current situation, forced to leave their forests behind and to adapt to a sedentary life of misery, poverty, loneliness, famine, and persecution within narrow and isolated communities. An enhanced urge for indiscriminate sex was possibly the only diversion left to these marginalized and brutalized people. Random promiscuity could also be viewed as an easily available remedy for a burning need for comfort. Closeness, skin and human contact, no matter how fleeting and superficial, offered warmth to a needy, ill-treated people who were exploited and marginalized by everyone save members of their own communities.

Julio reported that the police had become suspicious about twin infanticide in the community but used it merely as an excuse for all sorts of abuse of their own. According to Julio, the suspicion about twins had first been ignited by a woman, whom I shall call Alicia, living in another community, who had run away some 30 years earlier with her husband and twins. Her community was particularly hostile to twins as its inhabitants feared that other women might have had twins by "contagion" with them. In order to save them she crossed the so-called Chaco *Impenetrable*, a part of the region covered by dense, thorny vegetation, and populated by all sorts of dangerous animals, ranging from jaguars to poisonous snakes. It took her months. Now she was "famous" as she had been invited to take part in a television program to talk about her adventure, but suspicion about twins had started. *Indios* living near towns had become wary. All the communities living near towns now kept a pair of twins to show to the police whenever the necessity arose. Returning from El Chaco, I asked about twins in a few settlements near the outskirts of the main town in the region and was invariably introduced to one pair in each place. They were all clearly "fake" twins, to be produced as evidence of "correctness" to a disinterested police force. Most were young men picked out and paired at random. One such pair, when asked for their birthday, declared discordant dates three years apart.

A few days after my drive with Julio, I visited the *campo* where the young mother who had abandoned the campo's grandsons now lived. I will call her Patricia and she was 18, though she would have looked much younger were it not for a hard, determined expression on her face. She was short and plump, not particularly attractive, and wore a bright red heavy sweater and a miniskirt. Someone from outside the community must have fed her and given her these clothes, as all the other women were skinny, wore almost nothing, and seemed to be freezing. When I told Patricia that I had seen her twins, she shrugged and said, "I wanted to be here. I had many arguments with my husband. I want to be free to go and live in town (meaning prostitution). I breastfed them for six months, as Julio and Paula asked me to. I did my duty but then left." While we were talking, all the women circled around her in a protective way.

Patricia then asked me with a worried look if it was true that mothers of twins were prone to having other twins, explaining "If I have other twins, I cannot work." I said this probably would not happen to her, as her twins looked identical, and only so-called non-identical twins have a proven tendency to recur in families. She smiled for the first time and never mentioned her twins again.

The women began to ask me lots of questions about contraception, some having heard that you could be given shots. Patricia was active in the questioning.

The *Indios* did not have any of the prenatal options open to women living in high-income countries. No pill or contraceptive of any kind and no safe abortions were available in the region. Abortifacients were more often than not lethal herbal compounds to be drunk or inserted locally. Violent external means, such as jumping on the stomach of the pregnant woman, hitting it with stones, or, inserting unclean metal tools into the womb, were equally deadly. Abortion among the *Indios* could be less safe than carrying a child to term.

In developed countries contraception and safe abortion have been paramount factors at the foundation of the so-called women's revolution. They have also been paramount factors in almost totally erasing abandonment of infacts and infanticide. The only form of safe contraception available to these *Indios* women was plain abstinence, *coitus interruptus*, or anal intercourse, which many considered against nature, not socially acceptable or to their taste. Condoms could not be found in the region and would anyway have been too costly for them.

Young Patricia, like so many adolescents worldwide, wanted to experiment with sexuality. Prostitution was a culturally acceptable means of both experimenting with sexuality and gaining an advantage from it. Patricia and all the other women, however, feared unwanted pregnancies, especially twins. By breastfeeding her twins, Patricia allowed them to live, but she otherwise saw them only as a hindrance to her freedom, "career," and search for "warmth." Despite having looked after her twins for several months and breastfeeding them, she considered it had just been her duty. After doing "her duty," she left her twins behind and did not miss them.

Some days later I reached the *campo* where Alicia, the "famous" woman who had run away from her *campo* and crossed El Chaco *Impenetrable* with her husband and twins, now lived. Possibly due to her appearance on television, where she narrated the escape from her village and crossing the *Silva*, her status in the community was very high. Although her husband was the *casique*, I was introduced to her first. I expected to see a maternal figure, but she looked cunning and secretive. When I asked to meet her sons, Alicia said, "Only one lives here. The other is in another *campo*." The son who lived with her introduced me to his wife and informed me proudly that she was a prostitute and from time to time still went "to town." He asked me in a commanding tone to take some pictures of them. The media had become important for this family.

Television has reached even some of the remotest corners of the world, allowing everyone to observe how westerners live. Among other things, they have noticed our growing need to show our face and to tell all sorts of details about our lives, including intimate and distressing ones, on TV shows. Recently a mother in Italy proudly announced her new pregnancy during a television show only two months after the atrocious death of her young son, for which she was being investigated. TV shows have become a sort of cheap form of global group psychotherapy and a means to obtain a fleeting and illusory moment of fame, thus participating in the world of celebrities, whose opinion on everything is now valued above everyone else's. Take for instance Angelina Jolie talking as an expert about Africa, after delivering safely in Namibia attended by a team of specialists flown in solely for her, or the global attention being brought on the tragedy in Darfour only after George Clooney mentioned it.

Indios watching us also seek some visibility for themselves. Being on television is the ultimate, but even a Polaroid snapshot will do. Alicia, by appearing on the television show, had now become the diva of her tribe.

Two days later I met her other son, whom I shall call Josè, in a distant *campo*. He looked identical to his twin brother, but he seemed gentler and kinder in nature. When I asked how long he had been in this settlement, he said, "As long as I can remember." I asked, "Does your mother often visit you?" He said, "No, she never has." The diva who had achieved fame for her brave attachment to her twins had in fact completely abandoned one of them. After a while, Josè introduced me to an old woman saying,

"This is my godmother. She brought me up when my mother sold me to her." Josè had not only been abandoned but sold.

My stay was nearly coming to an end when I visited a more remote and secluded *campo*. The settlement, which looked much wealthier than any other I had visited so far, was run by a plain woman in her mid- to late-thirties, whom I shall call Fernanda, and by her husband, a priest belonging to a Christian sect I had never heard of before. The priest was not around at the time, and, over the following days, I never detected any signs of his presence. Fernanda had no children. Pointing to the *Indios,* she said, "They are my children. I don't need any of my own." Her whole demeanor conveyed intransigence and fanaticism.

Fernanda knew of my interests, and she asked all the other women to gather around her. As usual, the women seemed suspicious and hostile toward me, but obediently they all squatted down. In the meantime Ramon played football with the children. There was not a single man around, and I was told vaguely, "They are out." Luis, a tall adolescent boy, however, sat near Fernanda, and from time to time they exchanged knowing glances. It was clear that Fernanda was intimate with Luis, who could almost have been her son. She started talking in a tone of voice that was intimidating and unwavering "I am sure that this camp is different from all the others you have seen. It is the best camp around with proper housing, proper care, and since I am a teacher, I also run a school. I know that you are interested in women and pregnancies. Let me tell you something straight away. I will never ever admit any contraception here. It is against the law of the Lord. There should be no limits to his grace. Contraception is beginning to be practiced in some *campos*, especially near the main towns in the region. They give them shots. There is still very little money for that, but it is beginning. We have money, but these women must follow the preaching of the Lord. I check on their periods every month, so I know if they are pregnant or not. If they abort spontaneously, they must call me and show me the evidence."

Usually I was tactful in challenging the behavior of the *Indios* and tried to refrain from making judgments, but I did not feel the same with Fernanda. I was both angered and disgusted by the absolute control she tried to exert over the lives of these women. I also felt outraged by Fernanda's double moral standards, so I said firmly, "You cannot control the lives of these women. How can you even check on their periods? And perhaps their sexual encounters, too?" Becoming defiant, she replied, "I control their sexual activity. They are not allowed to hide in the forest with their men. It must all take place right in front of me and with my permission." "Shame on you." I responded. "How can you do that? I call that voyeurism. You are a teacher, so you must know what I mean. Sex and contraception must be their choice. Stop meddling with their lives." She answered, "If they choose contraception, they can leave."

An old woman, whom I shall call Margarita, broke the ice by saying to me, "Come. Follow me, and I will re-name you." I followed her to get "baptized" in a beautiful corner of the forest overlooking the crystal clear waters of a small river, where she said, "I will name you The Big Solid Tree." Then she hugged me tearfully. Taking a small necklace made of some kind of dried seeds from her neck, Margarita put it around mine, saying, "This is for my daughter. Now you are my daughter." Moved, I tried to reciprocate by giving her my sun hat. Margarita looked ecstatic and hugged me again. Then she said that she had another present for me and gave me two small splendidly carved wooden shovels, one plain and the other spoon-like. The wood had a delightful smell of a mixture of rosewood and teak.

When I went back to Fernanda, she had regained some of her composure. The women started laughing when they saw "my mother" with her new hat, but Fernanda seemed annoyed and retreated to her cottage. In a moment the boy followed her. During the rest of my stay I hardly saw Fernanda at all. Once back from my assignment, I complained about her to a pro-Indios association, explaining what she had told me, but I doubt that any of my complaints were taken seriously. The association was tightly controlled by government forces and the elite of the country. The walls of its office were covered with geographic maps on which several communities had been crossed off. More land was going to be expropriated.

Besides my new "mother," another interesting and touching encounter took place on the same day.

A *Silvicula* family had come out of the forest just two years earlier and now lived in the *campo*. The *Silvicula,* apparently ferocious *Indios*, refused all contact with civilization and killed anybody who attempted to approach them, including the *Indios* who lived in the *campos*. The *Silvicula* lived within the "*Silva Impenetrable,*" meaning an impenetrable, dangerous forest thick with thorny acacias. Nobody had come back alive after encountering them, and whenever the *Silvicula* were mentioned during my stay, everybody seemed scared to death. All told me of the atrocities they were capable of committing, from cutting people up into chunks and eating them to shooting them with poisonous arrows or severing their tendons so they could no longer walk or run, thus falling easy prey to the many dangers of the forest. The *Silvicula* had gradually grown to mythological proportions in my mind.

Of the *Silvicula* family now living in the campo, only their daughter, whom I shall refer to as Umna, was there at the time, the rest having gone to collect honey some distance away. I had noticed Umna from the start.

She had a different build from the other women: very muscular and broad in the shoulders, in contrast with her long slim legs. She also smiled a lot and seemed quite friendly toward everyone, including me, in a shy kind of way. Another peculiarity had struck me. She kept moving her eyes all the time, as if affected by nystagmus, an oscillatory movement of the eyeballs. When I first saw her, I made a mental note to try to give her a neurological examination.

Seeing Umna now, I offered to examine her and was surprised by the gentleness with which she agreed. I wondered how she could be a member of such a ferocious group. Her eye movements turned out to be not nystagmus but spontaneous. They seemed to have the function of quickly scanning the environment in order to perceive any discrepant element that might signal a potential danger. The impenetrable forest that Umna had recently left behind was indeed filled with innumerable dangers, from huge thorns to wild animals and lethal snakes. Extreme alertness could be vital in this extreme environment.

During my stay, Umna followed me around like a tender and affectionate pet. Umna was nearly twice my size, but when I walked, I sounded like an elephant compared to the absolute silence of her steps. Umna moved on tiptoe with incredible speed and levity. Her dexterity of movement probably saved her as much as her fast-moving eyes from the many dangers of the forest. We may all have had the same capacities thousands of years ago, but they are now irretrievably lost.

Umna had a kind of sixth sense, too, for she had somehow picked up on my interest in twins. The day before I was due to leave, Umna took me to her orchard, a leveled-out piece of land where she had planted giant pumpkins, of which she was very proud. She brought along the two wooden shovels given to me by my adoptive mother, which she laid down on the ground. The she picked up two pieces of wood, nearly identical in size, and then put them on her stomach while making a wailing sound, to indicate that the sticks represented baby twins. Next she pointed to the *Silva* far away in the distance and started moving around on all fours, making hissing and roaring sounds while pretending to cut and blind herself with thorns, to show that life in the *Silva* could be dangerous indeed. Umna then laid the "twins" down gently, stroked them tenderly, and moved away, as if to say that the *Silvicula* abandoned their twins because there were too many dangers around for them to survive anyway. She took up the "twins" once again and, this time pointing to the settlement, pretended to put the "twins" to her breasts, grimaced in disgust, threw the "twins" away, and simulated the motions of intercourse. Afterward she dug a whole in the ground with my shovels, buried the "twins," and simulated intercourse again.

Tender Umna, who belonged to a tribe capable of eliciting terror in everyone, was able to make a distinction between the different motives that lay behind the tragic destiny of newborn twins. The *Silvicula* abandoned their twins out of sheer necessity, because the *Silva* was too dangerous a place to wonder around while carrying them, but the mothers felt pain for their act. The women outside the *Silva,* however, whom Umna observed just as accurately, gave up their twins out of fear of sexual abstinence and showed no signs of pain or grief. It occurred to me that when the *Indios* still lived in the Silva, life was difficult, but possibly less miserable and constricted than in the *campos*. The *Silvicula* needed no compensatory sex. The poor *Indios* had become addicted to it.

After spending ten days in the campo, I was sad to leave Umna, and she also seemed distressed. She called to me in her peculiar guttural voice and took me aside, making sure that Fernanda could not see us. She pointed to her nails, pretending to paint them with polish. Although I do not wear nail polish, I always bring some with me, knowing that women at all latitudes go mad for it. Umna was thrilled. She hugged me tearfully and then ran with her incredible speed and lightness toward the orchard. I keep a picture of Umna on my desk.

El Chaco was quite different from every other case I had witnessed. In Ethiopia mothers let "nature run its course" out of sheer necessity, because they could not carry twins around in their nomadic wanderings. They had to "invest" in those infants who were likely to survive and receive benefit from their meager resources, and twins hardly fit this category. In Madagascar mothers chose to abandon or drown their twins at birth out of sheer superstitious terror. Social pressures also influenced their decision. Not only were twins excluded from the community, but their mothers could be expelled as well. In the Chaco region, however, mothers did not fear twins as malevolent entities, nor did the society loath them. Twins were simply a nuisance. Infant twins were buried alive so as not to give up sexual pleasure. Society prized "hot" women, and came to considering their sexual urge stronger than their maternal drive. As the *casique* said, "Mothers cannot cope with twins and sex."

Yet I was not as shocked as I might have expected to be by the fact that mothers were killing twins in order to have sex. The *Indios* mothers seemed otherwise so utterly human to me. I never regarded these women as heartless "Medeas." *Indios* women were interested in more effective means of contraception, which they knew existed and were commonly used by white women, but they could not afford them. In our world, where contraception is easily available and affordable, women regard intercourse disconnected from pregnancy as commonplace. A satisfactory sex life is considered a healthy and important right.

Indios women had been deprived of everything else, from their habitat and their land to ordinary human rights. When I objected to Fernanda's controlling policy and to her double moral standards in matters of sex, my god-mother was grateful for my courage in speaking up. She named me "The Big Solid Tree" and gave me some wooden palettes as a gift, which, I didn't know at the time, were used by mothers to bury newborn twins, as Umna later indicated. Perhaps if their basic needs had been fulfilled and the *Indios* mothers had been given the option of safe contraception, these supposed "Medeas" would have started giving up their palettes and caring for their twins. In high-income countries women are hardly ever faced with this kind of choice.

Five years before going to El Chaco, I was confronted in another country, Guinea Bissau, with a different sort of aberrant behavior running against all our idealized views of motherhood. Guinea Bissau, a former Portugues colony, is a small West African nation that in those years had gone almost totally adrift. Ethnic clashes, war, mock elections, coups d'état, unbridled corruption, and increasing poverty had all contributed to the disappearance of a coherent state and any semblance of democracy in the nation.[3] Despite its gorgeous, varied landscape, including some magnificent islands, the nation had been crossed off the tourist map as a dangerous, "no go" destination.

In 1995 a colleague, whom I shall call Pedro, whose ancestors originally came from the region, came to work in Milan for six months as an obstetrician. Pedro wished to improve his skills in several advanced medical techniques, such as echocardiography, the ultrasound-guided analysis of fetal heart functioning.

Pedro attended the twin unit regularly, and we became good friends. His next destination was Guinea Bissau, which he knew well, having worked there for over three years. One day Pedro asked me, "Why don't you come too? I am sure you could help us. We have many mental problems, but we also have a big twins problem there. Twins are considered evil. As such, they are killed."[4]

This was especially true among the two main ethnic groups of the country, people who did not live in the middle of nowhere but in and around the capital. Twins were believed not to be human beings but to be malevolent entities generated by the impregnation of women by all sorts of dangerous living creatures, such as poisonous insects, snakes, or man-eating crocodiles. These creatures were thought to penetrate women when they bathed in the waters of the various rivers and ponds. Given their unnatural, nonhuman origins, twins had to be killed. Many prospective mothers of twins, knowing that it was safer for their own health to deliver at the hospital where Pedro worked, would deliver these twins and wait to go back to their villages to kill them. Other ethnic minorities in the country who lived farther away from the capital regarded twins as sacred, but women belonging to those groups came less frequently to deliver in the hospital because of the distance.

Before leaving, Pedro repeated his invitation, and two months later, I joined him. Though sparsely inhabited, with roughly 1,340,000 inhabitants, and rich in natural resources, the country was in a state of undeniable poverty. Life-expectancy was barely 49 years for men and 51 for women. Infant mortality was at a high of 12 percent. Of the population, 59 percent were illiterate, and the nation had no universities. Most people lived off agriculture and fishing, both practiced in a craftsmanlike manner, but the country relied on imported food for basic survival. Many of its inhabitants, or 45 percent, were declaredly animistic, but Islam was almost as strong among 40 percent of the population.[5]

I was based in the capital, Bissau, which was a pleasant, sleepy town very much unaffected by modernity. Contrary to the massive urbanization of many other African nations, Bissau was sparsely populated with only a quarter of the total population. Pedro and I worked in the maternity ward of a hospital there. Although the decaying building lacked any modern equipment, my colleagues were capable of doing miracles with the few resources available. During my stay many hair-raising deliveries took place in the hospital, and Pedro and his students invariably dealt with them with incredible skill.

In the few free evenings after work, when Bissau was almost solely illuminated by a gigantic moon and candlelight, we regularly met at the only restaurant in town, where we discussed ways of trying to foster attachment for twins among women who delivered twins. We assumed that if we could manage to help mothers establish an emotional tie with their twins, they would find infanticide abhorrent. As our first step we decided to prolong the mothers' stay in the hospital as long as possible in order to encourage maximum contact with their infants. The general prematurity of the twins gave us a good excuse to keep mothers in the ward. While they were hospitalized, I tried everything I could to involve the mothers, encouraging physical contact with the twins, teaching them massage, showing them the many capabilities of their infants, engaging them in their care, showing them how the twins responded selectively to their voice, and encouraging them to sing, talk to, and cuddle their twins. I often felt like a walking encyclopedia on bonding and attachment and tried to maintain an optimistic outlook, but could not fail to notice worrisome signs, such as only fleeting eye contact, no real bodily closeness, no talking, singing, or lulling of the twins to sleep, and never any questions about their health and future development.[6]

Parallel to this work, I decided to follow up on the twins who had already been dismissed from the hospital, as I wanted to ascertain the true rate of twin neglect and infanticide. Pedro gave me a list of 103 twin births dating back five years. All of these deliveries had taken place at the hospital, and the ethnic origin of the twins was specified for each birth. Pedro and his colleagues had collected all these detailed data over the years. This was something unheard of in most low-income countries. I decided to begin the survey with those ethnic groups who were known not to commit twin infanticide, totaling 21 deliveries, and to leave for last the two majority populations who allegedly executed twins, totaling 82 deliveries. Since the families could not be reached by post or phone, I visited them accompanied by a guide, whom I shall call Amadou. In total I called on 77 families, as the remaining families had moved to some other part of the country and could not be found. Most of these families, or 88 percent, lived in villages on the outskirts of Bissau. My survey took two weeks to complete.

The first 16 visits were encouraging. Four twins had died, but the fact that they had been born both prematurely, at less than 30 weeks, and growth-retarded, at an average weight of 1000g, made their survival dubious in any case. All the other twins were alive and well-tended. The minority groups to which these twins belonged valued twins and in some cases even sanctified them. Twins were believed to be mediators with supernatural forces, which only they could placate. As such, they received special offerings that ranged from shells to lollipops, they were offered the best servings of food, they wore special clothing, and they were granted special privileges. For instance, twins were the only ones allowed to climb sacred trees and thus be closer to the sky.

My most successful case was a set of triplets who had recently been delivered at the hospital. Whereas in most low-income countries twins do stand a chance of survival, the majority of triplets do not. These triplets were born six weeks prematurely, and their mother had very little milk. However, I managed to obtain from Europe special formulas, bottles, and diapers, all adapted for premature infants. The mother was carefully instructed on how to deal with the infants, boiling their water when preparing their formulas, following a feeding schedule, preventing diaper rashes, and becoming aware of possible complications. When I visited the triplets at age two months, they were doing well and had put on weight.

Advising third-world mothers on the use artificial milk is a very sensitive issue, as, according to UNICEF, children who are not breastfed are exposed to a 25-fold increase in the risk of death, and each year 1 million and five hundred children die as they are artificially fed.[7] The main reason for such holocaust is malnutrition, as many families are too poor to give their children the prescribed doses due to the cost, and so they dilute them. The second reason is the lack of hygiene, the water added to the formula is often far from purified, and sterilizing bottles and teats without a stove and disinfectants is virtually impossible. The inevitable consequences of this lack of hygiene are intestinal infections causing lethal diarrheas. With triplets, however, unless one finds another woman willing to breastfeed them together with their mother, there are no other options available.

The visits to the 61 pairs belonging to the alleged infanticidal groups were a more upsetting story. The villages where they lived were not far from the main road running across the country and in some cases were actually built alongside it. Almost invariably the dwellings were located in the proximity of a magnificent centenary baobab or an equally stunning kapok tree. I am always spellbound by these trees, whose beauty and majesty can be awesome, and they are frequently considered sacred all over Africa.

On approaching these villages, I invariably noticed numerous lucky charms implanted in their huge roots. Tangles of metal were meant to attract evil like a powerful magnet, snarls of cord were intended to imprison evil as in a fishing-net, and empty, crushed upside-down beer bottles, pieces of broken glass, and acuminate nails were all meant to scare off evil forces with the threat of a potential peril. Inside the villages, where I saw more charms, there were also many sacrificial places like small huts and altars, most of them exuding a dark reddish-brown substance, almost certainly blood.

The villagers contrasted sharply with the poverty-stricken inhabitants of the rest of the country, dressed as they were in new and modern Nike-like gear. All were well-nourished and extremely well-built. Their oiled skins were free from the innumerable parasites and infections affecting others. Most of the younger men spoke some English. It was clear that these people ruled the country. Seeing them, one could almost feel that they belonged to the right side of the world. Men, women, and children alike, however, had a hard defiant look. When asked about the twins on my list, they smiled boldly and invariably replied, "We have no twins. They all died." Seven mothers whom I knew from the hospital proudly declared that their twins were now in another country, a circumlocution often used to indicate death without actually naming it, thereby avoiding the dreaded possibility of unleashing more death. All seven women told me they were pregnant again.

In one village a young man illustrated the destiny of the twins more vividly, using sign language. He raised a single arm vertically, then spread out both arms horizontally. One arm represented singletons, both arms twins. The two outspread arms meant that twins could only lie horizontally, like the dead. Singletons, on the contrary, could stand upright and move about among the living.

On my way back to Bissau after completing most of my grim follow-up, I spotted a pair of young twins living in a nice hut beside the road and stopped the car. The twins were not on my list, as they had not been delivered at the hospital, but they belonged to one of the infanticidal groups. The twins were chubby, looked well cared for, and were dressed in immaculate white garments. They must have been at least one year old. I began to think that there could be hope for some twins.

While having dinner later with Pedro and a lay priest, whom I shall call Massimo and who had lived in the country for many years, I talked about my visit to the villages. They did not seem surprised about the grim destiny of twins, as it was common knowledge that twins were killed. And when I described the plump twin boys in their spotless condition, they shattered my remaining hopes by saying, "White is the color of death." Twins were often tended well for years to be used as sacrificial animals at a later date when the community needed to ingratiate the spirits or placate adverse forces. Nobody saw any difference between twins and goats. Some twins were sold to tribes from neighboring countries when they felt the need for a human sacrifice. The words of those mothers who affirmed that their twins were in another country now took on a more sinister meaning.

All the trafficking in children were blamed by locals on Europeans and their demand for organ transplants. But there were no means to kill a twin and have its organs transplanted in this country. There were no freezers. There were no sophisticated operating theatres. There were no planes to transport the twins or their organs to reach their destination in time to be transplanted. And no twins could have been flown off alive on the few international planes leaving Bissau or its neighboring countries without being noticed. The real truth was that organs and fresh blood were needed for local human sacrifice.[8]

While waiting for immolation, most twins were subjected to all sorts of atrocities. Collective "ethnic" rape was just one of these outrages. Massimo had witnessed such episodes, one of which was particularly horrific. He had been tending to the irrigation of some fields when he saw a pair of twins, a girl and a boy seven or eight years old, who were playing by themselves. Massimo knew the twins, having met them with their father, who had often helped him carry out his engineering projects. Suddenly a herd of villagers appeared, who encircled the twins and tied them to a tree, led by the twins' drunken father. Their mother was also present, as were their older brothers and sisters, and many other women, all of whom were urging on the men. A collective anal rape of the children began. At the end of the orgy both twins were butchered. Massimo, looking tearful, concluded, "I could do nothing to help. All the men were brandishing huge machetes. I hid behind a tree. All I could do was just give their poor remains a decent burial."

Not even Pedro had been aware of this kind of atrocity. He had imagined that all twins were killed at or near birth, when attachment to them was still weak. Our attempts to foster attachment toward newborn twins now seemed hopelessly and pathetically naïve.

Not even more educated and economically favored people were immune from this practice. As in other parts of Africa, several kingdoms still operated within the nation, where nobles and kings owned most of the land and held many privileges. Soon after returning to Bissau, I visited one community where a noble woman had given birth to a pair of twins and who was on my survey list. The nobles looked quite modernized. They lived in proper houses with television sets and bathrooms fitted with taps for running water, though these taps and televisions were for display only, since electricity and running water were virtually nonexistent in the country. Both women and men had adapted a western style of clothing. The women were impeccably made up and had cropped hairstyles.

The mother of the twins, I will name her Leila, was in her mid-thirties and met me in her home with several other nobles. Leila looked particularly elegant, clearly having just visited the only hairdresser in town. She also seemed to enjoy a special standing within the community, for she did most of the talking. After offering me tea in a proper teacup, Leila explained to me the role of her group in society, saying, "Since we are nobles, we always have to set an example for the others." When I asked about her twins, she first said, "We have nothing against twins. It is all superstition and ignorance, but the populace believe them to be evil." Then she added impassively, "As you know, I had twin daughters. They drowned in the nearby river. They were five. Then no more children came." Not the slightest emotion passed over her arrogant, stony face.

Just as in Madagascar, noble mothers in the country, who had given birth to twins, were no longer allowed to have children. Their noble wombs forever tainted by the twins could have contaminated all future progeny. Contrary to Madagascar, however, these noble women could afford to buy contraceptives, which they obtained from neighboring countries. Leila confirmed this prohibition saying, "You are not allowed to have children after having twins. I know this is plain superstition, but I had to set an example. You cannot rule over the population unless you are prepared to sacrifice something. Life is full of compromise. After all none of my subjects knows that I am on the pill."

Later I was taken to the river where her twin daughters had "drowned." The river ran between green, gently sloping riverbanks. It would have been extremely difficult to simply fall or slip into the river. While looking at its muddy waters, I was told by Leila that strange, humanlike fish swam in there: "They usually swim in pairs and have faces like us." I found myself thinking that these supernatural, mermaid-like creatures swimming in pairs might be ghostly projections of dead twins reemerging from the murky unconscious of their "noble" mother. The twins whom she drowned in the river were a human pair, and they may even have looked like her. Yet in order to kill the twins and to set an example for her group, Leila had to regard her own children as nonhuman, mere fishes having to return to the water from where they came. Leila, however, also had to drown all her love and sacrifice, humanity and feelings that had existed inside her, as testified by her stony, hardened expression and her lack of emotions when reporting her twins' death.

After so much gloom, I wanted to end my survey on a hopeful note. The last case on my list was a beautiful young woman, I will call her Sky, who had delivered her twins at the hospital. While hospitalized, she had formed an immediate bond with her lovely twin boys, and her attachment continued to be strong at home. She often brought them to the hospital, where I met her after several months, and she never failed to inoculate her twins or to check on their growth. Sky became strongly attached to me as well. When I set out to visit her for my final survey her twins were almost one year old.

Sky was married to a king who had 46 other wives. The king was an ugly, wrinkled old man but apparently kind and bright. Due to his privileged condition, he owned plenty of land and goats and he could afford to keep as many women as he wanted. Sky was one of his younger wives. His kingdom lay at the end of a dazzling, tree-lined gravel road not far from Bissau. When I arrived, the king was regal in his kindness to me. He introduced me to his older, higher-ranking wives and to his innumerable progeny. Then he showed me around his huge palace, a complex built of hardened mud and straw. I was particularly struck by a circular courtyard with many doors opening into it. A strange conical structure towered in the middle of the courtyard, almost entirely occupying the space. The king explained that this was the courtyard of the wives. Behind each door he kept a young wife of childbearing age in a small room. Every evening he chose one to his liking and spent the night with her. When I asked about the conical building, he said, smiling, "This is the house of the fetish. It protects us all."

I asked if I could visit it, to which he replied, smiling craftily, "It has to be opened with caution. I cannot open it for you now. The unsealing needs preparation. However, if you promise to come back in a fortnight with anti-malaria tablets—I mean Fansidar—I will open it for you." We struck a deal: I would bring Fansidar, and he would open the door. Fansidar was particularly precious, because it was almost totally unavailable in Bissau, and the king suffered badly from malaria.

During all this time, I wondered where Sky was. So far she was nowhere to be seen, and I assumed that she might have been behind one of the many closed doors. When we went out of the compound, I finally saw her and was shocked. She looked and was treated like an outcast. Her clothes were all torn, and her breasts were bare. She was plastered with dust and mud. A white smear covered both sides of her beautiful face. I suddenly remembered that white was the color of death and took the smear to be an ominous sign. Sky carried her twins, one in her arms and one on her back. She was pregnant again. In sharp contrast with everyone else in the "family," Sky lived outside the compound and was prohibited from entering it. At one point the king hit her with a stick, shouting, "I have been patient enough with you. But now you know what you have to do." Looking terribly sad, Sky did not say a word but just half-glanced at me as she quickly went away.

When I asked the king about her, his lips were sealed. Instead of talking about Sky, he started a long tirade against the hypocrisy of our occidental mores. "All men have lovers in your world but pretend to be faithful and monogamous. Here we are just open about it. We marry them and give them status. Women are much happier this way."

A fortnight later I went back, bringing Fansidar as promised. I also hid in my bag some clean clothes for Sky and the twins. This time, however, Sky was inside the compound, together with the rest of the family. She was properly dressed and spotlessly clean, but her twins were gone. The king, noticing my quizzical glance, said, "The twins died a couple of days ago." Sky looked the other way, pretending to ignore me.

The king asked me about the Fansidar, which I gave to him. Then I reminded him of our deal. He smiled triumphantly, flaunting his Fansidar, and said, "I cannot open the door of the fetish for you. The opening needs sacrificial blood. I never allow anyone into it, especially women." I felt silly.

In a gesture of generosity, however, the king took me for one more look at the house of the fetish. When I noticed freshly coagulated blood before the tightly sealed entrance, my wish to go inside faded instantly. I knew what I would find behind that door. When we went back outside, Sky and all the other wives and children had moved somewhere else. The king now seemed in a hurry to send me back to Bissau, and I felt a real desire to get away.

In the evening, feeling terrible, I told Pedro what I had seen. I wondered whether my interest could have accelerated the death of the twins. Might I have been able to bargain my Fansidar for the twins? Pedro replied, "Don't feel guilty. They would have died anyway, and there is nothing we can do in a country gone totally adrift like this."

In this nation twins were not killed at birth, as in other countries. Many of these women had delivered their twins in hospital and had taken care of them, albeit reluctantly, in all sorts of ways for months or years, but still they did not hesitate to relinquish them when the time came. Attachment ought to have been secure and love strong enough by then, thus preventing these mothers from slaughtering their children.

After returning to my country I was haunted by the horrors I had witnessed in that nation, and I could not make sense of them. Jospeh Conrad's *Heart of Darkness* often came to my mind.[9] Kurtz, his dark hero hidden in the mists of the forest covering a murky tropical river, had lost all his inhibitions, committed all sorts of atrocities and, like many blood thirsty dictators, he had bewitched and mesmerized a frenzied crowd who followed him. Conrad, however, made it clear that Kurtz and his followers were not an isolated phenomenon, but something that could have happened anytime and anywhere under the right circumstances.

The more I distanced myself from the events, the more I saw that darkness pervaded not only this particular nation, but also the past of humankind as well as the contemporary world. Opening an atlas was enough to make one realize how many hot spots were indicated and how many wars, ethnic clashes, and racial cleansings were still raging around the globe. Heart of darkness was a part of our common human nature since the dawn of mankind and was likely to erupt when people blindly follow the diktats of their group.

In committing infanticide these mothers exemplified the enormous strength of social influences. These women were ready and even proud to sacrifice their twins in order to obey the laws of the group. No atrocity deterred them. The elegant and noble Leila drowned her twin daughters in the murky waters of the river simply to set an example to her subjects. Even gentle Sky, who tried to resist social pressures, in the end obeyed the dictates of the tyrant king, since she could no longer stand being alienated from the courtyard of wives.

Maternal love, considered the most sacred bond of all, could break down when society ordered it. No attachment was strong enough to withstand marginalization from the herd. Only a few brave rebels may have had the courage to face condemnation and persecution for not conforming to the crowd.

According to Herodotus, the Greek historian considered the father of history, the Greeks founded the notion of the civilized world in contrast with the barbarians who were regarded as qualitatively different "others."[10] Throughout the centuries the "other," the "different," though living among society, has been viewed as a nonhomogeneous human being that cannot be integrated into the group, as they are considered capable of infecting and threatening the community. As such, the other has to be wiped out and destroyed as a scapegoat. In this West African nation twins were considered as different, outside the herd, qualitatively different others engendered by evil forces, who might endanger the community, and as such they had been exterminated without remorse or grief.

Freud, writing of the events leading up to the horrors of World War II, described the masses following blindly atrocious social dictates as being just like primitive herds.[11]

Freud explained how evil harbors within us all in our more or less unconscious mind. We wish to deny our inclination to be cruel and less than saintly, preferring to believe that we are all good, all white, while others are all black, all bad. Evil is commonly and conveniently split off onto someone or something else, a scapegoat, which then has to be erased and exterminated in the illusion of freeing ourselves from it. In many societies twins serve as handy scapegoats.[12] Given their "difference," all badness is split off onto them, and they then have to be exterminated. Twins are viewed as the evil, the black, the Jew, the Rom, the Tutsi, and the Indio of these societies. All sins are pinned on them, freeing others from evilness. By eliminating these carriers, the society finds cohesion and peace for itself.

Even mothers of twins were not free from the stigma affecting their twins and could equally become the "others." Gentle Sky was humiliated and shamed in all sorts of ways. It would have taken exceptional noncon-formity for her to accept becoming an outcast from the community where she was forced to live, the only community that she would ever know.

Human scapegoating, as tragically highlighted by the words of Massimo, the lay priest in Bissau, can also take on the quality of collective frenzy, with everyone willing and excited to take part. The entire crowd surrounding the poor twins tied to the trees chorally incited their sodom-ization and dismemberment. Even the twins' brothers and sisters took part, to say nothing of their mother. Mothers and siblings could fall in with the general consensus and become torturers in their own right. Human scapegoating knows no bonding of family, just as it knows no bonding of country or race.

Chapter 10

One Gender and One Only

The real extent of twin infanticide cannot be known. In countries where it is practiced, social controls are lacking, the population census is inaccurate or unreliable, birth registers are approximate, and mothers have no access to prenatal care and seldom deliver in hospitals. It is not even possible to know how many women were pregnant to start with and how many live infants were delivered. On the other hand communities can be very cohesive in their determination to avoid problems and make their own rules and laws like small, separate states. Should a governmental agent go round the villages asking how many twins were born in the last ten years, the whole community would circle around a mother, whose twins had died in unnatural circumstances, denying the event. Typical answers would be "No twins in the last 20 years." or "Yes, there was a pair of twins, but they moved very far away." Occasionally someone indicates a single born and says that he or she was a twin but the other died and nobody would enquire any further.

The selective disposal of only one twin is even more difficult to demonstrate and also easier to conceal. When selection is based on the physical disadvantage of a given twin at birth, it may be justified, with a grain of truth, on the basis that one twin simply could not make it. It is equally likely that the birth of twins may be denied. The mother may reemerge from the generally secluded scene of the delivery with only one child, pretending that a single baby was born. In both instances no one will ever know if the "scene of the delivery" was also the "scene of a crime." Many single children may well have started out as twins.

Several motives lie behind this extreme form of preferential treatment. Some motives are shared with dual twin infanticide, while others are not. The physical inability of mothers to cope with two infants may lead them to dispose of the weaker one. Superstitions about conception may also doom just one twin. In many areas of the world, ranging from numerous regions of Africa to the islands of the Pacific, one twin is believed to be the reincarnation of an evil deceased ancestor. Nasty uncles, vicious in-laws, wicked mothers—all these tormented and tormenting souls—have a special preference for reincarnation in just one twin. We all look for family resemblances in our children at birth, but in some developing countries the wrinkled face of an unfortunate newborn twin may inspire the entire community to exclaim, "This must be uncle D coming back!" or "This must be mother-in-law X returning to earth!" The poor twin has to pay dire consequences for its avowed resemblance to the ill-favored relative. Similarly, one twin may be considered the incarnation of an evil spirit and the other not.

From the heights of our scientific knowledge we now have rational explanations for the supposedly different "incarnation" of such twins. The intrauterine environment is never identical for twins and can in fact be markedly unequal for them, which explains the remarkable differences between twins at birth. The placenta of one twin may be smaller than that of the other and thus supply fewer nutrients. One twin may suffer from complications during pregnancy, such as showing ominous cerebral blood-flows or being what is called hydropic, displaying an accumulation of fluids in body tissues and cavities, while the other may not. One twin may finish up in a particularly unfortunate position, tightly adhering against the uterine wall, causing its head or limbs to be misshapen. The most remarkable differences are caused by so-called twin-to-twin transfusion, where one twin may be big and purple red and the other winkled, small, and deathly pale.

As a result, at birth one twin may look like a chubby cherub from heaven, while the other like an alien creature or an old, wrinkled little man with spindly legs, just like "bad old uncle D" when he was alive. If none of the current scientific knowledge were available to us, we too would still be explaining these striking differences by the most outlandish theories.

Scientific knowledge about twin pregnancies has become available and widespread only recently. In the past, savants and intellectuals interpreted the differences between twins in the way that many illiterate people still do.

During the last half of the nineteenth century the so-called doppel-ganger, the German word for a double, commonly applied to indicate a so-called evil twin, became very familiar in European literary circles. Robert Luis Stevenson's classic tale of Dr Jekyll and his uncanny and evil double, Mr Hyde[1], Mary Shelley's "Frankenstein,"[2] Dostoyevsky's "The Double"[3] are just a few examples of fictional doppelgangers.[4]

When confronted with nonfictional doppelgangers, less erudite populations take fright and consequently dispose of the uncanny, supposedly evil twin.

The selective disposal of just one twin for superstitious and eugenic reasons was confirmed to me during the same year I was working in Northern Kenya. When heading toward the huge wasteland around Lake Turkana, I stopped for a day or two in Marsabit, a small town at the crossroads between the no-man's land of Lake Turkana and the mountainous area past Mount Kenya. Marsabit was a former vacation resort, with a splendid history of being the gathering place of the cream of white society up to the end of colonial times in 1963.

Presently many assorted ethnic groups converged there, from the Kikuyu to the Rendille, the Borana, and the Masai. Many Somalis also found their way to Marsabit.

Upon my arrival in the town I went to visit two missionaries, whom I shall call Father Carlo and Father Mauro, and who had been running the archdiocese for some 40 years. These old priests had devoted their lives to the indigenous population, and their knowledge of Africa with its many problems was unique. I wanted to ask them about local customs, to facilitate my work in the Lake Turkana region.

When we came to the subject of twins, the missionaries told me that in this area usually just one twin was killed. Occasionally the selection was based on their physical state, one twin being smaller and more disadvantaged than the other. But superstition also played its part in the choice. Often one twin was thought to be the reincarnation of a nasty deceased ancestor or, at times, an unearthly intruder, and thus killed. The priests said, "It is just like Castor and Pollux, the mythological Dioscuri finally reunited in the Gemini constellation, one of divine origin and the other perishable. Some myths are fairly universal." However, gender was another paramount reason for selecting one twin and not the other. Some ethnic groups preferred girls and others preferred boys, according to which gender could be exchanged for cattle, camels, or goats. Other groups, like the Muslim, considered girls inferior on cultural and religious grounds.

According to the missionaries, the infanticide of just one twin was a huge, though hidden, plague. It probably accounted for thousands of twins, if not more, being killed each year. The priests condemned the phenomenon but somehow also absolved it. As one said, "When you live as these people do in utter poverty, sometimes you make decisions that we would not make back home."

Given my interest in twins, the priests asked me if I would like to go around Marsabit with a guide next morning looking for twins. I accepted willingly.

My guide turned out to be a skinny old fellow, called Charlie by me, who went around barefoot but wore an English tweed outfit that seemed totally discordant with his disheveled appearance and the desolate surroundings. While we wandered along the muddy roads of Marsabit, Charlie poured out his miserable history to me. He had indeed seen better times. When Marsabit was still a holiday resort, a rich English lady had fallen in love with him and taken him back to England with her. As he recalled those days, "I had everything—a dream." Then he admitted, "African men are a bit restless. She found me in bed with another woman, and that was that." All that remained of his former fortune was his suit.

While we looked for twins, Charlie explained, "Only the Muslims keep their twins. They are proud of them. They want to outnumber everyone. Twins speed things up. All the rest just keep one." Roughly ten thousand people lived in Marsabit, but we were able to find only ten pairs of twins, and their parents were indeed Muslims, not animists like the rest of the local populations. The twins ranged between 5 and 13 years in age.

Muslims took care of their children, no matter whether twins or not. All were well nourished, clean, and well dressed. Twins were considered a blessing and a special gift from god. Twin boys however were particularly cherished and their mothers were proud of them. Twin boys attended a Koran school, while twin girls did not. Twin girls did not look physically neglected, but nobody seemed to pay much attention to them. They were busy with household chores and were even asked to work for their brothers.

When we left, Charlie told me that all girls had been subjected to genital mutilation. As Father Carlo and Father Mauro had said, girls could be considered inferior on cultural and religious grounds.

The differential treatment of these twins typified the widespread bias against half of humanity based solely on gender. In many areas of the world gender is the paramount reason for the termination of one or both twins. Termination based on gender is not confined to twins and can affect all newborns, but twins highlight how radical such a bias can be and how early such discrimination can begin. In opposite-sex pairs, the male is given a hearty welcome, while the female is disposed of, and if the twins are girls, both are killed. Gender alone makes all the difference right from the start. The massive scale slaughter of females is acted out in countries ranging from Pakistan, China, India, Bangladesh, and Nepal to Taiwan, South Korea, and North Africa. So called gendericide has been referred to as the biggest single holocaust in human history.[5]

Ultrasounds and amniocentesis have made it possible to detect gender well before birth. Ultrasounds have played a key role in developing the field of prenatal medicine.

In several developing countries the main use of ultrasounds has undergone an alarming change. It is not used for fetal reduction due to the risks of a higher multiple pregnancy, not for fetal selection based on some severe malformation or defect, but rather for fetal disposal based on gender.

The Nobel prize winning economist Amartya Sen was the first to call public attention to the phenomenon of "missing women" in 1990.[6] According to him more than 100 million females were missing at the "call" especially in India and China. Amartya Sen's original figures have been called into question in other studies reporting higher or lower numbers; however, the undisputable fact remains that all were quoting millions of missing females. Amartya Sen saw a solution to the genocide in offering women education, health care, family planning, and work opportunities.[7]

The phenomenon of female infanticide is as old as many cultures and generally reflects the low status accorded to women worldwide.

In India male preference is especially strong and deep-rooted among the Hindus, for whom it was sanctioned by the so-called Manu Codex dating back to the fifth century BC, granting females no independent status and thus forcing them to spend all their lives under the guardianship of their fathers, husbands, and sons.[8]

These ancient laws, albeit unofficially, are still alive in several parts of India, where sons are looked upon as a type of insurance, providing the income, doing most work in the fields, remaining in the family circle once married, and looking after their parents into old age and even lighting the fire at their cremation. Females, on the contrary, leave the family when they marry, and parents have to pay large dowries for their weddings or else social disgrace and embarrassment inevitably follow.

Girls, however, are missing even in some of the richest areas of the country, especially if their birth follows that of another girl, thus reflecting a deep and pervasive cultural bias. According to UNICEF, female fetuses account for 99 percent of the abortions performed in Mumbai and Delhi.[9]

Among other Indian provinces, Rajasthan is renowned for being one of the main regions having this sad record. With its beautiful palaces, temples, and fortresses, Rajastan is considered India at its best and has become one of India's main tourist destinations. However, Rajastan has one of the subcontinent's lowest life expectancies (45 for men and 47 for women) and literacy rates (36 percent for males and 12 percent for females).[10] Its land is very varied, and in parts it is dry and inhospitable, and in the northeast Thar Desert bordering Pakistan, it is almost totally barren.

I had been to Rajasthan in the early 1970s, when, to the dismay of my parents, I had taken a year off to do my internship in a hospital in Delhi. There I met another medical student I shall call Asha, of whom I became extremely fond. We kept in touch down through the years, and one summer when she came to Italy, I took her on a trip around my country. In 1998 she reciprocated my hospitality by asking me to visit her in one of the main towns of Rajasthan, where she was in charge of a maternity hospital. The hospital was big and efficient, and spotlessly clean. Ultrasounds were used routinely.

All hospitals in India currently refuse to tell parents the sex of their children when it is revealed with ultrasounds or amniocentesis, since sex tests have been illegal since 1994 and pre-implantation embryo selection based on gender since 1998. However, not one single claim has been brought to the attention of the courts.

Asha herself tackled the subject of selective female termination. In Rajastan there were plenty of private clinics to give parents this information. Sophisticated second-hand equipment was also readily available on the net, and no huge investment was needed. Portable ultrasounds made it possible that they reach even remote areas.

Some doctors traveled from village to village with their equipment, but this was only for the wealthy or the middle class. Asha told me, "The poor resort to the same old means at birth. They kill the girls."

When Asha and I went for walks outside the hospital, she pointed out signs to me advertising ultrasounds. They could be seen almost everywhere but were especially plentiful in this district full of medical practitioners. Asha explained, "They can make a fortune out of this."

When I asked Asha about twins in particular, she said, "Male twins stand a chance, but not females. It is the usual gender bias. Nobody wants females." The key problem, she added, "is the question of dowry. It is bad enough to have to pay for one marriage. Nobody wants to pay for two. Until the custom of dowries is abolished for good, females will continue to be exterminated, and female twins doubly so."

Asha offered to take me to visit some twins living in different environments. First we called at an upper-middle-class home in the rich area of town. When we rang the bell, a plump woman opened the door, holding a fat baby. The woman was covered all over in gold, from her richly embroidered sari to the bracelets and rings on her fingers, nose, navel, ankles, and toes. When she noticed that I was looking at the child, she proudly announced, "He is a boy." She invited us in to have some tea. Two servants brought out an entire patisserie along with the tea.

After we sat down, the woman said, "I know Asha did not approve of this, but my son was a twin. Asha would not tell me the sex of the twins. Having twins was bad enough, but I could not afford having one of the wrong sex. I went to a private doctor to find out, and one was a girl. We decided to terminate. An injection in her heart, and that was that." No guilt or sorrow showed in the woman's voice. Throughout our visit she continued to chatter garrulously, praising the virtues and joys of her only son.

After our departure, Asha commented, "You see it is as simple as that, like going to the supermarket and choosing to put down the cheaper brand. Males are valued, but females are considered a burden on family and society." Asha herself was proud to be the mother of three daughters and her pride was a clear indication of how higher education and a rewarding job could affect maternal views.

The next visit was to a woman living in a poorer area of town. She hugged Asha tearfully, and they spoke together in her dialect. After we left, Asha explained, "This woman was also expecting twins. Her husband forced her to have a scan in order to know the sex of the twins. He paid a huge amount of money for it to a private doctor. One twin was a girl. She didn't want to dispose of her, but he was adamant—either selective termination or divorce. Basically she had no choice or say in the matter. She still mourns her twin girl. Not all women make this decision light-heartedly, but husbands, families, and friends all force them." Women were scorned, humiliated, and divorced if they were not able to give the family a son.

That same evening Asha and I dined in a restaurant in a magnificent old Palace set on a small island in the midst of a Lake and talked about female abortion and infanticide. Asha had made a survey on the number of females disposed of in general, but she had no idea how many of these females were twins. Asha suspected twins to be a problem in their own right. A proper survey of missing twins and of missing twin females would have taken months to complete, but we decided to plan a rough, prelimi-nary assessment of our own into missing twin females. We took out pencils and paper and discussed matters deep into the night. Before we left, Asha said, "Most females are wretched in Rajastan. Sometimes in my imagina-tion this beautiful region with all its gorgeous art, buildings, and lakes is one vast graveyard of female newborn babies. Ultrasounds have added unborn females to the graveyard. Palaces like this one where we just had dinner have the feel of funerary monuments."

The following morning we began by examining the files of all twin births registered in the hospital in the previous ten years. Out of 570 twins born at the hospital, only one-fourth were girls. At least 280 twin girls were missing.

Asha and I next surveyed the files of all the twins who had been scanned or had amniocentesis at the hospital and whose mothers had never subse-quently returned. Though gender was never disclosed to the parents, it was noted down in the files. We wanted to find out how many twins had been aborted outside the hospital, and how many of those who had survived were females.

The data were vast, and we could not possibly have visited or contacted all the families. We decided to concentrate on four nearby districts, so Asha contacted 130 women asking them how the twins who had been detected with ultrasounds at the hospital were doing.

Only 40 twins were alive, and out of these just 11 were females. Not only females, but also twins were possibly discriminated and terminated.

The mothers were fairly direct in talking to Asha about the twin issue.

Twins in themselves were considered a burden and were disposed of. The main reasons given were "Twins are more difficult to handle" "Twins are expensive" "Twins are tiring" "Only pigs and cows have twins" "Imagine breast-feeding twins! In the end your breasts look like empty sacks. I don't want to be rejected by my husband." Fatigue, financial concern, and aesthetic considerations were the prominent reasons for terminating twins in general, and even more so female twins.

The "female problem" was even more openly discussed. Females were considered a catastrophe, not a burden. Only two mothers coming from very low-income families viewed females as potential assets, giving as their reasons, "Girls start working very early" and "Girls bring money home." How the money was earned was left unclear, but Asha felt sure that it was from prostitution. All the other mothers mentioned the enormous costs involved in keeping females as opposed to keeping males. The three most expensive ceremonies for girls involved naming and ear piercing, which went together, reaching puberty, and especially marriage and dowry.

On top of the expense involved, all mothers were preoccupied with their daughter's virginity, because a girl who lost her virginity before marriage was worth less than nothing. The comments were "A daughter needs to be married off as soon as she starts having her periods," "Females have to be married at puberty in order to save them from the lustful eyes of men." "Loss of virginity casts a shadow on your family." "The family loses its reputation." Economic problems and impeccable reputation were stronger than any maternal drive.

Only 15 mothers were clearly upset at having disposed of their twins and 10 of losing a female twin, but all had been forced to go ahead with it by their husbands and by social pressure.

Most mothers, who had been unable to afford prenatal selection, were frank about their methods of committing female infanticide. A common method was to feed the baby girl the milk of the yellow oleander shrub or the paste of its berries. Death was assured within an hour. Boiled water with paddy grains brought about death, preceded by convulsions and vomiting within half an hour. Other poisons were tobacco paste and pesticides. Suffocation was widespread. The girl's nose and mouth were pressed or covered with a thick wet towel. In wintertime mothers left their girls naked in some open space in the house until the bitter cold did the job.

This grim cursory assessment left Asha and me feeling depressed. When it came time to leave the country, I was sad to say good-bye to Asha, but by then I also viewed Rajastan as a huge graveyard filled with female infants and possibly with twins.

A "female problem" is not restricted to less developed countries. The maternity hospital where I work has given me the chance to become acquainted with many couples from China. With the fall of the Celestial Empire in the 1930s, Chinese migrated abroad in large numbers and settled in various countries. A sizable Chinese community grew up in Milan, where they inhabit an area known as Chinatown. Some of the Chinese immigrants there are of more recent arrival and are frequently illegal immigrants.

Italian regulations are protective of maternity, giving all pregnant women, including illegal immigrants, the right to be treated by the national health service. Once pregnancy is over and the child, or twin children, are six months old, the illegal mother must be sent back to her home country. By then, however, mothers will usually either have acquired official status or faded back into the hidden population.

A few years ago, a young Chinese couple came to the maternal-fetal department of the hospital. Ms Lee, as I shall call the mother, a tall, pretty, and nicely dressed woman in her mid-twenties, could hardly speak any Italian. Mr Lee, her husband, though far from fluent, could at least communicate in a rudimentary way. We started a scan, which revealed twins. I showed the couple the twins on the screen, whereupon Ms Lee started to cry silently, while her husband smiled, looking peculiarly calculating. The parents came back regularly for their prenatal visits and during each scan exhibited the same puzzling behavior: Ms Lee cried and Mr Lee smiled, until finally I asked another expectant Chinese mother to act as an interpreter. She seemed embarrassed by what she heard Ms Lee say and finally blurted out, "The woman must feel homesick." I suspected that a different story had been lost in translation, but had no clue to what it might be. Despite the father's persistent inquiries at every visit, we could not tell the twins' sex, because they refused to open their legs. Finally at 25 weeks one twin unmistakably showed that she was a female. Because the twins shared the same placenta and the same amniotic sac, they were undoubtedly monozygotic, and thus the other twin was certainly a girl. On hearing this information, Ms Lee suddenly smiled, while Mr Lee looked tense and angry. This stark change in behavior, which lasted until the birth, roused my curiosity. I had managed to establish a rapport especially with the mother, albeit purely eye-to-eye contact, so that as she approached term,

I suggested paying a home visit once the girls were born. Ms Lee looked pleased, and both parents agreed.

Three months after the delivery I went to visit them. The couple lived in a large, modern building on the outskirts of Milan, and their small flat was immaculate. When I arrived, Ms Lee was playing with the girls, looking delighted. Mr Lee immediately asked me to examine the twins. When the checkup was over, he plied me with questions on how to handle them, including everything from pacifiers and diapers, to medications, vaccinations, and vitamins. Possibly as a token of gratitude, he then managed to explain in a variety of ways, by drawing, talking, gesticulating, and finally showing me a bunch of airline tickets, his strange behavior at the hospital.

Twins escaped the so-called one-child per family policy introduced by the Chinese government in 1979, and they were more than welcome and very much in demand, as families could get "two for the price of one" and thereby fulfill many people's dream of having more children. I had thought that all twins were welcome in China independent of their gender, but as Mr Lee explained, this rarely applied to females, who were abandoned, neglected, murdered, and left in so-called orphanages from where no child emerged alive.

The fact that male twins were considered a blessing in China had resulted in the trafficking of twin infants to affluent parents in China. Monozygotic twins were especially desirable, because their similarity guaranteed there had been no foul play. Two infants born more or less at the same time but coming from separate parents could be faked as nonmonozygotic twins. So much money was paid for twins that young couples could make huge profits out of the sale and postpone to a later date the birth of a child for themselves. This kind of trafficking explained the smiling, calculating eyes of the young father and the tears of the young mother when first told of the expected twins. Mr Lee was already counting the profits from selling the twins, while Ms Lee was despairing at the thought of giving up her twins. The revelation of their being girls suddenly changed the situation, inasmuch as girls were not in demand and had no market value. The parents then reversed their behavior, Mr Lee showing disappointment and Ms Lee, happiness.

Mr Lee, however, was not someone who gave up easily. He explained to me that as soon as he had heard of the expected twins, he had contacted some relatives and through them a rich couple in China who desired children, and offered them his twins. In order to complete the transaction, he had asked to be sent airline tickets for the whole family, as well as half of the adoption fee up front. He justified this demand by claiming medical expenses that did not in fact exist, because pregnancy care is virtually free in Italy. When Mr Lee subsequently found out that the twins were girls, he did not tell the adoptive couple. Instead he sent them neutral reports on the twins, and Polaroids of their scans along with their growth charts. Once the girls were born, he told the Chinese couple that the hospital was to blame for the mistake and then disappeared with the tickets, the money, and his family in the Milanese suburbs. This is how I learned that twin boys were accepted and welcome in China, but twin girls were unwanted.

A tradition of female abandonment and infanticide existed in China long before the foundation of the People's Republic in 1949.

In The Book of Songs, dating back to 700–1000 BC we read[11]:

> "When a son is born
> Let him sleep on the bed,
> Clothe him with fine clothes.
> And give him jade to play with.
> When a daughter is born,
> Let her sleep on the ground,
> Wrap her in common wrappings,
> And give her broken tiles for playthings."

In China sons traditionally cared for their parents into old age and only they could perform the religious rituals for easing the deceased parent's transition into the afterlife.

Sometime later, I received even more startling evidence of the Chinese attitude toward twin females. After performing the last scan of the day at the hospital, I was about to go home. It was dark outside, and my colleagues had already left the unit, except for one nurse, with whom I was chatting briefly. We suddenly noticed two breathless Chinese people, a pregnant woman and her husband, running toward us down the corridor. The woman, whom I shall call Ms Wang, looked very pregnant and was panting heavily. We told them to sit down and asked what the matter was. Ms Wang spoke almost no Italian, but Mr Wang could make himself understood. This difference is typical of many first-generation Chinese immigrants. The women are often employed as cheap labor within the Chinese community and live in cramped workrooms with little or no contact with the outside world, so their chances of learning Italian are practically nil. Men, on the contrary, work outside the home, especially in catering and small-scale commerce, and pick up the language. Once children go to nursery school, they too begin to speak Italian well and fast. Often children are brought to the hospital to act as their mothers' interpreters.

Mr Wang told us outright, "We want to abort a child." Thinking that Ms Wang looked far too advanced in her gestation to allow for that, we asked Mr Wang when the delivery was due. He answered, "In one week."

The nurse yelled, "We cannot do that! You should have thought about that before. It is not permitted by law."

Mr Wang's face reddened, and he looked angry enough to explode, when his wife pointed to her hugely distended belly and pronounced in Italian, possibly the only words she knew, "Two. Boy and girl."

Then Mr Wang exclaimed, "We only knew that one of the twins was a girl two days ago. Before then she kept her legs well-crossed. Now we want to kill her, but not the boy." We tried to calm down Mr Wang, explaining that it was not possible to terminate such an advanced pregnancy, nor was it possible to terminate a fetus selectively because of its gender. He only became more threatening, saying, "We are Chinese citizens. Law is on our side. We can chose to abort a female right up until the very last moment." We didn't know what was allowed by Chinese law; however, no explanation that he was in a foreign country and had to follow the local laws could convince this belligerent man, who then started kicking the desk while shouting in his own language.

At the same time his wife kept pointing to her tummy and repeating mechanically, "No, girl. Girl, no" as if these words would be enough to convince us. To avoid the risk of getting beaten up, we finally had to call in a male nurse.

In the meantime I had managed to contact an interpreter and a social worker who arrived on the scene. While the parents remained adamant in their determination to kill the girl, the social worker proposed a less radical solution. The twin girl could be given away for adoption. The parents signed all the necessary papers without the slightest hesitation.

Most Chinese attending the clinic behave quite differently. The fact that the one-child policy does not exist in Italy, combined with effective contraception, the active role of women in society, and the guarantee by the state of schooling through university, seems to have affected the mentality of many Chinese.

The majority of parents living in Italy are quite happy to have girls, and are thrilled to have twin girls.

But western women, too, occasionally have to face difficult choices by selecting one—or more than one—twin and deciding to terminate it before birth. Even so-called identical twins may be different in terms of malformations and chromosomal defects. For instance, one twin may have a severely malformed heart or may suffer from Down Syndrome and the other not. When only one twin is affected, ultrasounds give parents the option of selectively disposing of it while continuing the gestation of a healthy singleton. This safe but painful choice can be carried out during the first half of pregnancy. Ultrasounds have made it possible to shift to the early prenatal stages the choices that less privileged women can only have at birth.

The same applies to the option of fetal reduction, whereby a so-called higher multiple pregnancy involving triplets, quadruplets, or more is reduced to one twin with a lethal injection of potassium chloride into the heart of those fetuses chosen to be terminated. Higher multiple pregnancies can occur spontaneously, their rate being calculated at 0.11 per 100 pregnancies,[12] but in high-income countries they are increasingly the result of poorly managed fertility treatments. The incidence of multifetal pregnancies has increased greatly since the introduction of ovulation-inducing drugs in the early '60s. Depending upon the medication, the incidence of multiples ranges from 7–9 percent with clomiphene citrate (Clomid) to 39 percent with human menopausal gonadotropins.

Higher multiple pregnancies carry with them enormously increased risks for both the mother and the fetuses. Extremely premature children, ranging from 23 to 27 weeks gestation, being the most common and obvious. By reducing a higher multiple pregnancy to a twin or singleton pregnancy, the risks are reduced and the surviving twin fetuses are given better chances of a favorable outcome.[13]

Fetal reduction is never based on gender. The twin fetuses to be reduced are generally selected on the basis of bigger or smaller size. However, more often than not, differences cannot be detected or are, anyway, minimal. Fetal reduction is almost always perceived by parents—and by those performing it—as a kind of Russian roulette, evoking a giddy sense of randomness and precariousness in all those involved. It gives each and everyone the feeling that he or she is a near miss, a product of pure chance, reminding us that had our parents simply made love on a different day we may not have existed at all. Furthermore, no matter how rationally this painful decision is made, a sense of agonizing guilt persists in the parents, who see the survivors as a constant reminder of the dead.

It is difficult for us to imagine what a mother or a surviving twin may feel when the difficult decision has to be taken at birth in different countries and under difficult circumstances.

Chapter 11

Abuse and Neglect

Child abuse and neglect are not contemporary innovations, as we often tend to think. A general attitude of cruelty and indifference toward children is as old as the hills.

According to the historians Philippe Ariès, George Duby, and Lawrence Stone, children only began to take on emotional value toward the end of the nineteenth century, when child mortality and birth rates started to decline, fostering a surge of strong emotional bonds between children and their parents. Falling birthrates also made individual children more precious.[1,2] Parents loved and valued their children even before then, but protected themselves against the emotional pain of early loss by adopting a more callous and aloof stance.

Colin Heiwood, another historian, regards childhood to be, to a considerable degree, a social construct and function of adult expectations, which changes over time and varies between social and ethnic groups within any society.[3] In many developing countries, where mortality below the age of five is still staggeringly high, even now parents do not dare to emotionally invest a great deal on their children, especially in those children who are less likely to survive. Suspension of attachment to the very young is also reflected in their frequent lack of social status. Twins, given their frailty, can often be taken as a good example of such emotional distancing.

Only in 1872 did the English Legislature pass the first Infant Protection Act and in 1884 the London Society for the Prevention of Cruelty to Children was finally founded. In the United States the Society for the Prevention of Cruelty to Animals was founded in 1866, even before the approval of laws protecting children in 1874. Under those laws a child asking to be removed from her family because she was cruelly beaten was finally allowed shelter in an institution, but only on ground that "she was a member of the animal kingdom" and could therefore be included under the laws against animal cruelty.

In her work *"Pricing the priceless child,"* the sociologist Viviana Zelizer says that the worth of American children changed radically between the 1870s and 1930s.[4] Children were no longer regarded as cheap labor or an insurance policy for their parents' old age, but were mainly conceived to fulfill emotional needs, the desire for self-perpetuation, and just plain love. Child labor laws and compulsory education were consequently endorsed. An increasing idealization of childhood and of motherhood began simultaneously to permeate society.

Glorification and idealization have continued to the present. Parents invest enormously in the few, precious children they produce and family life revolves around them in an unprecedented way with children influencing many of its main decisions, ranging from buying a bigger car to deciding to live near the best schools. Society too is apparently child-centered, with continuous worries about children's education, health, and safety, and an invasion of children' images portrayed like little cherubs, paralleled by celebrities flaunting perfect babies, blissful, even sexy, pregnancies, and an endless stream of love.

Children and their parents, however, are caught up in a net of contradictory meanings as these beatific attitudes conflict sharply with other societal policies and views.

Women have joined the labor force en masse. Public programs of child welfare, however, still have not been devised, and work is organized without regard for parenthood. Motherhood is generally more protected in Europe. In the workplace, however, having children is largely regarded as a personal preference that should not be encouraged.

Women who work are made to feel guilty by the "bad mother" mystique ascribing to mothers all future emotional problems of the child. Guilt is further enhanced by the pounding campaign on the paramount importance of the first three years of life, implying that mothers have to be there and available at all times. Disturbances ranging from depression to so-called psychosomatic disorders are considered to be rooted in early "traumata" from which there can be no rescue or salvation. Prenatal psychologists are currently extending traumata to detrimental maternal states of mind during pregnancy. Working mothers are consequently laden with anxiety and guilt.

Stay-at-home mothers on the other hand are made to feel left out from the mainstream of society by a culture that openly praises motherhood, but in fact looks down on it and still does not attribute it the dignity of paid work. Fostered by many contradictory voices, ranging from that of childhood experts, to those in the press and movies praising both the intrinsic worth of the career girl as well as the idyllic contentment of the all-devoted mother, odious *"Mammy Wars"* have broken out.[5]

Nobody can live up to such confusing and contradictory ideals, and the unfortunate result is that children can become a burden and be viewed as obstacles to fulfillment or having a career, or as economic burdens, or even as impediments to marital happiness. Needless to say, burdensome children are more likely to be exposed to abusive conduct.

According to the U.S. National Committee to Prevent Child Abuse, child abuse and neglect by parents are the most devastating problems affecting the welfare of children today, and in the United States alone more than three children die each day as a result of parental maltreatment.[6]

Overwhelmingly, however, as the writer Sara Ruddick says, mothers want to keep their children safe, to protect them from illness, accident, and violence. Mothers want to foster their children's capacity for joy and train them to behave in ways acceptable to their social group whose approval they desire.[7] As she says "Whatever goods a mother desires for her children, her effort to provide them is work." In the case of young twins one would want to add "extremely hard work" from the very beginning.

Most twins are loved dearly by admirably nurturing and caring parents, bring enormous joys to their families, and they inevitably grow up happily.

Young twins, nevertheless, create special problems and challenges, often requiring almost heroic efforts and determination. Caring for two infants is quite unlike caring for one child, and not all mothers can cope with this enormous endeavor, to the extent that twinship is now considered a risk factor for abusive and neglectful conduct by various organizations, including governmental and academic institutions.[8,10]

Many mothers of twins join multiples clubs or support groups, which is considered instrumental in helping to maintain good mental health. The sheer number of twin associations, twin clubs, self-help groups, and hotlines for parents of twins rapidly flourishing worldwide all testify to the burdensome and potentially dangerous aspects of caring for young twins without help.

So far only postnatal neglect and abuse of both physical and psychological nature have been found to affect twins to an inordinate degree, although the precise extent has not been quantified. My impression is that twins may also be subject to increased prenatal abuse. Matters should be investigated further in order to ascertain the extent to which twins are a special target for maltreatment starting in the womb. Problems can start at the fetal stage.

In 1993, I undertook a study of maternal responses to twin pregnancies in the maternity unit where I work. Changes in reactions were observed from announcement to the end of gestation. The study covered 200 pregnancies, corresponding roughly to the number of pairs of twins born yearly in the hospital. In the study, 139 pregnancies were spontaneous and 61 were the result of assisted reproduction.

The first reactions to the news were invariably extreme. Mothers displayed elation and idealization on the one hand, plain despair and loathing on the other. Just as they would in other cultures, twins did not elicit any gray tones.

Initially all women who had other children or had family problems of any kind burst into tears, voiced utter despair, and contemplated abortion. The most frequent exclamation was, "How can I cope with two?" Only 6 mothers out of 49 belonging to this subgroup were pleased about the news. Eventually the majority of initially despairing mothers adapted to the thought, decided not to abort the twins, and, despite comprehensible and inevitable ambivalence, were ultimately pleased with their brave decision. Just 5 mothers went ahead with their plans.

A patient of mine, whom I shall refer to as Ms F, a woman in her early thirties, already had three children. She and her husband had planned to stop there. When she found out that she was pregnant again she resigned herself to the fact that one more was not going to make a big difference. When she was told that she was expecting twins she started to cry, saying "I cannot cope with two. I am tired. I have no help. We have no money. One more child could have been hardly okay, but two is not possible." Then she asked about the procedures to abort the twins. However, Ms F came back a month later for another scan saying that she had decided to continue with her pregnancy. She commented, "God or nature don't seem to be very helpful, however I will do my best to bring these two up. My husband is not very helpful either, he is never there, but I better stick to him. Nobody would fancy a woman with five children." The twins were born with a caesarean and she asked for a ligature of her tubes. When I visited her a month later she showed me her lovely twins saying, "I am exhausted, sometimes I feel like strangling them, but I know that children grow up fast. They are gorgeous, aren't they? You remember I wanted to abort them? I was in despair. I can't even think about that now."

In contrast, women who had no children or who had resorted to fertility treatments of any kind were elated. Their exclamations ranged from "My wildest dreams" and "A pure blessing" to "This is so unique!" and "A big family all in one go!" Twins can be exceptionally valued and idealized especially when they are born to mothers who left reproduction to the last minute and to parents who had to resort to fertility treatments in order to conceive a child.

For all these first-time mothers the elation lasted until pregnancy became inevitably heavy to bear or some complication intervened.

After mid-pregnancy most mothers were already looking and feeling as if they had reached full term, and even minor ailments such as breathlessness, difficulties in digestion and sleep, backache, frequent micturition, swollen feet and legs, and uncontrollable itching, all contributed to make pregnancy very hard and full of discomfort. All mothers now expressed ambivalent feelings and 15 mothers openly rejected their twins. Comments were, "I can't stand this any longer," "I don't care about them any more," "Please could we accelerate their birth? Premature babies can be handled, but I will die if I have to continue enduring this ordeal." Twins were equated by these mothers with malevolent entities invading the mother' body. They were associated with parasites, bloodsuckers, demons, and invaders.

Additionally, fetal complications such as growth retardation or ominous blood-flows skyrocketed all concerns present even in uncomplicated pregnancies.

As another patient whom I shall call Ms G, a mother whose twins were both affected by severely stunted growth and whose prospects according to all medical parameters looked quite grim, commented, "I thought of pregnancy as a blissful state in which my children were protected by my body. I knew it is all an illusion, but one has to forget about death in order to carry on with life. Now I have death in my mind and my body no longer feels protective, actually it feels like a grave. I am not an anxious person, but anxiety never leaves me now. I don't want to prolong the agony when I know that their chances are so low."

Whenever maternal complications also intervened, pregnancy became a heartbreaking physical and mental ordeal.

By 22 weeks, a patient whom I shall refer to as Ms H, was already finding pregnancy too much. She suffered from piles, varicose veins had made her legs swell considerably, gall bladder stones caused continuous itching, and her abdomen was hugely distended. She complained, "I hope this will be over soon, can't you accelerate their birth?" When advised that 22 weeks was far too soon she moaned, "But how can I be asked to endure all this?" When at 32 weeks she had to be hospitalized due to high blood pressure, Ms H broke down and wept saying, "This is inhumane. How can I be asked to endure this torment? Please help me get rid of these two. I feel invaded and I want a cesarean now." A caesarean was performed two days later as her blood pressure rose even further and the twins were showing signs of suffering. Ms H, however, seemed to be able to forgive all the pain and discomfort she had suffered. Whenever she was visited in later years, she was very affectionate toward her twins. All the discomfort suffered during pregnancy, however, was not forgotten. The twins were nicknamed "my torturers," claiming that they had started tormenting her from the womb. Had she been a less mature, loving woman, she could have become a real tormentor of her twins.

Besides expressing hostile or strongly ambivalent feelings, 24 mothers displayed conducts amounting to more or less conscious physical abuse. These mothers "forgot" to take important drugs, lifted heavy weights, planned long drives for holidays, engaged in spring-cleaning, failed to turn up for check-ups, and ate less in the belief it would help maintain their figures. Incredibly, 26 mothers fell down the stairs squashing their stomachs.

Another patient, whom I shall call Ms I, a woman in her forties who had resorted to innumerable attempts at IVF before finally getting pregnant, came to the hospital after falling down the stepladder twice in a spurt of spring cleaning. She was all bruised and her husband was worried for the twins. He said, "They seem to have stopped moving." We performed a scan, and reassured him that the twins were doing fine. Mr I was relieved, but his wife declared, "I was hoping to push them out as I can't stand this any longer." Unlike Ms H, when the twins were born, she was not able to either forgive or forget. The twins became the prime target of all the ills in her life. As she often said, "Before getting pregnant my life was happy. I was a beautiful woman. Then I had this crazy idea of starting a family. I want my body back. I look like a cow now. It is all their fault. I want to go back to what I was, to my previous life. I want to erase them. I wish I had squashed them when I fell during pregnancy." Her husband was becoming sexually estranged, and she moaned "We were a couple before. I want my husband back. They are taking him away from me." She paid no attention to the twins, and, apart from feeding them, left them alone all day long in their cradle without even changing them.

A few mothers went even further than that, as in the case where prenatal abuse took the form of drinking. In eight cases and on repeated occasions colleagues asked, "Have a thorough look at these twins. As you can see, they do not move at all." Absolute lack of motion within the span of a careful ultrasonographic checkup can indicate the beginning of a problem or be a more ominous sign. Whenever this happened, I observed the twins for a lengthy period of time, one hour, while at the same time checking other important parameters, such as blood-flows. These measures were not necessary to make an accurate diagnosis. Often going near the mother was enough. Her breath, her acrid body odor, and her general behavior all gave her away. The twins were drunk!

One could do nothing to help and had to wait until the mother had sobered up to see if the twins were also sober and had started moving again. Movements are no guarantee, however, that no brain damage has occurred.

South Americans abound in my twin unit, and they like to give baby-showers, a celebration imported from the United States. The first one to which I was invited came as a shock. A patient, whom I shall call Ms Paloma, was five months pregnant and was expecting opposite-sex twins. She had invited quite a number of friends. All, including me, brought double presents for the twins, but the other guests also brought an impressive amount of alcoholic drinks, especially beer but also whiskey, vodka, and rum. Since I drink virtually nothing at all, when the toasting started, I asked for a Vodka, which I rapidly substituted for water in the kitchen. After the first few drinks, people explained to me the true nature of the ceremony. Whenever the father opened one of the numerous parcels he had to take one drink. If after a while he was still on his feet, other drinks were added. The aim of all this drinking was to knock him unconscious. This profound drunkenness had the ritual purpose of making the father identify with the neonate, so as to comprehend its feelings and ultimately become attached to it. Neonates are notoriously similar to the drunks in that they cannot stand up, reason or talk coherently, and often waver between a comatose sleepy state and wakefulness. The identification did not stop there. According to the ritual, the father had to become drunk enough to lose control of his bowels and his bladder. A huge diaper was kept ready for him. Only at this point was he no longer forced to drink. A large pacifier was now inserted in his mouth, thus further increasing the identification with the neonate while bringing to an end his dangerous drinking. I had been told, however, that in the case of twins mothers were often made to join in the drinking until unconscious. When my hostess also began to drink and everyone applauded, it was clearly time for me to leave.

When I saw Ms Paloma a few days later at the hospital, I warned her about the dangers of alcohol for the twins. She remonstrated, "But this is part of our culture. We can take better care of neonates if we feel and behave like them again. With twins you need both parents, one for each and the ritual has to be repeated on at least two different occasions." Sadly, when the twins were born, they were both found to suffer from a full-blown fetal alcohol syndrome.

The cultural roots of the ritual probably went back to the kind of shamanic ceremonials that were widely practiced in the region from which the twins' parents came.[11] In order to empathize with their patients and have enlightening visions about them, the local shamans took substances that put them in an altered state of mind. These substances ranged from alcohol to special mushrooms or leaves. When intoxicated, shamans fell to the ground, curled up in the fetal position, and often claimed to have visions taking them back to their prenatal and neonatal past. From this regressive state they emerged reborn, capable of being in touch with their patients' ailments and feelings.

The psychiatrist Carl Gustav Jung, founder of analytical psychology, was also a student of other cultures, and was particularly interested in shamans and their hallucinogenic trips. He considered regression as a prenatal, undifferentiated state of mind, which he called "the matrix of creation," as a necessary precondition, a voyage one had to undertake in order to be able to get in touch with our collective unconscious.[12] The overwhelming majority of South American parents, however, did not behave in this way at their baby showers, where people drank only soft drinks.

If prenatally twins can stretch their mothers bodies to the limit, postnatally they can be extremely stressing and taxing. The psychological and physical impact of twins on their caretakers during the early years of their lives is overwhelming.

In my longitudinal 1989 study of 30 pairs of twins starting from prenatal life to age six, where postnatal home visits were conducted fortnightly, the arrival of twins usually felt like a tornado hitting the house.[13] Everybody's life was turned upside-down beyond their wildest imaginations. All the tricky aspects of looking after a newborn child were exponentially increased. Lack of sleep and consequent fatigue affected all mothers. As one commented, "It feels like being forced to work on an assembly line twenty-four hours a day. You finish with one, and here comes the other. When they overlap, you just feel like screaming and tearing your hair."

Fathers too were exhausted. Save some lucky few, in order to earn more money they had to increase their workload, and requested—but rarely got—uninterrupted sleep. When they came back home in the evenings, they were immediately put on some task ranging from going to the supermarket, to boiling bottles, and lulling one twin to sleep. All commented, "I get some rest only when I am at work." Mutual misunderstandings piled up. All marriages go through a transition period when a child is born, and sometimes the transition can be quite hard. Marital difficulties, however, are known to be particularly frequent in families with twins.

Mr L bitterly resented his wife's complaints and once told me, "She is here all day enjoying the twins' company. I miss out on that. I work my fingers to the bone, but my wife doesn't realize that." Ms L screamed, "As from tomorrow I will go back to work and you will stay at home!" In a moment they were both screaming, and when the twins joined in the noise it became deafening. The Ls were soon separated.

Mothers resented having to give up work and being confined at home. The arrival of twins was considered as an intolerable limitation of their freedom and an equally intolerable demand for sacrifice. As a patient, whom I shall call Ms M, said, "I can't stand the lack of social contact. All I hear is their screams. I want my freedom back, I no longer can decide to come and go, actually I cannot even decide when to go to the toilet or shampoo my hair in peace."

Apprehension about the children, altered physical shape with the consequent fear of losing beauty, fitness, erotic value, and ultimately the love of their companions, all caused these women great misery. Twenty-two mothers suffered from depression. Mothers who had undergone assisted reproduction were hit particularly hard. The idealization surrounding these pregnancies, which was always especially high, meant that mothers came down to earth with a bump when confronted with the endless task of caring for two infants.

Maternal depression, marital difficulties, fatigue, and isolation are all factors easily conducive to abusive and neglectful conduct. In my study 11 cases, or almost a third, displayed compromised parental behavior. Screams, sudden explosions of rage resulting in physical punishment, and harsh "educational" measures, such as confining the twins inside dark rooms or making them skip meals, were all noticed. Threats of other extreme punishments were voiced, such as knifing, strangling, poisoning, scalding, and defenestrating. The outbursts occurred especially when the twins cried, were unwell or hungry, soiled themselves, or were rebellious during the toddler stage.

As the writer Sara Ruddick points out, children are utterly dependent on their caregivers. Yet they often respond to care in ways that are frustrating and enraging: bursting into temper tantrums at the supermarket, splattering food on the floor, running out in the street. From the beginning, children are especially vulnerable to assault by their own parents, by exhausted, angry people who love them.[14] Comprehensibly, overworked mothers of twins and poor or single-parent mothers are particularly affected.

Propelled by pervasive idealization, we seem to have forgotten anything but the bright side of motherhood. Problems are more than doubled in the case of young twins.

Mr and Ms N, who had been married for several years, had decided to postpone having a child until their family business was firmly established. In the meantime they had enjoyed a fairly unencumbered life. They often traveled on business to China and Japan. They also had a wide circle of friends and often went out to the movies and dinner. But when Ms N was approaching 40, they decided to try having a child. The difficulties proved innumerable, which only made Ms N more obsessed with the idea of getting pregnant. Nothing was left untried, including countless attempts at IVF performed in foreign, lucrative, and unscrupulous facilities. When

Ms N finally came to my clinic, all her life revolved around what she called "the problem." As she said, "If I solve the problem my life will be perfect. Otherwise it will be a total catastrophe. It all depends on the problem." Ms N was encouraged to seek psychological support and to consider adoption as her obsession was now all pervasive and risked destroying her life, but instead she went to yet another clinic. When she reappeared two months later, she was elated. She was expecting twins and wanted us to follow up on her during the pregnancy. Her husband was elated too. He held her hand throughout the checkup, frequently stroked her face gently, and seemed utterly in love with her.

Ms N's pregnancy was initially complicated by only minor problems, such as itching and piles, which nevertheless made her life an ordeal. Then hydramnios, an excess of amniotic fluid, set in, and she could hardly breathe, eat, find a comfortable position, or sleep. She was huge and exhausted. At checkups her husband looked at her with a mixture of fear and disbelief.

When I visited her a few months later, Ms N was severely depressed and was utterly uninterested in the twins, a boy and a girl. She said, "Before I was free. Now I am confined to my home. I have nobody to talk to and not even a minute of respite. It's just continuous demands. When one stops, the other starts." Following my suggestion, she hired a babysitter, but could not stand the presence of another person in the house. As she said, "I was used to being by myself." Her marriage was also collapsing. She resented her husband's relative freedom, and there were bitter quarrels all the time. I referred her for psychiatric help, but she did not accept it, saying "It's all their fault."

The conditions in which the twins lived were also worrisome. She kept them in a cot, which resembled a cage, and never spoke or played with them. The twins appeared dopey, and I suspected that she was adding some tranquilizer to their formulas in order to keep them quiet. As she admitted, "I only love them when they are asleep. They look like angels then." I had the ominous feeling that she would have loved them even more had they slept an eternal sleep, but it was difficult to intervene, because the twins were apparently well-fed, clean, and generally physically healthy. I requested a home visit from a social worker, who said that unfortunately we had no grounds for taking action. Abuse that was purely psychological was difficult to demonstrate. The suggestion of looking for traces of tranquillizers in their blood was dismissed, as we needed a court order and, as the social worker said, "We will never get one."

Four years later Ms N's marriage had ended. By then she was perhaps slightly less depressed, but the twins lagged behind in all developmental milestones, from walking to talking. They attended special classes and were each assigned a remedial teacher throughout primary school. Subsequently I lost touch with them.

Abusive conduct was not exclusive to families who had undergone assisted reproduction; however, given the extreme idealization surrounding these pregnancies, the families were hit especially hard.

The anthropologist Nancy Sheper-Huges suggests, challengingly, that the current epidemic of child abuse may represent, in part, a paradoxical effect of the suppression in our societies of the former, traditional pattern of selective neglect directed toward babies seen as ill-fated for survival.[15] However, as she says, a careful distinction needs to be made between allowing certain neonates to die for economic and societal reasons or because the infants are seen as hopelessly unfit to live in a traditional society, and the hostile battering of a child in a modern industrialized society. The two patterns are not only distinct but nearly mutually exclusive. They represent the difference between cultural norm and cultural pathology, between human exigency and malicious intent.

Young twins represent a realm in which such distinctions may occasionally be blurred.

Yet twins, given all the hardships they usually entail, can also testify to the formidable extent of maternal love.

A patient, whom I shall call Ms O, was an attractive woman in her late twenties, who already had one child when she was told that she was expecting twins. Pregnancy had been planned, but not for two, and Ms O took the news rather somberly commenting, "My husband will have to work hard, and I will have to work hard too." Complications started early. At 16 weeks the twins were found to suffer from twin-to-twin transfusion syndrome. Ms O was submitted to repeated, at times weekly, amniocentesis in order to try and redress the balance of amniotic fluid between the twins. Ms O tolerated the whole ordeal stoically, but was terribly worried and distressed about the twins as she had been told that their chances of survival were low. Twin-to-twin transfusion syndrome has a poor prognosis when it starts early in pregnancy. Her husband was never there with her because, as she said, "He now works night and day to save money for them, but we will make it. All that matters is their health." Unfortunately, when she came for her 20-week scan, the heart of one twin was found to be malformed. We arranged a consultation with a specialist who said that the twin's serious malformation required repeated and complex surgery once born. Ms O was devastated. From then on her husband accompanied her. When she reached 30 weeks, the twins showed ominous signs and an emergency caesarean was performed. Both boys had to be detained in the intensive care unit for over a month and Ms O came to the clinic twice a day, making long trips. As she said, "I cannot move near the clinic, as my eldest son needs me too." One twin was finally dismissed, but the other had to undergo its first operation. Ms O now split her time between home and another hospital. She looked exhausted. As she said, "I hardly have time to sleep and eat. But all that matters is their health." We kept in touch telephonically. She told me that she was helped by a neighbor when she was out, but once back home had to cope with the children and their demands and with all sorts of household chores. More surgery ensued and the twin twice suffered a cardiac arrest, luckily without consequences. As she commented, "Now my life is pervaded with worry and anxiety." Yet more pain and anxiety was added. When the twins were one year old, Ms O phoned me asking for a consultation. She told me crying that her husband was leaving her. As she said "Probably all this is too much for him and he is seeing another woman." Yet Ms O continued to cope stoically with the circumstances. But four years later this sad story had a happy ending. The twin survived his last and most dangerous operation. Mr O reunited with his wife, and they all came to see me. Mr O commented, "My wife has been heroic. I left her all alone in the middle of the turmoil, but I could no longer cope with the fatigue and the anxiety. I admire her for her formidable capacity to love, her generosity and her forgivingness. She has coped with impossible circumstances and even managed to raise our children as well." Ms O smiled, and just added "I don't know how I have been able to make it, but love was my greatest prop. I love my family and my twins. Life without them would be unthinkable."

Chapter 12

Till Death Us Do Part

Down the centuries, twins have been associated with a host of myths. Male-female pairs have featured almost universally in creation myths, serving as the original couple who gave birth to all humanity.

Particularly notable is the creation myth of the Dogon, an African population living in Sudan and Mali, reported by the French ethnologist Marcel Griaule in 1948. In a series of unforgettable conversations, Ogotemmeli, a blind old Dogon, explained to Griaule the religious ideas of his population.[1] According to the Dogon's creation myth, a primeval god first copulated with the earth, who gave birth to four pairs of opposite-sex twins, and these incestuous pairs fathered the human race. Men in turn then began to produce single offspring, but duality was essential to maintain the natural order based on the fusion of masculine and feminine traits, and to avoid what Ogotemmeli described as "the permanent calamity of single births," each infant was born with twin souls, one male and one female completing and complementing each other as couples do.

Traces of this ancient belief are still present in our current attitudes toward twins, whom we tend to view as a pair and a unit. As twins grow, we expect them to feel especially close at all times, as if united by a mystical and pure bond.

Most twins indeed share a unique bond, which they themselves declare to be very special and unmatched by any other link.

In a series of 40 interviews with adult twins contacted through advertisements in various magazines in 1994, when asked about marriage, 34 twins declared, "At first it was difficult," and the most frequent comments were "Compared with the relationship I have with my twin, I did not experience the same closeness in my marriage." "Communication in particular was hard, as it required effort. With my twin words were often not needed, we simply understood each other." And "Adjustment to marriage was complicated, as I expected a special intimacy, and I became very demanding."

All twins found it difficult to part from their co-twins. However, ten twins also expressed relief and ambivalence. As one female commented, "My relationship with my twin brother was holding me back. I relied on him and he relied on me, for a while we became a closed unit, and we didn't make any effort to live fully." Another female declared, "Parting was difficult, but especially in retrospect I realize that my life was stunted and my marriage enriched me enormously." A male said, "People imagine only closeness and perfect understanding, but I often hated my twin, and my marriage freed me."

In the popular imagination, however, twins are constantly experiencing closeness and perfect understanding. Additionally, male-female twins embody the fantasy of the perfect marital couple, as well as the perennial search for a twin soul. As in the Dogon mythology, the theme of incest hangs around this type of twins.

Some ethnic groups still regard opposite-sex twins as the ideal, original couple, to whom everyone yearns to conform, with the consequence that opposite-sex twins are pushed toward incest.

During my contact with the gypsies whom I visited weekly as a doctor in their settlements, I was made to believe for quite a while that opposite-sex twins were just considered as ordinary siblings. Once the gypsies had learned to trust me, however, and to treat me with familiarity, they offered to show me their pictures. Gypsies love to have their picture taken, and all families have heaps of photos taken on special occasions in particular, such as birthdays and marriages. Among the many photographs I was shown were five pairs of young male-female twins dressed in bridal costumes and French kissing. Their parents told me that they had asked the twins to pose in this way as husband and wife simply for fun.

Then one day I was invited to a large party where loud music was playing and everybody was dancing and drinking. The five pairs of opposite-sex twins I had seen in the pictures were also there, four of them now approaching puberty. All the pairs still wore bridal clothes and behaved like lovers, kissing and dancing to the motions of intercourse. Everyone else laughed and clapped their hands while making such drunken comments as: "They are getting there. Soon they will be able to make love to each other." or "You lucky ones. Nothing like fucking your twin sister, pure perfection." Or "Look at them. This is just a preview." I was later told by my best friend among the gypsies, that one boy in the camp was actually the result of the union of an incestuous pair. His parents lived together but could not be officially married because Italian law forbade such marriages, so the boy had been declared the son of some other couple.

Gypsies live in very tight communities, and inbreeding, including marriage between close relatives such as first cousins, is the rule. Incest is also frequent, including intimate mother-son relations. In their close communities everybody watches everybody else, all know when incest takes place, and rumors and gossips begin to circulate. The incestuous pair is laughed upon, with such remarks as "You are a mother-fucker, a real one!" or "You pig, leave your daughter alone." Incest, however, is regarded as a transient phase preceding marriage, and is seemingly only morally condemned. The sole openly accepted exception is incest between twin brothers and sisters, considered the most sublime form of all unions, and substituting marriage.

During a few subsequent visits I met the incestuous twin pairs again, four of whom were now living *more uxorio,* like husband and wife. Two of the twin girls aged 14 were already pregnant. As soon as gypsy girls reach puberty, they are taken out of school and married to barely adolescent boys. The marriage is not recorded until the partners are 18, when Italian law permits it, by which time the couple may already have several children registered in someone else's name. Whenever I saw the two pregnant twin girls, I felt saddened and powerless. Once, two gypsy men and a woman noticed my reaction and approached me to say "*Gadjè* are stupid! You miss so much in life!" then I was told again, "Nothing like fucking your twin sister."

Throughout history brother-sister incest was a prerogative of royalty and nobility in many places ranging from Egypt to the African region of the Great Lakes, and to the Pre-Columbian South American empires.[2] The custom had both political and economic significance, because wealth as well as power had to remain within the family. Familial intermarriage was practiced until the beginning of the last century by dynasties such as the Hapsburgs who ruled over Austria and Spain. I wondered whether the "children of the wind" had picked up this custom from the many places they crossed and transformed it into a superior form of union to be enjoyed by just a few privileged twins. Or perhaps the practice epitomized the irresistible temptation to break the *gadjè* rules. Gypsies love to cause a stir and to be provocative, and much of their culture now rests on breaking the laws of the "stupid *gadjè.*" This often gets them into trouble and elicits further suspicion and hatred of them, fostering an ever-increasing marginalization, which in turn makes the gypsies cling even more to their illicit behavior. Their nomadic spirit is reduced to sudden, almost symbolic migratory acts. With the coming of spring, gypsies take off in their caravans and circle the town or visit some relatives, breaking any possible work contract and disrupting all attempts at schooling. Their freedom, sense of rhythm, incredible musical talent, and explosive joy are confined to their "pagan" gatherings, which stir complaints from their neighborhood. Incest, too, is no longer a secret, and social systems are beginning to take active steps to control it. Those who were once called the children of the wind for their extraordinary freedom and capacity to move and absorb different cultures now seem stuck in an unsolvable dilemma, living against society and yet permanently inhabiting it.

Even if I had continued working with the gypsies for many more years, I am sure that my twin mystery would not have been solved. Gypsies have no written records, and they love to shroud their customs in a veil of secrecy.

In most other populations incest is one of the strongest taboos, and the incestuous aura surrounding male-female twins can have weighty consequences. In Java and Bali, Indonesia, for instance, male-female twins are believed invariably to commit incest.[3,4] The Balinese assume that they are already doing so inside their mother's womb, while the Javanese think that they will become incestuous in adult life. As a result, until fairly recently opposite-sex pairs were doomed to death for breaking the incest taboo with these allegedly illicit activities. As in ancient Egypt, only twins of royal origin were spared. Although better law enforcement and the tourist trade have changed the fate of this type of Indonesian twins, the villages where they happen to be born still sometimes have to undergo extensive purification ceremonies to purge their intrauterine sin. In some parts of Bali the mothers, too, will have to go through purification rites for having allegedly sheltered incestuous activities inside their bodies during pregnancy. Curiously some prenatal psychologists have somehow restored the Indonesian myth of intrauterine incest, albeit for all pairs of twins, not just opposite-sex ones. Convinced that twin fetuses can already establish complex emotional ties in utero, these psychologists go so far as to claim that the twins first "embraces" and "kisses" may be observed with ultrasounds at 86 and 92 postmenstrual days, respectively.[5] See figure 12.1.

Besides these ramblings of so-called experts, the incestuous aura surrounding male-female pairs is currently reflected in other areas.

I have taken countless photographs of twins in many areas of the world, including my own country and Central Park, New York. Recently I looked back over these photos focusing on male-female pairs. Most of these pairs, or 88 percent, were dressed, as young children, like little brides and grooms. When the twins reached school age, the habit stopped, save for special festivities, when 40 percent of twins were again made to wear bridal costumes. By adolescence all male and female twins had become "unseen," in that they were clearly differentiated in their gendered bodies and clothing.

Figure 12.1 This carving from an old temple in Java illustrates ancient beliefs associated with opposite-sex twins. The carving is shaped like a uterus. Inside, opposite-sex twins depicted as adults wear bridal costumes, implying incest in the womb. The two small statuettes at the base of the "womb" are newborn twins incapable, like all neonates, of committing incest, which will be reenacted later in life.

In my 1989 study of twins from prenatal life to age six, where opposite-sex twins made up 15 sets of twins, their parents generally considered these twins as the ideal, self-sufficient progeny. Their thoughts ran, "Now that we have one of each sex, we don't need to try again. Our family is complete." Male-female pairs were experienced as complementing and completing each other, just as couples do.[6]

The psychology of opposite-sex twins has been investigated by the French psychologist Reneè Zazzo. Zazzo considered them an ideal model for studying the dynamics of couples governing all human relationships, including married life. He thought that male-female pairs in particular could help us understand the incest taboo and the many facets of love.[7] He found that 15 percent of males and 46 percent of females from opposite-sex twins opted for celibacy, a choice that he considered to be psychologically determined, in that no marriage partner could grant the same degree of mutual, unspoken understanding offered by the co-twin.

Claire Salvy, another French psychologist who studied opposite-sex twins from adolescence to old age, found that those who were married considered the deep sharing of emotions to be the most essential element in a marriage. Male-female twins who were still adolescent looked only for friendship and camaraderie in the other gender, not seduction, which felt especially alien to them. As adults the majority of these twins (87 percent) lived far from each other, but they were as prone as monozygotic twins to experience special empathy toward one another. Most (89 percent) reported experiencing extrasensory perception in the form of unusual pain and crippling anxiety, as if the other was in some kind of danger.[8]

Despite their parents' initial extremism in differentiating between the male-female roles, these adults felt that their own personality represented a unique blend of characteristics belonging to both roles. The blending was made vivid to me one day in Rajastan, where I saw a strange pair of young opposite-sex children with their parents. Both children were dressed luxuriously in a way that made them look curiously androgynous. The boy had long hair and wore a sari-like skirt on top of his trousers. The girl's hair was cut short, and her clothing mixed traditional female and male elements, from a frivolous hat and frilly top to trousers and gym shoes. Their parents, who were evidently upper-class with expensive clothing and a limousine, noticed my perplexity. They smiled and explained that the children were twins and that male-female pairs were almost comparable to hermaphrodites. "They personify masculine and feminine blending together in a unique way. As they grow, they are capable of understanding the other sex in a unique way." Incest was not an issue, as it is not in most opposite-sex twins. The Rajastani parents underlined in their own way the unique feature characterizing this type of twins: mutual understanding of each other and of the opposite sex, treated in a compassionate, brotherly and sisterly way.

Unlike French psychology, behavioral geneticists have hardly ever taken male-female pairs into account. Research in the field has concentrated instead on same-sex pairs, in order to erase the inevitable gender variable in comparing monozygotic and dizygotic twins. Recently, however, opposite-sex twins have been rediscovered over the question of whether the masculinization of female fetuses or the feminization of male fetus occurs in the human species, as it does in other animals. Cattle breeders are familiar with the so-called freemartin effect in which the female of opposite-sex twin calves is born with the external genitalia of a female but with ovaries that are seriously altered. This condition results in the infertility of the female, while the male, called a freemartin, functions perfectly as a bull. The freemartin effect is due to placental vascular connections in the cow whereby male hormones are transferred to the female co-twin in utero. Human opposite-sex twin fetuses, which have different and separate placentas, have no such vascular connection to produce this effect.

Other animals that share the same placenta and vascular connections, like cows, are currently being investigated. According to Nancy Segal, a researcher in the field of behavioral research, female mice "positioned between males in the uterus are heavier and more aggressive than females positioned between females." In addition male gerbils "positioned between two females sire smaller litters, are less likely to impregnate females, and are less likely to elicit scent-making by females."[9] Here too hormonal transfer in utero would seem to be the cause.

The leap from cows, mice, or gerbils to humans is a big one, and the difficulties in proving hormonal transfer in our species are for the moment insurmountable. Yet a scientific myth may be on the horizon for opposite-sex twins. It is suggested that their gender differences might be erased or exchanged in utero by hormones producing a kind of hermaphroditic physical condition. So far, however, we have no evidence of this exchange with consequent hermaphroditism in humans. This claim is just the opposite to what researchers like Salvy or the Rajastani parents have noted, that years of shared living and mutual understanding are required to produce a kind of harmonious, hermaphroditic mental blending.

Same-sex twins, whether monozygotic or not, are free from this alleged danger of hermaphroditism, but they are encumbered by different myths and taboos that overwhelmingly concern male twins. In the antiquity, male twins were represented as the originators of towns rather than of the human race, the most famous example being Romulus and Remus, the founders of Rome. Often these twins had been exposed at birth and allegedly raised by animals. Exposure was based on reality. Twin exposure and infanticide were widespread worldwide.

Another aura that haunts same-sex twins is the possibility of incest and homosexuality. In my 1993 study of initial parental reactions to the news that they were expecting twins, nobody mentioned the homosexuality-incest scenario. When male pairs were positioned pertinently, I heard only the odd comment on homosexuality, such as, "They will become fags. Who cares! We will love them anyway." The gay movement has done a lot to free homosexuality, especially male homosexuality, from all sorts of prejudices and condemnations. Incest, on the contrary, seems so unthinkable as to be totally denied. Fetal females were excluded from both taboos. The non-protruding nature of female genitals purified them in utero and no parent mentioned future lesbian scenarios.

When the twins were visited in their home after birth, the differences between the child-raising practices of same-sex and opposite-sex twins were evident. During the first year, all twins might occasionally be made to share the same cradle, but the habit soon ceased for all opposite-sex twins whose parents began to treat them as ordinary siblings. No such constraint was placed on same-sex twins, who continued to be regarded as a pair. They could share the same bed or hop into each other's bed as long as they wished. They were frequently asked to kiss and hug each other. Even mutual masturbation was not forbidden. Several parents gave me their own videos of their twins, whom they liked to film unawares as they awoke, in the act of embracing and fondling each other's genitals. When the twins were caught in the act, everybody smiled or even laughed, and nobody mentioned homosexuality, let alone incest.

In some other areas of the world, both taboos are openly acknowledged and lived out. In 1991 I was working in the Indonesian part of Papua, then called Irian Jaya, in a stunning valley with a river running through it. I had been asked to visit the local populations in order to report on their needs for sanitation. The valley was gorgeous—green, untouched, surrounded by mountains with spectacular views. The main town was a sleepy place, without paved roads and with wooden huts for houses. The focal point of the town was an open-air market where modernized natives wearing T-shirts and trousers, and speaking some English, mixed with naked people from the valleys expressing themselves in their dialect and selling the vegetables they had grown and pigs they had reared in the mountains.

Things may have changed by now, but at the time the natives living outside the town were still pretty much untouched by civilization. All males were naked, save for a dried gourd of many shapes and sizes that they wore on their penis. Each man had a collection of gourds, including several with a small fur tip. Women were bare-chested and wore a fiber skirt. Men were generally itinerant, going around from village to village trading wood, potatoes, pigs, and other goods, including females. Women were more stationary. They worked all day in the fields, using rudimentary axes and their own hands, and when dusk set in, they walked back to their village. All young children were looked after by the women while working. They carried the infants on their back, together with sweet potatoes and occasionally piglets, in a special net attached to their head. When I first saw a woman with that net, I thought how impossible it must have been for her to carry twins.

In the villages I had to deal with all sorts of diseases, ranging from malaria to skin cancer, goiter, and chest complaints. Children were particularly affected. Nights were chilly, and all suffered from chronic bronchitis, if not pneumonia or tuberculosis. The natives also had infected scars on various parts of their bodies, whose nature I could not understand at first. Then I realized that during the chilly nights everyone gathered close to the fire, and when they fell asleep, they often fell into the fire, burning their skin.

I had an interpreter with me, a young local man with a wild pig tusk in his nose, whom I will call Jim. He had left his village to seek a different life in town, but he often went back to the mountain chain where the natives lived. Everyone knew him, especially the women, because Jim was a womanizer. He listened to women, played with their children, paid them compliments, brought them gifts, and in the end invariably ended up in the bush with some girl.

Despite the presence of an interpreter, verbal communication was not easy. Natives expressed themselves mainly through body language, and I began using it too. Their dialect was simple, and I soon picked up some words, although words could have different meanings attached to them. The first word I learned was mother, which also meant anything connected with the idea of motherhood, such as pregnancy, delivery, and breastfeeding.

My contact with the women was initially difficult. They were reserved and shy, especially with strangers. They slept in separate huts with young children and pigs. Except for Jim, nobody seemed to take much interest in women. Pigs, on the contrary, were highly valued, and women breastfed piglets as well as their own infants.

Initially when I was with the women in the villages, they sat close to each other, watching me in absolute silence, and did not allow me even to go near them. I was regarded as a potentially dangerous stranger. Jim explained to me that women were often raped by nearby tribal groups, who invaded their villages. Long, ferocious, retaliatory wars would then ensue.

Matters changed for me one day when an elderly woman approached me, touched my breasts, and slipped her hand inside my trousers. Then she went back to the others and whispered something to them, whereupon they all let out their familiar cry, a kind of Wawawa which sounded like barking dogs. The cry was used to express all sorts of feelings such as pain, sadness, and excitement, but in this case it meant satisfaction. Having ascertained, despite my short hair, small breasts, and trousers, that I was a woman, the other women were no longer afraid, though still shy. Rumors traveled fast, and the news that I was a woman soon spread to other villages. Gradually I came to be respected as a kind of witch doctor. The locals attributed any disease to evil magic, and my cures were interpreted as potent countermeasures against it.

After the first few busy days, I began asking about twins, who were generally brought up separately. One twin was regularly given away, as women could not cope with working in the fields while carrying and breastfeeding two infants simultaneously. The "adoption" might take place within the same community, but more often than not one twin was handed over to some barren woman from a neighboring village. Though the twins were raised apart, they generally kept in touch by visiting and playing with each other.

In my wanderings from village to village, children always followed me. One late afternoon when dusk was approaching and I was sitting by myself on the grass at the edge of a beautiful wood, suddenly two young boys joined me. They had probably been following me all along. The boys were clearly identical twins, although one still lived as if in the Stone Age, going around completely naked save for a small penis gourd. The other twin, who had been adopted by a more modern family on the outskirts of the town, wore a T-shirt, short trousers, gym shoes, and a cap. He also spoke some English. The modernized twin explained to me that he often climbed up into the mountains to play with his twin brother. The link between them had not been broken either by distance or by divergent cultures. From then on the twin boys joined me nearly everyday.

A few days later I asked Jim what happened to twins when they grew up. He told me that twins seldom married. When they reached manhood, they reunited and shared the same hut. He took me to see one such pair, two skinny fellows who were no longer young. They looked identical except that one wore a lot of feathers and flamboyant leaves on his head, while the other did not, wearing only the usual penis gourd. Unlike Europeans, natives who showed off a lot of plumage had been the least successful in life and were trying to compensate for their relative failure with impressive displays of finery. The twin who did not flaunt any finery was highly regarded and treated like a chief. The twins held hands and fondled each other in a loving way, as if they were married. Jim confirmed the impression by commenting, "They need no wives. They are married to each other. I mean they have sex together." Male homosexuality was simply accepted and considered natural among the natives.

Another day, as Jim and I were walking along a gravel road through deep tropical forests to reach a distant village, suddenly out of the forest came four young adult men belonging to a distant pygmy group. All were completely naked, save for the usual penis gourd. Each of them held up a huge leaf as an umbrella, to protect them from the frequent rain and scorching sun. After we repeatedly exchanged greetings, they showed curiosity about me—my hair, my clothing, the color and texture of my skin. To my surprise, I noticed that two of the men were sharing the same pair of gym shoes, one fellow wearing his shoe on the right foot, the other on the left, and the shoes were both falling apart. Clearly someone had dumped them somewhere. Through Jim, I asked the two men the meaning and purpose of this strange act of sharing. The choral answer was, "We are twins!" Having recently reunited, the twins were sharing their one and only pair of shoes as a sign of their affection and of the special link uniting them. The twins were also holding hands. My guide noted matter-of-factly without further comment, "They are also married to each other. Twins do that."

Other non-twin homosexual unions, though common, were generally casual and sometimes even on the spur of the moment. When two men disappeared into the forest holding hands, everyone knew why and merely giggled. Stable, lifelong homosexual unions, though by no means unique to twins, were a constant feature of twin marriages.

Following these encounters with twin unions, which had so far been between men or boys, I became inquisitive about twin girls. Yet whenever I raised the subject, everyone became close-mouthed. Only one couple living in a village near the town showed me their own little girl, still suckling at her mother's breast, who they told me was a twin. Both parents grew vague when asked about the whereabouts of the other girl. Clearly I had brought up a touchy issue, and the entire clan became evasive or withdrew into silence, as the locals usually did when some secret rule or taboo was mentioned. Jim told me that besides this couple, no one else in the mountains had given birth to twin girls as far back as anyone could remember. Only in town were there two pairs of twin girls. This made me wonder if in the mountains adoption was ever practiced for girls. It was more likely that one of the twins had been disposed of.

On the whole, women and girls were treated no better than the pigs with which they slept, but everyone rejoiced when singleton females were born because females had a market value for the natives, in the sense of being considered pricey exchange goods. I could never find out why twin girls were not similarly welcomed, and whether their doom had any hidden, superstitious significance. Nor could I find out if marriage among male twins also stemmed from some secret custom and had a hidden meaning, as the secretiveness of the natives made me suspect. Sometimes I dream of going back to the beautiful valley for a longer stay to get some answers to these questions, but not for that reason alone. I loved the valley with its gentle inhabitants who, despite their reputation for being ferocious warriors, were extremely tender to me. Since the time I was there, many things have changed. The natives have repeatedly rebelled against Indonesian domination and fought for their independence, which they have not yet obtained. Possibly many of my patients, including the incestuous homosexual twins, are dead by now, wiped out by disease, fanaticism, or thinly disguised extermination.

Several years after visiting the area I witnessed another blatant infringement of the homosexuality-incest taboo. After working in Togo and Benin, I made a visit to Accra, the capital of Ghana, and its neighboring castles, which are beautiful but chilling reminders of the slave trade. While visiting the castle of Elmina, perhaps the most renowned in the area, I saw a pair of adult monozygotic twins dressed exactly alike in long blue-and white tunics. When I approached them, it turned out they both spoke some English, and we struck up a friendly conversation. They asked where I came from, my profession, and my reasons for being there. The twins lived together and invited me to their house, which was set in a poor area nearby. Entering their home felt like entering an anthill, for a communal court- yard shared with other houses swarmed with people, all of them curious about me and thrilled by my presence. Once inside, the twins told me that they both were fishermen, used the same boat, and lived together like "husband and wife." All their neighbors knew this and took it as a matter of course. The twins mentioned that recently they had felt the urge to have a child. In unison they added, "You will see what we did." They whispered something to a woman, who quickly went out and came back followed by a young woman holding a pair of newborn male twins. The fishermen explained, "She is our wife. We gave her official status by marrying her. Now she can do what she wants." Unmarried and childless women had no standing, but now that the woman had married and given birth to twins, she could have gone back to her community, leaving her husbands and children behind, without being frowned upon, as all that mattered was the completion of a social obligation. I looked closely at the babies who were identical. The fishermen smiled and commented proudly, "Now we have one each." I thought to myself, "God only knows who the father is." In their case not even DNA analyses could have revealed the paternity.

Monozygotic twins fathering monozygotic twins with the same woman was a genetic dilemma. Monozygotic twins carry the same genes and when they conceive a child half of their genes mix with half of those of their spouse. The fishermen, however, had copulated with the same woman, thus making it impossible to ascertain paternity.

The fishermen, however, were far from thinking about DNA analysis. They asked me to take some pictures of them, each proudly holding one of the babies. I thought that the infant twins were lucky to have such doting fathers. The young woman also seemed happy about the whole arrangement. She had been hired to produce a much wanted child, the fishermen were thrilled when she delivered twins, and once breastfeeding was over, she could return to her community, but with a new and loftier status. See figure 12.2.

Nobody else seemed to be outraged, even though in Ghana homosexuality was frowned upon and men of some wealth bought themselves as many wives as their finances permitted, to flaunt their virility. Twins were different, however, and were allowed to break the rules. When I asked why, the answer from the fishermen was, "Twins are special. They are married to each other from the very beginning and some end up living together as

Figure 12.2 These West African twins have found an arrangement by temporarily marrying the same woman, who has given birth to twin girls. The woman will go back to her village, but with the status of being married and fertile. The twins will continue living together bringing up their own twin girls.

husband and wife later in their lives." Male twins were allowed to be inces-
tuously homosexual. When I wondered whether twin females were allowed
to live out their incest similarly, the answer was "No." Women were
regarded as truncated if childless and not properly married to a man.

In many other areas of the world, male homosexuality, though officially
condemned, was nevertheless a reality. Female homosexuality, though
rarely contemplated even as a possibility, was also frequently lived out.
Recently a pair of Philippine monozygotic twin girls came to my maternity
hospital in Italy. The twins were young, age 24, and newly wed, but they
wanted to get pregnant soon. My colleagues told them to come back in a
year's time if they had been unable to conceive by then. The girls were
tearful and disappointed, complaining, "A year is too long. We need a
baby now!"

I spent some time trying to talk to the twins, who were holding a big
wedding album. When I asked them to show me the pictures, they bright-
ened up. All the photos showed only the two girls in their wedding gowns.
No husbands were included in any picture. I looked up and said, "You
married each other." The women smiled and replied with a sigh of relief,
"That's exactly it. We just needed a name to try artificial insemination.
You know people gossip. But it has to be quick. We have little money, and
we don't like to do it with men. We wanted to marry each other. It is
difficult for twins to be apart." Since I never saw the women again, I
imagine they got what they wanted.

The phenomenon of twins of all genders ending up "wedded" to each
other may thus be more common than we think. Marriage may not necessarily imply sex but simply the decision to share their lives. Twins often
find each other's company superior to any other kind of companionship.

The most daunting idea for many twins is in fact the separation from,
or even more so the loss of, their co-twin. Joan Woodward, an English
psychotherapist whose twin sister died in childhood and who conducted a
study on twin loss by interviewing over 200 bereaved European twins,
found that the most prominent feature of the loss was a deep and disturbing sense of loneliness. Twins admitted to feeling truncated, amputated, or
halved. Only a few felt relieved at having broken free from a link that they
experienced as a tightening chain, preventing them from living their own
lives to the full.[10]

Besides often unbearable pain, the death of a co-twin can be difficult in
other ways. Twins who lose a twin can have problems relating to others.
They may look for their lost twin in a marriage partner, expecting to find
the same degree of mutual dependency and understanding. The death can
create such overpowering loss anxieties that the twins prefer not to face
marriage, closeness, or deep attachment to anyone. The dead twin can

become so idealized as to make the survivor feel that nobody else could measure up. Or twins may find it difficult to be alone. Still others may fight their loneliness by filling their lives to the brim, so as never have to experience any void.

The uniqueness of twin loss has led to the formation self-help groups for lone twins, where they can voice to other halved twins all the sorrows that they feel nobody else could properly understand. There are also more up-to-date ways of grieving for a twin. A Philippine woman in her early forties, whom I shall call Ms Ramos, was referred to my hospital because she was expecting twins. She was overjoyed with the news. When asked if twins ran in her family, she said "I was a twin. My twin died of an accident twenty years ago. They will be like the two of us all over again." Next time she came to the unit, Ms Ramos brought along a big photo album to show to me. In every picture a duplicated image of herself, a "virtual" twin, had been added by computer. She said, "We were identical. I often go to a photographer and ask him to do what we call a fantasy. My sister is with me. I can have her whenever I want." When her twins turned out to be a boy and a girl, Ms Ramos was disappointed but added cheerfully, "Never mind. I never feel lonely with my album."

When I worked in the Philippines in 1994, I realized that this sort of duplication, locally called fantasy, was pretty widespread. Fantasies could be seen hanging on the walls of many photography shops. Given my interest in these pictures, I was introduced to a young woman, whom I shall call Juliet, whose monozygotic twin sister had recently died in a car accident. Juliet had gone straight to a photographer, and her room was now full of pictures of herself next to her virtual sister, the computerized reproduction of her own image. As Juliet said, "I don't miss my sister any more. I can have her with me, even when I grow old." As with Ms Ramos, the digital camera and the computer had brought back to life her dead co-twin and almost erased her grief.

My most moving encounter with the unthinkable pain involved in the loss of a co-twin took place again in the gorgeous valley in Western Papua on a beautiful evening two days before I was due to leave. After working all day visiting natives in the valley, I was sitting on the grass admiring the beauty of the surroundings. Suddenly a feeble moaning sounded to my left. I turned round and noticed an extremely wrinkled old man, who may actually have been younger than I, and seemed to have materialized out of nowhere. People in the valley walked incredibly silently and swiftly, their feet adhering like suction cups to the steep and slippery ground. After the initial fright, I made contact with the old fellow by offering him a cigarette. I always carried some tobacco with me, knowing that the locals were crazy about it. Their life-span being barely over 40 years, I thought a cigarette would do them no harm. As the old man smoked, he continued to moan and look sad. Then he showed me his left hand, where the first joint of two of his fingers had been cut off. He continued to moan and cry for a while, then hugged me repeatedly while singing a melodious and rhythmic but melancholy tune. The locals, who had a good musical ear, often sang such songs. Finally, as suddenly and silently as he had appeared, the old man left. See figure 12.3.

Jim, who knew the man, later told me that in order to communicate the pain they felt over the death of loved ones, the locals severed off their own fingers one by one. Only the thumb was regularly spared for some reason which was not explained to me. So far, however, only women and especially young girls had been described as undergoing this kind of mutilation.[11,12] The old man had a twin, whose death was for him the most excruciating pain of all. He had severed two of his fingers following his twin's death to show that he felt truncated and dead without his twin.

Twins worldwide claim to feel truncated and halved when they lose their co-twins.

Figure 12.3   This old Papuan man severed off two fingers when his co-twin died. The severing of fingers, usually only done by young women, indicates pain at the loss of a dear one, as well as having a "placatory" function. The dead will be pleased with the sacrifice and not envious of mutilation. However, this man apparently was not afraid of his twin, just truncated by his death.

In that valley rumors spread swiftly. Knowing of my interest in twins, the old man had come to see the white "magician" in the hope that, like Zeus in ancient Greece, I could bring his beloved twin brother back to life, or else allow him to be reunited with his twin up in the sky, as Castor and Pollux were forever linked in the stars of Gemini. When I did not fulfill his hopes, he left.

Conclusion: Bringing It All Back Home

I no longer dream of Africa as I did as a young girl. My idyllic and naive vision of working as a doctor abroad has changed. Remarkable people still operate all over the world, but significant foreign aid is becoming increasingly difficult. On one hand, workers are increasingly restrained by governments demanding absolute control over their actions, complete adherence to their own codes of conduct, and utter silence on any misdemeanors. On the other, dubious associations, incompetent workers, and absurd projects mushroom at an astonishing rate and are given the green light. Aid figures favorably on any curriculum, elicits universal excitement, and a lot of glamour is attached to it. Elegant delegations attend innumerable meetings in sealed-off luxury hotels. Posh ladies used to ask their husbands and lovers to open antique shops and boutiques for them, now they set up NGOs.

In the meantime, extreme poverty and extreme inequality dominate the world. More than one-third of humanity has no access to medical care and no human rights whatsoever.[1] Many more are only slightly better off. This disparity is not due to any particular virtues or sins. Only sheer luck decides if one is born on the right side of the world, with the right color of skin, the right gender, and the right class. As many unfortunate twins demonstrate, even being born a few kilometers apart can make all the difference between life and death. Within the same country, twins are spared in some regions, worshiped in others, and ruthlessly killed in yet others.

The realm of maternity and motherhood is one of the main divides separating developed areas from developing areas of the world.[2] When maternity includes twins, the gap is often unbridgeable.

Motherhood has become a choice in the developed world, where sex is now separated from pregnancy. Biology is no longer destiny, and women can choose when and whether to reproduce. Although various forms of abortion and birth control have been used since the dawn of mankind, safety and reliability are only recent accomplishments. Due to these advances and other societal changes, women now have access to higher education, can pursue engrossing careers, and enjoy a carefree sexual life. Nevertheless, the lifestyle of mothers continues to differ profoundly from the lives of women who do not have children, to say nothing of men. As for mothers of twins, an abyss separates their lives from the lives of ordinary mothers.

Despite these differences, high-income societies continue to idealize motherhood. Sacred, angelic, all white, and idyllic views dominate. The maternal instinct is often unreservedly taken for granted. The underlying assumption is that mothers are people with no further identity, who find their main gratification in the constant company of young children, attending to their needs only. The isolation of mothers, confined to their homes looking after children all day long, is taken for granted, and so is the idea that maternal love is selfless, unconditional, and all-encompassing.

Though idealized publicly, motherhood is not valued socially. Women gain no credit for being mothers and are caught in a net of contradictory messages. Raising children may be the most important job in the world, but as Ann Crittenden pointed out, "you can't put it on a curriculum."[3] Paradoxically, in order to have the right to some esteem, women have to choose a path other than motherhood. Women may be approaching equality in many fields of work, but motherhood still lags behind. And for the mothers of twins their work is simply unpaid slavery.

Several societal phenomena encourage the idealization of motherhood. An abundance of experts flood mothers with impossible rules about the skills of parenting. As Judith Warner points out, experts warn us that none of the cooing, crawling, floor play, bonding, talking, or singing works unless it is done with unconditional and uninterrupted pleasure. Experts claim that children can be made bright and successful if only mothers try hard at all times to maintain connection through eye contact and face-to-face interactions. Babies must be breastfed on demand up to 90 times a day and never be left alone for more than a few minutes.[4] These rules include premature babies and therefore also many twins.

These standards are impossible to attain by any mother and are doubly so for the overstretched mother of twins. As a result, guilt and anxiety have become pervasive among mothers. Mothers of singletons feel at fault even for going to the toilet, while mothers of twins are desperate at being unable to maintain constant eye contact and face-to-face interaction with two children.

This distress may seem paradoxical, as humanity has never known a safer time for children. Many childhood diseases have been eradicated or have become treatable, and children are healthier than ever before. The poisonous mixture of guilt and anxiety instead derives from our idealization of motherhood and the accompanying belief in its omnipotence.

The myth that most problems can be traced back to the early relationship with one's mother stems from a wealth of psychoanalytic literature. Like most men of his day, Freud was actually quite ignorant about women, whom he called "the dark continent."[5] His writings have since been vulgarized and distorted to fit in with views that would have been quite alien to his inquiring mind, and they continue to be read as a contemporary bible, outside their historical context.

Equally disturbing are the derivations of the so-called attachment theory, introduced by the psychiatrist and psychoanalyst John Bowlby in England in the late 1950s, which claims that separation from the mother at an early age can result in serious problems later in life.[6] His writings, too, have been taken out of their historical context and made into all-encompassing universal truths. A disturbing contemporary notion propounded by his followers and causing maternal nightmares is "trans-generational transmission," whereby not only what your mother did but also what your grandparents did can make your children vulnerable to all sorts problems in an endless chain of anguish. As experts say, the nursery "is full of ghosts."[7,8]

Anxieties have lately been introduced even into the womb by the radical wings of prenatal psychology. Ultrasounds, which have made it possible to study fetal behavior in utero, show that fetuses move a lot, rapidly alternating between cycles of activity and of rest. Prenatal psychologists have mistakenly equated fetal motions to wakefulness and hence to consciousness, thereby transforming fetuses into sentient beings expressing all sorts of emotions.[9] But fetuses in fact are not awake, save for brief periods during the very last stages of pregnancy. Fetal motions are spontaneously generated within the primordial nervous system and have other important functions, such as providing essential stimulation to the nascent fetal brain that fosters its development.[10]

Prenatal psychologists have added a quality of anxiety to fetal motions. They regard hyperactive fetuses not as experiencing a perfectly natural cycle of turbulent motion but rather as being bombarded by obnoxious maternal emotions. To equate fetal motions with anxiety-driven states inundates already stressed pregnant mothers with further worries.

Fetal behavior has taken on wider significance in connection with the issue of abortion. Antiabortionist movements promote their cause by bringing fetal motions into play. They equally connect fetal motions, in a crescendo of charges, with wakefulness, consciousness, and ultimately sentience, leading up to the equation of abortion with infanticide. Twin fetuses are cited to reinforce this view. Mutual stimulation by twin fetuses elicits several types of movement, which are said to support the conclusion that twins have complex social and emotional interchanges, further reinforcing the equation of abortion with infanticide. Human interactions, however, just like wakefulness, belong only to life after birth and are not present in life before birth. Fetuses are progressively preparing to enter a social world, but a proper social dimension is extraneous to what is basically a solitary fetal life. Twins are not alone inside the womb, but the overwhelming majority of them inhabit different amniotic sacs, which are separated by various layers of thick membranes. Other considerations apart, it is difficult to envisage how complex social interactions could be carried out across all these barriers. Yet antiabortionists, to say nothing of popular culture, in books, posters, and cards, persist in figuring twin fetuses as hugging each other and kissing as if twins shared an idealized link that originated during their joint stay in the womb.

The intrauterine life of twins is far from idyllic and is actually fraught with peril, sometimes lethal. The risks of spontaneous abortion and stillbirth are greatly increased in twin pregnancies. In these cases the claim that twin fetuses are miniature adults socially interacting with each other makes many unfortunate mothers feel that they have lost mature children. Furthermore, many mothers fear having caused their twins' death by not protecting them properly. The fact is that anxiety has always been a natural part of motherhood. Starting from conception, mothers cannot protect their children from all dangers, yet they are driven by experts and society to believe they can control their children's fate by quasi-magical ways of thinking. A perfect upbringing resulting in perfect children will protect them from all ills.

Besides mothers, children themselves are idealized by society, adding to the confusion of mothers. Children are portrayed as innocent, pure, charming little cherubs, filling one's life with endless delight. Strong pressure from society obliges mothers to love children in public and to fake unlimited enthusiasm toward them. Twins in particular have become a parental dream, as they set up a complete family in one go. Such a dream is particularly important for those women who have postponed reproduction to the last minute. Fantasy, however, soon rubs up against the harshness of reality. Young twins can simply drive you mad by screaming at the same time or running in opposite directions in the street.

During pregnancy all women oscillate between feelings of euphoria and depression. On one hand, pregnancy is the tangible sign of an active, mature sexual life, giving the mother a feeling of completeness, self-sufficiency, worthiness, and self-esteem. On the other hand, pregnancy produces nostalgia for youth, anxiety over the loss of freedom, fear of a kind of slavery, and dread of losing one's beauty, agility, erotic value, as well as the love of one's companion. As Naomi Wolf poignantly says, once you are a mother, you cannot also be a heartbreaker, a rock-and-roller, or a lonesome traveler.[11]

Babies bestow unique joys, but these joys are never limitless and free from an undertow of ambivalence. As Adrienne Rich reports, "My children cause me the most exquisite suffering of which I have any experience. It is the suffering of ambivalence: the murderous alternation between bitter resentment and raw-edged nerves, and blissful gratification and tenderness."[12] Mothers of twins are overwhelmed by these feelings. Once past the initial stages, a twin pregnancy becomes a physical ordeal. Mothers often perceive their twins as malevolent, demonic foreign bodies invading all their physical space. Twins are described as parasites, leeches, and vampires. Driven by physical torment and psychological anguish, mothers can even attack their twins through self-destructive acts, such as becoming intoxicated or deliberately taking a fall.

Medical advances have enormously reduced the risk of fatalities during delivery for both the mother and the baby, although it is difficult to break the long association between childbirth and death that has been a part of women's experience since the dawn of mankind. Mothers fear delivery. For mothers of twins, however, lurking terrors of falling ill and dying are not totally unrealistic, because twin pregnancies and deliveries involve so much greater hazards than singleton ones.

Breastfeeding is the sole postnatal function clearly linked with gender. For centuries affluent women refused to suckle their infants, handing them over to wet nurses and frequently not even bothering to visit them for months. Recently, bottles and formulas have freed women from this biological imperative. Medical evidence, however, has shown the presence of protective antibodies in maternal milk. This piece of evidence has been transformed into a life-and-death sentence, reinforcing social pressures and launching the campaign "Breast is best" by both medical and non medical gurus. As a result, women have been pushed back to the breast. Many mothers find breastfeeding pleasant, as it allows them closer contact with an infant while he or she is quiet, but for mothers of twins, breastfeeding takes on a different quality. It is impossible to enjoy peaceful, intimate contact with one twin while the other is screaming frantically. Furthermore, mothers of twins often cannot produce enough milk for two, and twins, being born prematurely, may also need reinforced formulas, which are enriched with vitamins, minerals, or fatty compounds. The inability to breastfeed causes enormous anxiety and guilt in these mothers, who fear endangering their already growth-retarded and fragile infants.

Leaving work is often imperative for a parent of twins because not all families can afford a rotation of nurses, nor are child-minders, neighbors, or even grandparents always willing to offer help with two. One of the two parents generally has to stay at home, and it is overwhelmingly the mother. John Bowlby encouraged this view by arguing that fathers are secondary in their children's lives, especially during the first year, and only become important at later stages. His followers, however, transformed this statement into a biological law to be applied in all circumstances.[13] Fatherhood has been stripped off from males who have been more than willing to accept the sole role of breadwinner. Currently young men are beginning to question this rigid stereotype and to participate in the care of children, but there is still a huge gulf between the amount of work put in by men as compared to women.

The birth of twins accentuates the role of the father as breadwinner and of the mother as caregiver. Men staying at home to look after their children are considered oddities who risk losing their jobs. Because fathers generally earn more, losing their salary is objectively more burdensome to the family economy, and it is often a luxury that cannot be afforded in the case of twins when all expenses are doubled. Fathers frequently have to take up extra work in order to meet the costs, while mothers continue to have to choose between career and motherhood. Mothers are overwhelmingly the ones who clean, wash, take children to the doctor and the park, help them with schoolwork, and, generally speaking, do the dirty work.

In order to conform to the equal rights recognized by many other European nations, Italy introduced a law in 2000 that allows both mothers and fathers to take parental leave while retaining 100 percent of their salary during the first months of their children's life. A maximum of 20 men opted for this program. In the successive months of parental leave, when the salary is cut to 70%, no men took up the chance. So far Scandinavian fathers are the only ones to score well on parental leave. Scandinavian countries are little affected by the mentality of the overpowering nature of maternal attachment. These countries were also the first ones to introduce what still are the best parental leave laws. Not even in Scandinavia, however, do 100 percent of men choose to stay at home.

Fathers involved in ordinary child care selectively engage in play and social activities rather than in physical tasks such as changing and feeding, but fathers of twins are heavily involved as caregivers from the very beginning. Caregiving is enforced by circumstances rather than by choice. As soon as they enter their homes, fathers are handed one twin and made to change diapers, warm bottles, or load the washing machine. Men resent their double tasks, and women resent their double load as caregivers as well as their new confinement in the home. Bitterness arises on both sides, leading to increased marital problems. In the early stages fathers generally feel too guilty to leave their mate to cope alone with two young children, but as soon as the twins achieve some independence, divorce ranks high among the parents.[14]

As a result of these various strains, twins are subject to abusive and neglectful behavior to an inordinate degree. At one time, favoritism was the rule in families, when the eldest male inherited all and other children were sent away to the army or convent or married off against their will. Today favoritism exists in more subtle ways, especially for twins, despite the contemporary myth that children can be treated exactly the same. At birth not even twins display the same temperamental inclinations. One can be adorable and the other bossy, one can be prudent and the other reckless, one can be easygoing and the other difficult. Favoritism toward one over the other, while vehemently denied, is generally the rule in an unintended reaction to an overwhelming situation. By choosing one twin and trying to eliminate the other, mothers unconsciously attempt to create a singleton situation.

Abusive or preferential treatment of children conflicts with the idealized view of motherhood, especially the idea of maternal instinct as a free and natural flow of love. The French philosopher Simone de Beauvoir was the first to openly question the existence of maternal instinct.[15] Since then, among others, the anthropologist Nancy Shepher-Huges,[16] the primatologist Sarah Blaffer Hrdy,[17] the philosopher Sara Ruddick,[18] and the historians Philippe Ariès,[19] and Edward Shorter[20] have all cast doubt on the existence of such an instinct. As Elizabeth Badinter puts it, motherly love is not a given but a gift.[21] Maternal love as a human feeling is uncertain, fragile, and imperfect. Affection may or may not be present. Love may be great or it may be negligible. The different forms in which it is expressed can range from positive to negative, passing through zero along the way. Huge differences exist not only within families, but also within different countries, different regions of the same country, and within different strata of the population.

For the overwhelming majority of the world's population, who are poor, nothing much has changed for hundreds of years in the realms of maternity and child care. Motherhood and sexuality are still connected, because contraception and safe abortions are mostly unavailable to them or too costly. According to the United Nations Population Fund (UNFPA), Niger, considered to be the poorest country on earth, provides only 4 percent of all women with access to any means of contraception. Many other countries rate only slightly above this appalling figure.[22]

Religious and cultural beliefs are less responsible for this situation than one might think, for as soon as women from these countries migrate, they ask for contraceptives, seek abortion, and even have their tubes tied. The number of children per family quickly drops to two or three. Immigrant mothers who have twins generally stop at that point. Exposure to another culture has made them free to use birth control.

In many low-income countries girls begin their reproductive career in their teens, often as soon as puberty starts. At the age of 25 a woman may already have five children, having lost three or four others on the way. This was justified in the past when everybody's life expectancy was short, and may even be justified now in places where life expectancy continues to be appallingly brief. Furthermore, maternity gives women the only standing they have. Neither romantic love nor freedom of choice enter into marital arrangements, as parents, elders, and sometimes even horoscopes have the primary say in picking the right candidate. Many girls find themselves traded off to older men, whom they must learn to tolerate.

Women and men everywhere are increasingly leaving their villages and rural zones for the city. These urbanized citizens are often incredibly poor, isolated, and malnourished. Villages are far from being havens of friendliness and cooperation, but towns lack even the flimsy cultural and emotional bonds of villages and are host to millions of people living in utter moral and material poverty. Other emotional bonds can be formed in shanty towns, but poverty, and criminality prevail. Manila, Port Moresby, Dacca, Calcutta, the suburbs of Rio, Karachi, and Nairobi are just a few examples of uncontrolled urbanization and the living nightmare it has become.

Once in town, bleak and predictable scenarios can present themselves. Women have children by different men. These men, addicted to alcohol and other substances, are capable only of impregnating and beating women and then vanishing, leaving the mothers alone to care for their children. As women say, "men come and go," and the burden is left entirely on the mother's shoulders. HIV continues to escalate, destitute and infected mothers start drinking, and children are abandoned in the streets.

Pregnancy is a perennial danger for these women. In some developing countries women have a one-in-seven risk of dying during their fertile years from complications linked with pregnancy and delivery. Contrast them to Swedish women, who run a one-in-thirty-thousand chance of dying during pregnancy and delivery. Prenatal care is not a right and not even something heard of for the overwhelming majority of the world's population. Only the rich have access to it, since they can pay for it. Sophisticated technologies for monitoring both maternal and fetal health are available in only a few private centers. For all others, iron supplements, urine tests, and measurements of the blood pressure are nonexistent.

The risk for a twin pregnancy and delivery in low-income countries has not been calculated, it is certainly at least double that in high-income countries, which explains why so many twins are considered bad luck. One frequently hears the curse "May you become a mother of twins!"

Women discover they are pregnant with twins only at the time of delivery, the same as women did in high-income countries in the pre-ultrasound era. However, even then western women received better prenatal care. Twins were often detected with stethoscopes, revealing two heartbeats instead of one, and X-rays were taken to determine whether the mother's pelvis was large enough for a spontaneous delivery or a caesarean was required. In contrast, the pelvises of many teenagers living in the developing world are often not wide enough to permit mother and infant to emerge unscathed from the delivery. The women deliver alone or assisted by untrained elderly women, whose only instrument may be a rusty knife to cut the cord, often causing lethal tetanus infections that could be easily avoided with a simple vaccination. Only 16 percent of women living in low-income countries are assisted by even minimally trained staff.

Should complications arise, women in Sweden who do not live near high-tech medical facilities are immediately transferred to one by helicopter, however, in low-income countries women may have to be transported on a wheelbarrow to the nearest hospital. The journey along gravel roads may take days to complete and be altogether impossible during rainy seasons. Those who live in town go to hospital on foot, but they may be turned away if they cannot pay. In any case they often find themselves in a filthy environment, where hygiene and comfort are totally lacking. Cats, rats, and cockroaches run around the delivery rooms. A caesarean, if feasible at all, is a catastrophic event. Should massive bleeding requiring a blood transfusion occur, mothers have to bring their own donors, hoping that the blood groups will match and that the blood of the donor is not infected with some kind of hepatitis or HIV. One in six children born at such hospitals dies during delivery or soon after. Of surviving infants, 15 percent die before reaching the age of 1. Although statistics for twins are again not available, prematurity, growth retardation, and other complications are certain to skyrocket these grim figures.

Postnatal care does not exist at all in most areas of the developing world. Children are malnourished to the point of starvation, and at worst this can cause death. Chronic malnutrition, however, can also lead to stunting and render children highly vulnerable to innumerable diseases. Uncorrected visual, hearing, and other defects can all lead to impaired scholastic and social functioning. For twins, however, this may be looking too far into the future. In developed countries many twins sometimes have to undergo quite prolonged stays in Intensive Care Units, where all their vital functions are monitored and vital parameters corrected and aided in order to ensure survival.[23] Despite all this, not all twins do make it or make it without many problems.

Postpartum care is also unavailable to their mothers. Whether pregnant or not, women work incessantly, far more than men. They work at home, in the fields, in minor trades, or on the streets, trying to raise their children with almost no income. Africa and other countries are largely dependent on this informal economy of women working in precarious, underpaid jobs. Should the women fall ill or the police harass them, they find themselves without any source of income. Most are already undernourished, having to scavenge for food. Many end up with only their bodies to sell. In their moral degradation, quite a few women even sell the bodies of their children.

Although maternity gives women their only standing, mothers are valued solely for their generative powers, not for their nurturing skills. As soon as infants are weaned, the next pregnancy starts, and both in villages and towns the infant is left to wander alone or in the care of slightly older children. To be a good mother means to have healthy children, who can soon become part of the labor force and enter the reproductive chain. In shanty towns, participation in the labor force may mean begging, child prostitution, theft, or other petty crimes. Children soon leave their shacks to live in the streets, where their peer group takes on paramount importance. In order to be accepted by their group the children have to go through initiation ceremonies, such as sniffing glue. Mothers lose track of these children.

Both in villages and towns the only power women have is over their own children, especially their infant children. Given their fragility and incapacity to survive alone, infants come last in the social ranks. In many areas of the world children have no status until they reach adolescence or puberty. Because infant mortality is so high, children are not even given a proper name until they are at least one year old, when their mothers can start to hope they might survive.

Infanticide is often a form of late contraception, which does not pertain to twins alone, although twins, given their greater fragility, are particularly liable to it. Those infants chosen to die are generally not given a proper burial and are just left behind, thrown in dumps or the bush, with no name, cross, or any other sign to indicate where they have been left. For their mothers, these infants are comparable to early fetuses, nonsentient beings, whose survival is assessed in a rational way in the developed world. We have early diagnostic techniques, such as CVS, amniocentesis, and ultrasounds, to determine the children we decide raise or discontinue. Mothers in the developing world have none of these techniques and can decide only belatedly, at birth, on which children they are prepared to bring up. Many twins do not pass the test.

One should not think of mothers living in developing countries who give up such babies as callous and incapable of love. They just want to conserve their resources for children who are likely to live. These mothers generally do not act on impulse, nor can they be described as deranged when they kill their twins. They acknowledge their impossibility of caring for two often frail, premature infants in a down-to-earth, matter-of-fact terms. By abandoning their twins in the bush, they decide simply to let nature take its course and to concentrate their meager resources on worthier children, who are more likely to survive. Little emotional meaning is attached to a grim choice that their society does not question and in fact supports.

As the historian Lloyd de Mause reports, contemporary western societies seem oblivious to the past and have erased from the public consciousness many historical nightmares.[24] Mothers are now regarded as the natural bearers of a maternal instinct, motherhood has become sanctified and Medea has been reduced to a myth. Yet infanticide was the most frequent crime all over Europe from the Middle Ages until about 1800. Children had no rights whatsoever, not even the right to live. They were abandoned, neglected, employed for cheap labor, and submitted to all sorts of torture. It was only gradually over the course of centuries that children and their needs came to be the center of attention, and only recently we have even begun to value children as children. The status of children has finally advanced to a level equal to that of adults. Legal systems now generally hold that the inherent rights of children are not lessened simply because of their age, and parents may no longer claim to have exclusive control over their offspring simply because of biological responsibility for their creation. Yet despite our predilection for calling modern civilization "advanced," the crime of infanticide still has not disappeared from developed nations, and child-murder remains a statistically common crime. The idea of mothers being capable of harming their children runs counter to all views of motherhood and stirs up deep, largely unconscious fears. Initially we are all utterly dependent on our mothers even for simple survival, and this power can elicit almost instinctive panic in most of us. In high-income countries infanticidal mothers are generally excused as victims of hormonal turmoil, who are suffering from the shock of a delivery that put them temporarily out of their minds. When their infirmity is more pronounced, mothers are excused as being demented. Legal enforcement is generally lenient toward them, on the assumption that an emotional component governs such murderous acts. Mothers are rarely said to be lucid or matter-of-fact when killing their infants, but rather commit these acts when in a panic, enraged, driven to despair, overwhelmed by fatigue, or abandoned. A crime such as child homicide, which is felt to be utterly incongruent with the dominant understanding of femininity and motherhood, can be explained only with pathology. The few mothers who appear to have been lucid in their acts attract morbid curiosity, are regarded as evil and bad, and are punished harshly. Generally these mothers have to be kept separately in jail from other criminals, who feel entitled to punish them for having committed what everyone considers the most horrible and unnatural of all crimes.

Postpartum depression, so often mentioned in the courts of high-income countries as a reason for infanticide, seems to have reached epidemic proportions even outside the courts. Mothers of twins are hit particularly hard.[25] Postpartum depression seems hardly to exist in low-income countries. These latter women, perhaps more than very depressed, are often already desperate, but the reasons are different, such as having to scrape out a living, abandonment by their husbands, or being forced to hit the streets. In the developed world women feel acutely fearful and depressed at parturition, dreading the loss of whatever freedom or power they had in career or marriage. In developing countries women have never experienced these pleasures in the first place. One cannot mourn something one has never even possessed. For women living in low-income countries the most worthy achievement they can attain is to give birth to healthy children, for which everyone compliments them. Twins, who often do not fall in the healthy category, must pay a heavy price for their failure.

Superstitious beliefs also play a role in twin infanticide, which are at first more difficult for us to understand. It is widely believed that twins are unearthly creatures who bring bad luck. Yet twins truly can be bad luck. Even in the developed world twin units are increasingly a part of maternity hospitals because of the risks of pregnancy for both mother and twins. In developing countries mothers in fact die more frequently during a twin pregnancy and delivery. When they deliver twins, the babies are more often stillborn or die soon afterward. Twins are thus easily associated with death. Death in turn is not always regarded as a natural event that eventually affects us all, but may rather be seen as the result of the influence of malevolent forces. Twins, by "causing" death, including their own, become the very malevolent entities that have to be chased away.

Twins elicit bewilderment for other reasons. Their birth is unexpected. At birth, twins may look strange. One may be extremely bloated and red all over, and the other deathly pale. Their skin may be translucent, they may be hairy, or they may be covered with a greasy substance called "vernix caseosa." Their heads may look disproportionately big and their limbs unusually small. They may only let out feeble cries and be unable to suck vigorously, move their limbs, or hold their mother's gaze. These factors easily contribute to the impression of twins as being nonhuman and otherworldly. Their more frequent malformations, deformations, chromosomal defects, and various conjoinments, as in the case of Siamese twins, add to a whole range of reasons for considering twins both unearthly and bad luck. The superstition turns out to be not beyond anyone's comprehension.

Even taking the life of twins in order to continue having sex, as among the *Indios* communities, is not totally incomprehensible. The sex life of couples in the developed world decreases dramatically after the birth of any child, and more so after the birth of twins.[26] In high-income countries, women, however, have incomparably better lives. They generally do not suffer from hunger or cold or live in fear of extermination, and they have access to means of communication, family planning, health care, transportation, education, and support, which are unheard of among *Indios*. For these utterly poor and marginalized people their main, if not only, pleasure in life is sex and one cannot expect them to give it up easily for the dubious pleasure of nurturing sickly and probably doomed twins. The alternative choice of contraception, which many of them ask for once they know it exists, is denied to them on both religious and monetary grounds.

The delayed murder of twins in war-torn Guinea Bissau was the only ritual I could not stomach and it still haunts me. I cannot fully comprehend the reasons behind these murders, nor empathize with those committing them. Perhaps the mothers found their twin pregnancies so uncomfortable as to continue to attach evil to the twins for years to come. Perhaps the mothers never saw their twins as human beings at all, on a par with others in their tribe. But more likely the killings had cold-minded social and political roots. The ethnic groups involved in the twins' mass murder belonged to the ruling classes of the country, thought of themselves as a superior race, and were proud of their culture, which condemned twins. The sacrifice of twins as scapegoats for society's evils fostered the cohesion and superiority of the ruling group.

Cruelty toward the weak has always existed, and any pretext will suffice to give vent to one's sadism against any helpless scapegoat. Freud pointed out how frequently his patients expressed the fantasy of beating and torturing impotent children.[27] This kind of fantasy is accompanied by intense pleasure, often culminating in acts of autoerotic satisfaction. Greek myths on the Bacchante are full of intoxicating child homicides. The masses described by Freud during World War I took pleasure in their acts, and in the war-torn Guinea Bissau, eroticized pleasure was an important component in the sadistic butchering of twins. But nothing had prepared me for this horror, and writing about it still makes me cringe.

Equally difficult to comprehend is the setting off of twins for the pedophilia trade. Parents know they are condemning their children to agonizing deaths, and they do so for money. Again, one has to turn to history to comprehend these horrible acts. Until recently children were considered an economic investment and source of labor, and this labor included their widespread use for sexual purposes. Pederastic marriage between barely pubescent girls and old men in exchange for goods of any kind, from money to camels, is still a terrible reality worldwide.

Women have come a long way during the last century, though they have not yet reached equality with men. Paramount to their freedom has been the possibility of reproductive choice as well as safety during pregnancy and delivery. Abortion and ultrasounds have been important tools in fostering this autonomy and well-being of women. Like most tools, however, they are full of potential for both destruction and construction. As Herbert Aptekar says, "The axe fells trees but it also builds a house. Fire may destroy cities but it also cooks food."[28] The axe, fire, abortion, and ultrasounds all demand intelligent application, as well as recognition that they are simply tools. The same tools are being used against the "second sex" especially, but not exclusively, in India and China in the biggest gender cleansing operation in human history.

India has changed beyond belief since the days I worked in Delhi as a young doctor. Many women now receive an education, have a career, participate in the government, or even govern the country. Yet the bias against females noticed in the psychiatric ward during my first stay is still acted out in several regions of this huge country. Despite specific laws, millions of females are aborted just because they are the wrong gender. Twins per se are not welcome in parts of India, because they are considered a nuisance, costly, aesthetically unappealing, and dangerous to the preservation of maternal beauty. Therefore one of them is terminated before birth. In opposite-sex pairs the automatic selection of the female for termination brings the enormity of female discrimination fully to light. Females are not given the chance to take their first breath or let out a cry, while boys are cherished and allowed to see the light.

The perpetrators of this crime are generally mothers, whose choice is not determined by incapacity to feel empathy for a certain child. These mothers, having not yet seen their girls, decide to terminate them exclusively on the basis of gender—their own gender. Mother-daughter love is rarely a straightforward matter. It can be complicated by all sorts of negative feelings, especially envy and jealousy. Children's stories are filled with good, but dead, mothers and bad step-mothers, who vividly illustrate a split between the good, but abandoning, and the murderous mother who takes over and acts out all her wickedness. Snow White and Cinderella are just two fictitious examples of evil being perpetrated against daughters. In real life in India the mothers of female twins similarly do not identify in the least with their own gender. Having no hope of a better future for their daughters-to-be, they deny them any future at all.

These mothers are living in a society that has made them into utterly powerless, vulnerable victims. The majority can be rejected or abandoned by their own families, and they have no voice at all in matters of love. Anna Freud described a particular mechanism of defense mobilized by people in situations involving extreme cases of victimization, which she called "identification with the aggressor."[29] Faced with utter powerlessness against physical and psychological abuse, children can react in two basic ways. One is to say, "This will never happen again," and grow up knowing that this is one thing he or she will never do. The other reaction is to reenact the crime by identifying with the aggressor and victimizing of another child. As Anna Feud put it, "This type of identification is summoned by the ego to protect itself against authority figures who generated anxiety and the purpose of this type of identification is to avoid the wrath and potential punishment of the enemy… [The victim] identifies out of fear rather than out of love." Indian mothers follow the principle, "If you can't beat them, join them," and they collude with the entire society by aborting their female daughters-to-be. In the process they become invested with the powerful role of priestess to the sacrifice and preserver of the tradition.

Following the same principle, women are often the main preservers of other horrible traditions and the perpetrators of other crimes, such as genital mutilation and gender-linked torture of all kinds. The Chinese patients who came to the twin unit of the hospital where I work in my country also considered female twins a misfortune. Yet once exposed to a culture that increasingly values females by fostering their health, education, and equal rights, these mothers eventually changed their minds and welcomed their twin girls. Had the same twin girls been born back home, they would have faced the hideous fate of death at birth.

In developing countries the gap between the wealthy and the poor reaches staggering proportions. By striking all sorts of dealings with the rich, and supporting them for their own interest, people belonging to high-income countries are not foreign to, and foster or provoke, the misdeed. The rulers, including women, are educated, apparently modern, and incredibly rich. Their world includes financial ventures, the stock market, off-shore bank accounts, commerce, communication, travel, and leisure. The rich feel no shame or guilt about showing off their wealth. They own huge mansions, holiday retreats, custom-designed private jets, cars, and all sorts of up-to-date paraphernalia. The government and the army function like their private properties, as do the resources of their countries. With the odd exception, their possessions could guarantee a more than decent living for the entire population, but the rich live above the law and above human concern. A middle class also exists, including a few professional people, teachers, blue collar workers, and small entrepreneurs, who may privately complain about government corruption but are too enmeshed in the power system, or too afraid of it, to dare question it openly.

In contrast, the poor in these countries live in a Dantesque Inferno, lacking everything, even hope. They subsist in total obscurity but dread passing through life without leaving a trace. Even the most destitute often claim some kind of visibility, mesmerized by the rich, as the westerners are by Hollywood stars. To ourselves we are the most important people on earth, and the possibility that this importance is reflected by others with whom we can identify, if only in our imagination, provides some solace during a largely anonymous stay on earth. Waving our hands or bowing our heads when watching a black Mercedes pass through the crowd feels like a way of participating, if only marginally and vicariously, in an exclusive world of the powerful.

Voodoo regards twins as a similar bridge to the powerful gods, and the elders hold firmly to this traditional belief. For the young, however, twins may represent something more modern: they may be compared to Hollywood stars. In Togo and Benin, as well as in all other developing countries, the locals know a lot about how other people live in our global village. During colonial times they already had a very intimate glimpse into the lives and mores of those who ruled them. Currently knowledge has been extended and updated through access to various forms of media, the tourist trade, new churches, encounters with travelers and traders, and reports from immigrants visiting back home. Togo and Benin are also exposed to visits by wealthy Afro-Americans in search of their roots. In fact the locals know more about us than we know about them.

The importance of the media is becoming overwhelming worldwide and this means the locals, but especially the young, are exposed to the star system tool, with which twins have much in common. Like all stars, twins have a powerful visual impact. They wear elaborate clothing when all others may wear nothing but rags. Their names are changed to make them more catchy. Twins perform a central role in many ceremonies that are the equivalent of Oscar nights. They have their fans, who keep their relics. At the same time twins are democratic stars, appealing to even the poorest strata of the population, who can easily identify with them because most twins come from obscure families before reaching their local pinnacle of fame. Twins conform to the Hollywood stereotype of the common man or the girl next-door, representing a bridge between obscurity and fame that can never be crossed otherwise.

In some areas of the Cameroon twins are similarly put on a pedestal, but they pay a high personal price for the privilege. Their life at the top is terribly lonely. Twins are forbidden to mix with their peers and are not even allowed to mix with each other. Twins have no childhood at all. To others they are nothing more than a public image, being thrust into the limelight from birth. Their mothers are similar to movie mothers, who live out their own desires for privilege and status, single-mindedly making their twins fulfill their role as stars from day one, forever stunting their emotional growth and sense of fulfillment.

Apart from these countries where fame is lifelong, for twins growing up worldwide, the limelight they all seem to share tends to fade out of their lives. Some twins grieve over their previous fame and, albeit unconsciously, try to recapture it by behaving like doppelgangers. They continue to wear the same clothes, exhibit the same quirks, behave in synchrony, and plan their outings together. Female twins find it especially difficult to be falling stars, having attracted public attention since babyhood through their looks. Females are always judged by their looks. Female twins are judged by two sets of standards, those applied to all females and to twins alone, making it doubly hard to give up both their looks and the superficial aspect of their twinship. Although doppelganger behavior elicits the attention of passers-by, it makes adults appear freakish or pathetic, just like the fading stars in "Sunset Boulevard" who try uselessly to hang on to their withered glory. Opposite-sex twins and dizigotic twins are spared the consequences of such a fall from grace.

Adult twins throughout the world attract prurient curiosity for another innate reason, their sexuality. Twins, both males and females, are regarded as hot items, and having sex with twins is a common fantasy, though one that is not often fulfilled. Another fantasy has twins breaking one of the greatest sexual taboos, incest. Same-sex twins are often thought to add homosexuality to their incestuous activities, thereby infringing all of the sexual rules.

Such prurience has a lot to do with projecting onto twins our own unacceptable and dangerous thoughts, fantasies, and desires that are impossible to admit to ourselves. Denied thoughts and actions are attributed to someone else, so as to reduce the anxiety that they would otherwise elicit if we recognized them in ourselves.

Not all societies, however, share the same taboos. Homosexuality and incest are not universally considered unacceptable forms of conduct. Some cultures not only are tolerant but also foster this kind of behavior in twins. To regard such societies as simply barbarian would amount to yet another denial of thoughts that may lurk in the unconscious of us all, as well as ignoring all the differences in culture existing between different societies, affecting amongst other things our sexual and sentimental mores.

Twins at all latitudes find themselves uniquely subject to another powerful emotion, envy. Aristotle defined envy as "pain at the good fortunes of others."[30] Kant regarded envy as "a propensity to view the well-being of others with distress, even though it does not detract from one's own ... [Envy] aims, at least in terms of one's wishes, at destroying others' good fortune."[31] And the psychoanalyst Melanie Klein saw envy as "the angry feeling that another person possesses and enjoys something desirable—the envious impulse being to take it away or spoil it."[32]

The ties between twins, though marked by conflict, are universally considered to be the strongest, most perfect, and most enduring of all bonds. As such, they stir up envy. Prurient curiosity about twins is often aimed at spoiling their special bonds by reducing them to nothing more than a form of pornography.

The process of falling in love, though universal and existing since time immemorial, has not yet found a wholly satisfactory explanation. Freud linked it to our earliest experiences, which we tend to relive later in life as if they had been imprinted. The sociologist Francesco Alberoni thought that falling in love stems from a profound sense of dissatisfaction, which is finally overcome when we meet another person who fulfils our expectations.[33] Falling in love thus implies a profound and revolutionary break with the previous order. Many others consider falling in love to be a fundamental need, resulting from our yearning to overcome isolation. Why we fall in love with one person and not with another is still largely a mystery, but everyone agrees that falling in love is a temporary state, which may imply falling out of love once we have known our partner long enough for what he or she truly is. The honeymoon always ends. The fall can result in separation and divorce, but it can also develop into a more mature and realistic form of love that keeps the partners together "till death us do part."

The love between twins overcomes all these hurdles. Twins are already together at the big bang of conception, and they go on to share the womb and postnatal environment. No one can claim to have a better knowledge and understanding of another person than twins. As they grow, twins may lead separate lives, but many do not, as no other love can match their profound mutual understanding. A special link continues to unite them even when living on opposite sides of the world.

The bond between twins transcends even death. I have heard many people say, "I'd die for you" or "I'd die for her." But I have never in my whole life known of anyone else going so far as to sever a finger to exemplify the depth of his love. The old Papuan who showed me his mutilated fingers while singing a melancholy song cherished the vain hope that I could revive his strongest bond of all, that with his dead twin.

Notes

Introduction: A Personal Journey

1. William Wordsworth, "My Heart Leaps Up When I Behold," in *The Golden Treasury of the Best Songs and Lyrical Poems in the English Language*, ed. Francis Turner (New York: Bartleby, 1999), 332.
2. Alessandra Piontelli, "On the Onset of Human Fetal Behavior," in *Psychoanalysis and Neuroscience*, ed. Mauro Mancia (New York: Springer-Verlag, 2006), 391–418.
3. Clifford Geertz, *The Interpretation of Culture* (New York: Basic Books, 1973), 13.

1 Our Twins

1. Joyce A. Martin and Melissa M. Park, "Trends in Twin and Triplet Births: 1980–97," *National Vital Statistics Reports* 47, 24 (September 14, 1999): 1–2.
2. Thomas J. Matthews and Brady E. Hamilton, "Mean Age of Mother, 1970–2000," *National Vital Statistics Reports* 51, 1 (December 11, 2002): 1–3.
3. Selma M. Taffel, "Demographic Trends in Twin Births: USA," in *Multiple pregnancy: Epidemiology Gestation & Perinatal Outcome*, ed. Louis G. Keith, Emile Papiernik, Donald M. Keith, and Barbara Luke (New York: The Parthenon Publishing Group, 1995), 133–144.
4. Menken Jane, James Trussel, and Ulla Larsen, "Age and Infertility," *Science* 23 (1986): 1389.
5. Victoria Clay Wright, Jeani Chang, Gary Jeng, Michael Chen, and Maurizio Macaluso, *Assisted Reproductive Technology Surveillance* (Atlanta, GE: U.S. Division of Reproductive Health, 2004), 4.
6. Centers for Disease Control and Prevention (CDC), *2004 Assisted Reproductive Technology Success Rates* (Atlanta, GE: U.S. Department of Health and Human Services, December 2006).
7. Linda K. Kerber and Jane Sherron De Hart, *Women's America: Refocusing the Past.* 6th Edition (Oxford: Oxford University Press, 2003), 97.

8. U.S. Department of Agriculture (USDA), *USDA Annual Report on the Cost of Raising a Child* (Washington: 2001), 3.

9. Marcia A. Ellison, Selene Hotamisligil, Hang Lee, Janet Rich-Edwards, Suh-Cem Pang, and Michael J. Hall, "Psychosocial Risks Associated with Multiple Births Resulting from Assisted Reproduction," *Fertility and Sterility* 83, 5 (May 2005), 1422–1428.

10. Elizabeth R. Goshen-Gottstein, "The Mothering of Twins, Triplets and Quadruplets," *Psychiatry* 43, 3 (1980): 189–204.

11. Keith Thorpe, "Comparison of Prevalence of Depression in Mothers of Twins and Mothers of Singletons," *British Medical Journal* 302 (1991): 875–878.

12. National Organization of Mothers of Twins Clubs Inc, *Fathers Only Survey* (NOMOTOC Publications, Plymouth, MI: 2007), 5.

13. Jane Spillman, "Antenatal and Postnatal Influences in Family Relationships," in *Twin and Triplet Psychology*, ed. Audrey C. Sandbank (London: Routledge, 1999), 19–34.

14. Gillian Leigh, *All About Twins* (London: Routledge, 1989).

15. Nancy Bowers, *The Multiple Pregnancy Sourcebook* (Lincolnwood, IL: Contemporary Books, 2001), 1.

16. Francis Galton, "The History of Twins as a Criterion of the Relative Powers of Nature and Nurture," *Journal of the Anthropological Institute of Great Britain and Ireland* 5, (1875): 391–406.

17. For an outline of these studies, see Nancy L. Segal, *Entwined Lives: Twins and What They Tell Us About Human Behavior* (Hialea, FL: Dutton Press, 1999).

18. For an outline of these studies, see Elizabeth Bryan, *The Nature and Nurture of Twins* (London: Ballière Tindall, 1983).

19. Marjory Wallace, *The Silent Twins* (Harmondsworth, Middlesex: Penguin Books, 1986).

20. William Shakespeare, *The Comedy of Errors*, in *Complete Works of William Shakespeare, 1590–1594* (London: Wordsworth Special Editions Paperback, 1997), 166–186.

21. William Shakespeare, *Twelfth Night, or What You Will*, in *Complete Works of William Shakespeare, 1601–1602* (London: Wordsworth Special Editions Paperback, 1997), 641–669.

22. Robert Musil, *The Man Without Qualities*, First Publication: 1930–1942 (London: Vintage, 1996).

23. Rosamond Smith (alias Joyce Carol Oates), *Lives of the Twins* (New York: Simon and Schuster, 1987).

24. David Cronenberg, script writer and director, *Dead Ringers* (1988), Producers, MarcBoyman and David Cronenberg. Distributed by Twentieth Century Fox. Run time, 115 minutes.

25. Bruce Chatwin, *On the Black Hill* (New York: Viking Books, 1983).

26. Anne Geddes, *Pure* (Kansas City: Andrew Mc Meel Publishing, 2003).

27. Mary Ellen Mark, *Twins: Photographs and Interviews* (New York: Aperture Books, 2003).

28. Dimitrije E. Panfilov (ed.), *Aesthetic Surgery of the Facial Mosaic* (Berlin: Springer, 2007), 53.

29. Bernard This, *Naitre... et sourire* (Paris: Flammarion, 1983).
30. Renè Frydman, *l'Irrésistible désir de naissance* (Paris: Presses Universitaires de France, 1986), 182–183.

2   Voodoo Twins

1. Roger Brand, "Réalité anthropologique des Jumeaux et Culte Vodun au Sud Bénin," in *Des Jumeaux et des autres*, ed. Claude Savary (Geneva: Musée d'ethnographie, 1995), 216–233.
2. For a deepening of Voodoo, refer to the following. Marc Augè, *Le dieu objet* (Paris: Flammarion, 1988). Inès de la Torre, *Le Vodou en Afrique de L'Ouest* (Paris: L'Harmattan, 1991). Suzanne Blier-Preston, *African Vodun: Art, Psychology, Power* (Berkley: University of California Press, 1995). Judy Rosenthal, *Possession, Ecstasy, and Law in Ewe Voodoo* (Charlottesville: University Press of Virginia, 1998).
3. Edward Burnett Taylor, *Religion in Primitive Culture* (New York: Harper, 1958 [1871]).
4. For an analysis of trance and trance phenomena, see Brian Inglis, *Trance a Natural History of Altered States of Mind* (Boulder, CO: Paladin Books, 1990). Charles T. Tart, *States of Consciousness* (Washington: Backinprint, 2001).
5. For the role of fetishes in Africa, see Albert de Surgy, *Nature et function des fétiches en Afrique Noire* (Paris: L'Harmattan, 1994).
6. World Health Organization (WHO), *Maternal Mortality in 2000: Estimates Developed by WHO, UNICEF, UNFPA* (Geneva: WHO Publications, 2004), 2.
7. Daniel Lainé, *African Kings* (Berkley: Ten Speed Press, 2001).
8. For an analysis of the cheferie, refer to Adrian B. van Rouveroy van Nieuwaal, *L'Etat en Afrique face à la cheferie: Le cas du Togo* (Paris: Karthala, 2000).
9. Eric de Rosny, *L'Afrique des Guérisons* (Paris: Karthala, 1992), 33–45.
10. Joseph Breuer and Sigmund Freud, *Studies on Hysteria*. The Standard Edition 2, 1883–1895 (London: The Hogarth Press, 1961).
11. American Psychiatric Association, *Diagnostic and Statistical Manual of Mental Disorders, DMD-IV-TR*. Fourth Edition (Washington: American Psychiatric Association, 2000), 711–713.

3   Stone Idols

1. For a detailed analysis of the many causes of poverty even in potentially rich states, see Paul Collier, *The Bottom Billion: Why the Poorest Countries Are Failing and What Can Be Done About It* (Oxford: Oxford University Press, 2007).
2. U.S. Census Bureau International Data Base. Population Division, Washington, DC, *Country Summaries, Cameroon, 2000*.

3. For customs related to twins in the Cameroon, see René Gardi, *Monti e Popoli Sconosciuti del Camerun* (Milano: Bompiani, 1957).

4. Pamela Feldman-Salvelsberg, *Plundered Kitchens, Empty Wombs: Threatened Reproduction and Identity in The Cameroon Grassfields* (Ann Arbor: The University of Michingan Press, 2002), 9–18.

5. Arno van Gennep, *The Rites of Passage* (Chicago: Chicago University Press, 1961), 66–69.

6. For an extensive overview of West African secret societies and their function, see Frederick W. Butt-Thompson, *West African Secret Societies* (Berlin: Trubner Press, 2003).

7. Rene A. Spitz, *First Year of Life: A Psychoanalytic Study of Normal and Deviant Development of Object Relations* (Madison, CT: International Universities Press, 1966).

8. John Bowlby, *A Secure Base: Parent-Child Attachment and Healthy Human Development* (London: Basic Books, 1988).

9. American Psychiatric Association. *Diagnostic and Statistical Manual of Mental Disorders, DMD-IV-TR.* Fourth Edition (Washington: American Psychiatric Association, 2000), 583–589.

4 The Big Shock

1. For an overview of mentioned data, see Alessandra Piontelli, *Twins: From Fetus to Child* (London: Routledge, 2002), 22–27.

2. Ian Blickstein, "Maternal Mortality in Twin Gestations," *Journal of Reproductive Medicine* 42, 11 (1997): 679–760.

3. Mark Denbow and Nicholas Fisk, "Twin Pregnancies," in *Fetal Medicine,* ed. Charles H. Roddeck and Martin J. Whittle (London: Churchill and Livingstone, 1999), 863–877.

4. Agustin Conde-Agudelo, José M. Belizàn, and Gunilla Lindmark "Maternal Morbidity and Mortality Associated with Multiple Gestations," *Obstetrics and Gynecology* 95 (2000): 899–904.

5. Walter F. Ferguson, "Perinatal Mortality in Multiple Gestations," *Obstetrics and Gynecology* 17, 1 (1994): 101–103.

6. Virginia J. Baldwin, *Pathology of Multiple Pregnancy* (New York: Springer Verlag, 1994).

7. Sean P. Carr, "Survival Rates of Monoamniotic Twins Do Not Decrease After 30 Weeks' Gestation," *American Journal of Obstetrics and Gynecology* 163 (1990): 719–722.

8. Beryl R. Benacerraf, *Ultrasound of Fetal Syndromes* (Philadelphia: Churchill Livingstone, 1998), 231–240.

9. Kurt Benirschke and Peter Kaufmann, "Multiple Pregnancy," in *Pathology of the Human Placenta,* ed. Kurt Benirschke and Peter Kaufmann. Third Edition (New York: Springer Verlag, 1995), 767–778.

10. For an overview of perinatal and postnatal data, see Elizabeth Bryan, *Twins and Higher Multiple Births* (Londond: Edward Arnold, 1992), 89–110.

11. Richard E. Besinger and Nancy J. Carlson, "The Physiology of Preterm Labor," in *Multiple Pregnancy: Epidemiology, Gestation and Perinatal Outcome,* ed. Luis G. Keith, Emile Papiernik, Donald M. Keith, and Barbara Luke (New York: The Parthenon Publishing Group, 1995), 415–425.

12. Marelee C. Allen, "Factors Affecting Developmental Outcome," in *Multiple Pregnancy: Epidemiology, Gestation and Perinatal Outcome,* ed. Luis G. Keith, Emile Papiernik, Donald M. Keith, and Barbara Luke (New York: The Parthenon Publishing Group, 1995), 599–612.

13. Beverly Botting, Ian M. Davies, and Arthur J. Macfarlane "Recent Trends in the Incidence of Multiple Births and Their Mortality," *Archives of Diseases in Childhood* 62 (1997): 941–950.

14. Ibid.

15. Kurt Benirschke and Peter Kaufmann, "Multiple Pregnancy," in *Pathology of the Human Placenta,* ed. Kurt Benirschke and Peter Kaufmann. Third Edition (New York: Springer Verlag, 1995), 767–778.

16. Frank Falkner and Adam P. Matheny, "The Long-term Development of Twins," in *Multiple Pregnancy: Epidemiology, Gestation and Perinatal Outcome,* ed. Luis G. Keith, Emile Papiernik, Donald M. Keith, and Barbara Luke (New York: The Parthenon Publishing Group, 1995), 613–624.

17. Angelo Castiglioni, Achille Castiglioni, and Giovanna Salvioni, *Babatundé: la vita rinasce* (Varese, Italy: Edizioni Lativa, 1988), 50–51.

18. Ora Bomsel-Helmreich and Widad Al Mufti, "The Mechanism of Monozygosity and Double Ovulation," in *Multiple Pregnancy: Epidemiology, Gestation and Perinatal Outcome,* ed. Luis G. Keith, Emile Papiernik, Donald M. Keith, and Barbara Luke (New York: The Parthenon Publishing Group, 1995), 25–40.

19. Marshall H. Klaus, John H. Kennell, and Phyllis H. Klaus, *The Doula Book* (New York: Perseus Group, 2002).

20. Dana Raphael, *Being Female: Reproduction, Power, and Change* (Chicago: Aldine Press, 1975), 77–89.

21. Elizabeth Batinder, *L'Amour en plus* (Paris: Flammarion, 1980).

22. Donald Winnicott, "Transitional Objects and Transitional Phenomena," *International Journal of Psychoanalysis* 34 (1951): 89–97.

23. For a critique of the extreme wings of prenatal psychology, see Alessandra Piontelli, *Twins: From Fetus to Child* (London: Routledge, 2002), 41–51.

24. Helain G. Landy and Luis J. Keith, "The Vanishing Twin: A Review," *Human Reproduction Update* 4, 2 (1998), 177–183.

25. For a deepening of Mizuko Kuyo, see William R. LaFleur, *Liquid Life: Abortion and Buddhism in Japan* (Princeton: Princeton University Press, 1992). Helen Hardacre, *Marketing the Menacing Fetus in Japan* (Berkley: University of California Press, 1997). Mary Picone, "Infanticide, the Spirits of Aborted Fetuses, and the Making of Motherhood in Japan," in *Small Wars: The Cultural Politics of Childhood*, ed. Nancy Scheper-Huges and Carolyn Sargent (Berkley: University of California Press, 1998), 37–57.

5   Keepers and Outcasts

1. Lynn Thorndike, *History of Magic and Experimental Science* 1 (New York: Columbia University Press, 1923), 273–277.
2. Ibid.
3. Ibid., 514–515.
4. Bible. *Genesis* 25: 21–34.
5. Ibid., 27: 1–45.
6. Alessandra Piontelli, *Twins: From Fetus to Child* (London: Routledge, 2002), 22–27.
7. Ibid., 62–69.
8. For a discussion of the life and customs of the inhabitants of the Turkana region, see Philip H. Gulliver, *The Family Herds: A Study of Two Pastoral Tribes in East Africa, the Jie and Turkana* (London: Routledge, 1966). Alistair Graham and Peter Beard, *Eyelids of Morning* (San Francisco: Chronicle Books, 1990). Rada Dyson-Huds and Nigel Dyson-Huds, *Turkana Pastoralists* (New York: Rosen Publishing Group, 1996). Nigel Pavitt, *Turkana: Kenya's Nomads of the Jade Sea* (New York: Harry N. Abrams, 1997). Chieka Ifemesia, *Turkana* (Orlando, FL: Harcourt, 2009).
9. For deepening various aspects of shamanism, see Mircea Eliade, *Shamanism: Archaic Techniques of Ecstasy*. First Publication, 1951 (Princeton: Princeton University Press, 1994). Piers Vitebsky, *Shamanism* (Norman, OK: University of Oklahoma Press, 2001). Roger Walsh, *World of Shamanism: New Views of an Ancient Tradition* (Bristol, UK: Llewellyn Publications, 2007). Rebecca Stein and Philip L. Stein, *Anthropology of Religion, Magic and Witchcraft* (Needham Heights, MA: Alwyn and Bacon, 2007).
10. Sigmund Freud, *The Interpretation of Dreams*. The Standard Edition, 5.2 (1900–1901) (London: The Hogarth Press, 1961), 608.

6   Forced Adoption and the Sex Trade

1. For a general discussion about sex labor and migration, see Kamala Kempadoo (ed.), *Trafficking and Prostitution Reconsidered: New Perspectives on Migration, Sex Work, and Human Rights* (Boulder, CO: Paradigm Publishers, 2005). Kevin Bales, *Disposable People: New Slavery in the Global Economy* (Berkley: University of California Press, 2004).
2. George Knox and David Morley, "Twinning in Yoruba Women," *British Journal of Obstetrics and Gynecology* 67 (1960): 981–982.
3. For a good exposition of the history and customs of the gypsies, see Yan Yoors, *Gypsies* (Long Grove, IL: Waveland Press, 1987). Isabel Fonseca, *Bury Me Standing: The Gypsies and Their Journey* (New York: Vintage Books, 1995). Angus Fraser, *The Gypsies* (Chichester, West Sussex: Wiley, 1995).

4. For the holocaust and the gypsies, refer to Alexander Ramati, *And the Violins Stopped Playing: A Story of the Gypsy Holocaust* (London: Hodder and Stoughton, 1986).

5. For Dr Mengele's link with twins and his atrocities, see Lucette Matalon Lagnado and Sheila Cohn Dekel, *Children of the Flames. Dr Joseph Mengele and the Untold Story of the Twins of Auschwitz* (New York: Penguin Books, 1991).

6. Hillary Rodham Clinton, *It Takes a Village And Other Lessons Children Teach Us* (New York: Simon Schuster, 1996), 11–18.

7. For a critical analysis of the traditional village life, see Beth Blue Swadener, Margaret Kabiru, and Anne Njenga, *Does the Village Still Raise the Child?* (Albany, NY: New York State University Press, 2000).

8. For deepening the topic of child prostitution, see Siroj Sorajjakool, *Child Prostitution in Thailand* (Binghamton, NY: Haworth Press, 2002). Julia.O'Connell Davidson, *Children in the Global Sex Trade* (Cambridge: Polity Press, 2005). Kevin Bales, *Understanding Global Slavery* (Berkley: University of California Press, 2005).

9. Donald Winnicott, "Transitional Objects and Transitional Phenomena," *International Journal of Psychoanalysis* 34 (1951): 89–97.

10. Chou Ta-Kuan, *The Customs of Cambodia* (Bangkok: The Siam Society, 1993), 18.

11. T. Berry Brazelton, *Touchpoints* (London: Viking Press, 1992), 83–84.

12. Adrienne Rich, *Of Woman Born: Motherhood as Experience and Institution* (New York: W.W. Norton, 1985), 67–77.

7 Let Nature Take Its Course

1. Giacomo Corna Pellegrino and Gianni Morelli, *Enciclopedia Geografica* 12 (Milano: Istituto Geografico De Agostini), 172–187.

2. For issues of power linked with age and menopause, see Thomas Buckley and Alba Gottlieb (eds.), *Blood Magic: The Anthropology of Menstruation* (Berkley: University of California Press, 1988). Nancy Foner, "Older Women in Nonindustrial Cultures. Consequences of Power and Privilege," *Women and Health* 14 (1989): 227–237. Kathrin M. Yount and Emily M. Agree, "The Power of Older Women and Men in Egyptian and Tunisian Families," *Journal of Marriage and Family* 66 (2004): 126–146.

3. Marjorie Shostack, *Nisa* (Cambridge, MA: Harvard University Press, 1981), 167.

4. John Boswell, *The Kindness of Strangers: The Abandonment of Children in Western Europe from Late Antiquity to the Renaissance* (Chicago: Chicago University Press, 1998).

5. For a discussion on the interplay between traditional and western medicine, see Akin Makind, *African Philosophy, Culture, and Traditional Medicine* (Columbus, OH: Ohio University Press, 1988). Jan L. Slikkerveer, *Plural Medical Systems in the Horn of Africa* (London: Kegan Paul, 1990). Isaac Sindiga, *Traditional Medicine in Africa* (Nairobi: East African Education Publications, 1997).

Peter A. Winstanley, "The Approach to Treatment," in *Principles of Medicine in Africa*, edited by Eldryd Parry, Richard Godfrey, David Mabey, and Geoffrey Gill, 3rd Edition (Cambridge: Cambridge University Press, 2004), 1311–1337.

6. Herbert Spencer, *Principles of Biology* (London: William and Norgate, 1864).

7. Maria W. Piers, *Infanticide Past and Present* (New York: W.W. Norton, 1978), 16.

8. Ian MacGillivray, "Epidemiology of Twin Pregnancy," *Seminars in Perinatology* 10 (1986): 4–8.

9. For a discussion on the New Churches, see Melvin D Williams, *Community in a Black Pentecostal Church: An Anthropological Study* (Prospect Heights, IL: Waveland Press, 1984). Harvey Cox, *Fire from Heaven: The Rise of Pentecostal Spirituality and the Reshaping of Religion in the 21st Century* (Cambridge: Da Capo Books, 2001).

10. For gender inequalities in access to medical care, see World Health Organization, *Gender and Health Technical Paper* 98 (WHO Publications: Geneva, 1998), 16. Kathrin Strother-Radcliff, *Women and Health: Power, Technology, Inequality and Conflict in a Gendered World* (Needham Heights, MA: Allyn and Bacon, 2001). Farzaneh Roudhi-Fahimi, *Gender and Equity in Access to Health Care Services in the Middle East and North Africa* (Washington: Population Reference Bureau, 2006). Sheila Dinotshe Tlou, *Women and Health* (U.N. Womenwatch, May 11, 2007). www.un.org/womenwatch/daw/csw/tlou.htm

11. Gregory Bateson, *Naven: A Survey of the Problems Suggested by a Composite Picture of a New Guinea Tribe Drawn from Three Points of View* (Stanford: Stanford University Press, 1958).

12. Margaret Mead, *Male and Female*. First published in 1949 (New York: Harper Perennial, 2001).

13. For a description of life in the Sepik Area, see Nacy Lutkehaus Christian Kaufmann, William E. Mitchell, Douglas Newton, Linda Osmundsen, and Meinhard Schuster (eds.), *Sepik Heritage: Tradition and Change in Papua New Guinea* (Durham, NC: Carolina Academic Press, 1990). David Lipset, *Mangrove Man: Dialogics of Culture in the Sepik Estuary* (Cambridge: Cambridge University Press, 1997). Laura Zimmer-Tamakoshi (ed.), *Modern Papua New Guinea* (Kirksville, MO: Thomas Jefferson University Press, 1998).

14. Elizabeth A. Stewart, *Exploring Twins: Towards a Social Analysis of Twinship* (London: Palgrave Macmillan, 1999), 23.

15. Helen L. Ball and Catherine M. Hill, "Re-evaluating Twin Infanticide," *Current Anthropology* 37, 5 (1996): 856–863.

16. Graham Hancock, *Lords of Poverty: The Power, Prestige, and Corruption of the International Aid Business* (London: Macmillan, 1989), 32–33.

8   The Hold of Superstition

1. For slavery in Madagascar, see David Graeber, *Lost People: Magic and the Legacy of Slavery in Madagascar* (Bloomington, IN: Indiana University Press,

2007). Dominique Torrés, *Esclaves: 200 millions d'esclaves aujourd'hui* (Paris: Phébus, 1995). Gwyn Campbell (ed.), *Slavery: Abolition and Its Aftermath in the Indian Ocean, Africa and Asia* (London: Routledge, 2005).

2. Giacomo Corna Pellegrino and Gianni Morelli, *Enciclopedia Geografica* 12 (Milano: Istituto Geografico De Agostini), 218–223.

3. For superstition in Madagascar, see Suzanne Lallermand *Grossesse et petite enfance en Afrique noire et à Madagascar* (Paris: L'Harmattan, 1991). Joro Angano and Sakalava Tromba, *Mythes, rites et transes à Madagascar* (Paris: Kartala Editions, 1996). Lesley A Sharp, *The Possessed and the Dispossessed: Spirits, Identity, and Power in a Madagascar Migrant Town* (Berkley: University of California Press, 1993). Didier Mauro, et Emeline Raholiarisoa, *Madagascar: L'ile essentielle. Etude d'anthropologie culturale* (Paris: Anako, 2000).

4. James George Frazer, *The Golden Bough: A Study in Magic and Religion*. First Publication, 1890 (London: Dover Press, 2002).

5. Alan Dundes, "Wet and Dry, the Evil Eye: an Essay in Indo-European and Semitic Worldview," in *The Evil Eye: a Folklore Casebook,* ed. Alan Dundes (New York: Garland Publishing, 1981), 257–298.

6. David J. Rothman, E. Rose, T. Awaya, B. Cohen, A. Daar, and S. L. Dzemeshkevich et al., "The Bellagio Task Force Report on Transplantation, Bodily Integrity, and the International Traffic in Organs," *Transplantation Proceedings* 29 (1997): 273–945.

7. For peoples and customs in the Golden Triangle, see Paul Lewis and Elaine Lewis, *Peoples of the Golden Triangle* (London: Thames and Hudson, 1984). Christopher R. Cox, *Chasing the Dragon: Into the Heart of the Golden Triangle* (New York: Henry Holt, 1996). Grant Evans (ed.), *Laos: Culture and Society* (Bangkog: Silkworm Books, 1998). Patrick Bernard, *Peuples D'Indochine* (Fontenay-Sous-Bois, France: Anako, 1999). Het Bun Dai Bun and Hans George Berger, *Laos: Sacred Rituals of Luang Prabang* (London: Westzone, 2000).

8. Melanie Klein, *Our Adult World and Other Essays* (London: Heinemann, 1963), 305–308.

9. For aspects linked with twin pregnancy and delivery, see Alessandra Piontelli, *Twins: From Fetus to Child* (London: Routledge, 2002).

9 Heart of Darkness

1. Giacomo Corna Pellegrino and Gianni Morelli, *Enciclopedia Geografica* 12 (Milano: Istituto Geografico De Agostini), 176–179.

2. For customs related to the Indios inhabiting the Chaco, see Branislava Susnik, *Los Aborigenes del Paraguay: Approximacion a las Creencias de los Indigenas* (Asuncion, Paraguay: Publicaciones Museo Etnographico Andres Barbero, 1985). Elmer S. Miller (ed.), *Peoples of the Gran Chaco* (Westport, CT: Greenwood Publisers, 1999). Miguel Alberto Bartolomé, *El Encuentro de la Gente y los Insensatos* (Mexico City: Instituto Indigenista Interamericano, 2000).

3. U.S. Government, *21st Century Complete Guide to Guinea-Bissau* (White House: CIA Factbook, 2007)

4. For a discussion of customs and beliefs in Guinea Bissau, see Inger Callewaert, *The Birth of Religion among the Balanta of Guinea-Bissau* (Lund, Sweden: Lund Studies in African and Asian Religion, Vol. 12, 2000). Jonina Einarsdottir, *Tired of Weeping: Mother Love, Child Death, and Poverty in Guinea-Bissau* (Madison, WI: University of Wisconsin Press, 2004).

5. Boubacar-Sid Barry, Edward G. E. Creppy, and Estanislao Giacitua-Mario (eds.) *Conflict, Livelihoods, and Poverty in Guinea-Bissau* (Washington, DC: World Bank Publications, 2005).

6. For a description of bonding and attachment, see Marshall H. Klaus, John H. Kennell, and Phyllis H. Klaus, *Bonding: Building the Foundations of Secure Attachment and Independence* (New York: Merloyd Lawrence Books, 1982).

7. WHO recommendations on exclusive breastfeeding available at http//www.who.int/child-adolescent-health/NUTRITION/infant_exclusive.html

8. For the history and a discussion on the motives of human sacrifice, see René Girad, *Violence and the Sacred* (Baltimore: The John Hopkins Press, 1979). Walter Burkert, *Homo Necans: The Anthropology of Ancient Greek Sacrificial Ritual and Myth* (Berkley: University of California Press, 1986). Henry Hubert and Marcel Mauss, *Sacrifice: Its Nature and Functions* (Berkley: University of California Press, 1986).

9. Joseph Conrad, *Heart of Darkness*. First Edition: Blackwood Magazine, 1902 (London: Penguin Classics, 1994).

10. Herodotus, *The Histories* (New York: Everyman's Library, 1997).

11. Sigmund Freud, *Civilization and its Discontent*. Standard Edition 21 (London: The Hogart Press, 1930), 101–103.

12. For deepening the motives underlying scapegoating, see René Girard, *The Scapegoat* (Baltimore: The John Hopkins Press, 1989).

10   One Gender and One Only

1. Robert Louis Stevenson, *Strange Case of Dr Jekyll and Mr Hyde*. First Edition, 1886, in Barry Menikoff, ed., *The Complete Stories of Robert Luis Stevenson* (New York: Random House Publishing Group, 2002).

2. Mary Wollstonecraft Shelley, *Frankenstein; or the Modern Prometeus*. First Published in 1818 (New York: Simon and Schuster, 2004).

3. Fedor Mihajlovic Dostoevskij, *The Double*. First Published in 1846 (West Valley City, UT: Waking Lion Press, 2007).

4. For a discussion on the Doppelganger, see Robert Sterling, *The Book of Doppelgangers* (Rockville, MD: Wildside Press, 2003).

5. For the extension and modalities of gender inequalities, see Martha Crave Nussbaum, *Sex and Social Justice* (New York: Oxford University Press, 1999).

6. Amartya Sen, "More than 100 Million Women are Missing," *New York Review of Books* 37, 20 (December 20, 1990): 61–63.

7. Amartya Sen, *Development as Freedom* (Oxford: Oxford University Press, 1999), 189–203.

8. Patrick Olivelle (trans.), *The Law Code of Manu* (Oxford: Oxford University Press, 2004), 305–320.

9. UNICEF, "Women and Children: The Double Dividend of Gender equality," in *The State of the World's Children, 2007* (Geneva: UNICEF, 2005).

10. Giacomo Corna Pellegrino and Gianni Morelli, *Enciclopedia Geografica* 8 (Milano: Istituto Geografico De Agostini), 184–235.

11. Arthur Waley (trans.), *The Book of Songs: The Ancient Chinese Classic of Poetry* (New York: Grove Press, 1996).

12. Robert Derom , "The Epidemiology of Multiple Births in Europe," in *Multiple Pregnancy: Epidemiology, Gestation & Perinatal Outcome*, ed. Luis G. Keith, Emile Papiernik, Donald M. Keith, and Barbara Luke (New York: Parthenon Publishing Group, 1995), 145–162.

13. Mark I. Evans, Nelson B. Isada, Peter G. Pryde, and John C. Fletcher, "Multifetal Pregnancy Reduction and Selective Second-Trimester Termination," in *Multiple Pregnancy: Epidemiology, Gestation & Perinatal Outcome*, ed. Luis G. Keith, Emile Papiernik, Donald M. Keith, and Barbara Luke (New York: Parthenon Publishing Group, 1995), 359–366.

11   Abuse and Neglect

1. Philippe Ariès, et Georges Duby, *Histoire de la vie privée* (Paris: Seuil, 1985).

2. Lawrence Stone, *Family, Sex and Marriage in England* (London: Penguin Books, 1977).

3. Colin Heywood, *A History of Childhood: Children and Childhood in the West from Medieval to Modern Times* (Cambridge: Cambridge University Press, 2001).

4. Viviana Zelizer, *Pricing the Priceless Child: The Changing Social Value of Children* (Princeton: Princeton University Press, 1994).

5. Leslie Morgan Steiner, *Mommy Wars: Stay-at-Home and Career Moms Face Off on Their Choices, Their Lives, Their Families* (New York: Random House, 2006).

6. U.S. Department of Health and Human Services, *National Child Abuse and Neglect Data System (NCANDS) Child File, 2005*. Washington, DC.

7. Sara Ruddick, "What Do Mothers and Grandmothers Know and Want?" in *What Do Mothers Want?* ed. Sheila Feig Brown (London: The Analytic Press, 2005), 70–71.

8. Jessie R. Groothuis, "Increased child abuse in families with twins." *Pediatrics* 70, 5 (1982): 769–773.

9. Esther R. Goshen-Gottstein, "The Mothering of Twins, Triplets and Quadruplets," *Psychiatry* 43, 3 (1980): 189–204.

10. H.B. Nelson and C.A. Martin, "Increased Child Abuse in Twins," *Child Abuse and Neglect* 9, 4 (1985): 501–505.

11. For an exposition of shamanic practices in South America, see Alice Beck Kekoe, *Shamans and Religion: An Anthropological Exploration in Critical Thinking* (Long Grove, IL: Waveland Press, 2000). Anna Mariella Bacigalupo, *Shamans of the Foye Tree: Gender, Power, and Healing among Chilean Mapuche* (Austin: University of Texas Press, 2007).
12. Meredith Sabini (trans.), *The Earth Has a Soul: The Nature Writings of C.G. Jung* (Berkley, CA: North Atlantic Books, 2002).
13. Alessandra Piontelli, *Twins: From Fetus to Child* (London: Routledge, 2002).
14. Sara Ruddick, *Maternal Thinking: Toward A politics of Peace* (Boston: Beacon Press, 1989).
15. Nancy Scheper-Huges, *Death Without Weeping: The Violence of Everyday Life in Brazil* (Berkley: University of California Press, 1992).

12   Till Death Us Do Part

1. Marcel Griaule, *Dieu d'eau: Entretiens avec Ogotemelli* (Paris: Fayard, 1948), 24.
2. For deepening the topic of incest in preindustrial and contemporary societies, see Luc De Heush, *Essais sur le symbolisme de l'inceste royal en Afrique* (Bruxelles: Université de Bruxelles, 1958). Claude Lèvi-Strauss, *The Elementary Structures of Kinship* (Boston, MA: Beacon Press, 1969). Jack Goody, *The Oriental, the Ancient, and the Primitive: Systems of Marriage and the Family in the Pre-Industrial Societies of Eurasia* (Cambridge: Cambridge University Press, 1990). Nancy Thornill Wilmsen (ed.), *The Natural History of Inbreeding and Outbreeding* (Chicago: The University of Chicago Press, 1993). Fancoise Héritier, *Les Deux Sœurs et leur mère. Anthropologie de l'Inceste* (Paris: Odile Jacob, 1994).
3. Angela Hobart, Ruth Rasmeyer, and Albert Leeman, *The People of Bali* (Malden, MA: Blackwell Publishers, 1988), 96.
4. Fredrik Barth, *Balinese Worlds* (Chicago: The University of Chicago Press, 1993), 229.
5. Brigid Arabin, Ulrich Gembruch, and Jim van Eick, "Intrauterine Behavior," in *Multiple Pregnancy: Epidemiology, Gestation and Perinatal Outcome,* ed. Luis G. Keith, Emile Papiernik, Donald M. Keith, and Barbara Luke (New York: The Parthenon Publishing Group, 1995), 331–350.
6. Alessandra Piontelli, *Twins: From Fetus to Child* (London: Routledge, 2002).
7. René Zazzo, *Les Jumeaux, la couple et la personne* (Paris: Presses Universitaires de France, 1960).
8. Claire Slavy, *Jumeaux de sexe différent* (Paris: L'Harmattan, 2000).
9. Nancy L. Segal, *Entwined Lives* (Hialea, FL: Dutton Press, 1999), 44–45.
10. Joan Woodward, *The Lone Twin: A Study in Bereavement and Loss* (New York: New York University Press, 1998).
11. For a deepening of peoples and customs of West Papua (Irian Jaya), see Gilbert Herdt, *The Sambia: Ritual and Gender in New Guinea* (New York: Holt, Rinehart and Winston, 1987). Jane C. Goodale, *To Sing with Pigs Is Human*

(Washington: University of Washington Press, 1995). Susan Meiselas, *Encounters with the Dani* (Gottingen, Germany: Steidl Publishers, 2003). Pascale Bonnemère (ed.), *Women as Unseen Characters* (Philadelphia: University of Pensilvania Press, 2004).

12. Eric Lobo, *Esprits de Jungle: Irian Jaya l'univers iréel des Papous* (Paris: Romain Pages Editions, 1999), 34–35.

Conclusion: Bringing It All Back Home

1. World Health Organization, *World Health Statistics* (Geneva: WHO Press, 2006).
2. For a good overview on maternity in developing countries, see Kalpana Ram and Margaret Jolly (eds.), *Maternities and Modernities* (Cambridge: Cambridge University Press, 1998). Cynthia Garcia Coll, Janet L. Surrey, and Kaethe Weingarten, *Mothering Against the Odds* (London: Guilford Press, 1998). Cecilia Van Hollen, *Birth on the Threshold* (Berkley: University of California Press, 2003).
3. Ann Crittenden, *The Price of Motherhood: Why the Most Important Job in the World is Still the Least Valued* (New York: Henry Halt, 2001), 3.
4. Judith Warner, *Perfect Madness: Motherhood in the Age of Anxiety* (New York: Penguin Books, 2005), 12–17.
5. Sigmund Freud, *The Question of Lay Analysis* (1926). Standard Edition 20. (London: The Hogart Press, 1959), 4.
6. John Bowlby, *Attachment and Loss: Attachment* 1 (London: Tavistock Institute of Human Relations, 1966).
7. Selma H Fraiberg, Edna Adelson, and Vivian Shapiro, "Ghosts in the Nursery: A Psychoanalytic Approach to the Problems of Impaired Infant-Mother Relationships," *Journal of the American Academy of Child Psychiatry* 14, 3 (1975): 387, 421.
8. Peter Fonagy, Miriam Steele, George Moran, Howard Steele, and Anna Higgitt, "Measuring Ghosts in the Nursery: An Empirical Study of the Relation Between Parents Mental Representations of Childhood Experiences and their Infants' Security of Attachment," *Journal of the American Psychoanalytic Association* 41 (1993): 957–989.
9. For a critique of these ideas, see Alessandra Piontelli, *Twins: From Fetus to Child* (London: Routledge, 2002), 28–51.
10. Alessandra Piontelli, "On the Onset of Human Fetal Behavior," in Mauro Mancia ed. *Psychoanalysis and Neurosciences* (New York: Springer-Verlag, 2006), 391–418.
11. Naomi Wolff, *Misconceptions* (Woodston, PE: Anchor Books, 2003), 66.
12. Adrienne C. Rich, *Of Woman Born: Motherhood as Experience and Institution* (New York: W.W. Norton, 1985), 31.

13. For a critical review of these studies, see Ross D. Parke, *Fatherhood* (Cambridge, MA: Harvard University Press, 1996).

14. David A. Hay, "What Information Should the Multiple Birth Family Receive Before, During and After Birth," *Acta Geneticae Medicae et Gemellologiae* 39 (1990): 259–269.

15. Simone De Beauvoir, *Le Deuxieme Sexe* (Paris: Gallimard, 1963), 462–466.

16. Nancy Sheper-Huges, *Death Without Weeping* (Berkley: University of California Press, 1992), 410–412.

17. Sarah Blaffer Hrdy, *Mother Nature: A History of Mothers, Infants, and Natural Selection* (New York: Pantheon Books, 1999), 173–174.

18. Sara Ruddick, *Maternal Thinking* (Boston: Beacon Press, 1989), 9–11.

19. Philippe Ariès, *L'enfant et la vie familiale sous l'Ancien Régime* (Paris: Le Seuil, 1973), 313–317.

20. Edward Shorter, *The Making of the Modern Family* (London: Fontana, 1977), 226–228.

21. Elizabeth Batinder, *The Myth of Motherhood: An Historical View of the Maternal Instinct* (London: Souvenir Press, 1981), 10–13.

22. For issues and figures on maternal mortality, access to family planning and health care, skilled attendance at delivery, and infant death, see UNFPA, "Reproductive Health Fact Sheet," *State of World Population 2005* (New York, 2005).

23. Beverly Botting , Ian M. Davies, and Arthur J. Macfarlane, "Recent Trends in the Incidence of Multiple Births and Their Mortality," *Archives of Diseases in Childhood* 64 (1987): 941–950.

24. Loyd De Mause, *The History of Childhood* (New York: Psychohistory Press, 1974), 1–50.

25. Keith Thorpe, "Comparison of Prevalence of Depression in Mothers of Twins and Mothers of Singletons," *British Medical Journal*, 302 (1991): 875–878.

26. Robert Snowden, *The Artificial Family* (St. Leonard, Australia: Unwin and Allen, 1983).

27. Sigmund Freud, *A Child Is Being Beaten*. Standard Edition 17 (London: Hogart Press, 1919), 184–186.

28. Herbert Aptekar, *Anjea* (New York: William Godwin, 1931), 185.

29. Anna Freud, *The Ego and the Mechanisms of Defence* (London: Hogart Press, 1937), 109–121.

30. Aristotle (trans. George A. Kennedy), *On Rethoric* (Oxford: Oxford University Press, 1991), 121–124.

31. Immanuel Kant (trans. Annette Churtun), *Education* (Ann Arbor: University of Michingan Press, 1960), 24–25.

32. Melanie Klein, *Envy and Gratitude* (London: Hogart Press, 1946), 202.

33. Alberoni Francesco, *Falling in Love* (New York: Random House, 1983), 111–114.

Bibliography

Alberoni, Francesco. *Falling in Love.* New York: Random House, 1983.

Alistair, Graham, and Peter Beard. *Eyelids of Morning.* San Francisco: Chronicle Books, 1990.

Allen, Marelee C. "Factors Affecting Developmental Outcome," in *Multiple Pregnancy: Epidemiology, Gestation and Perinatal Outcome,* edited by Luis G.Keith, Emile Papiernik, Donald M. Keith, and Barbara Luke, 599–612. New York: The Parthenon Publishing Group, 1995.

American Psychiatric Association. *Diagnostic and Statistical Manual of Mental Disorders, DMD-IV-TR.* Fourth Edition. Washington, DC: American Psychiatric Association, 2000.

Angano, Joro, and Sakalava Tromba. *Mythes, rites et transes à Madagascar.* Paris: Kartala Editions, 1996.

Aptekar, Herbert. *Anjea.* New York: William Godwin, 1931.

Arabin, Brigid, Ulrich Gembruch, and Jim Van Eick. "Intrauterine Behavior," in *Multiple Pregnancy: Epidemiology, Gestation and Perinatal Outcome,* edited by Luis G. Keith, Emile Papiernik, Donald M. Keith, and Barbara Luke, 331–350. New York: The Parthenon Publishing Group, 1995.

Ariès, Philippe. *L'enfant et la vie familiale sous l'Ancien Régime.* Paris: Le Seuil, 1973.

Ariès, Philippe, et Georges Duby. *Histoire de la vie privée.* Paris: Seuil, 1985.

Augè, Marc. *Le dieu objet.* Paris: Flammarion, 1988.

Bacigalupo, Anna Mariella. *Shamans of the Foye Tree: Gender, Power, and Healing among Chilean Mapuche.* Austin: University of Texas Press, 2007.

Baldwin, Virginia J. *Pathology of Multiple Pregnancy.* New York: Springer Verlag, 1994.

Bales, Kevin. *Disposable People: New Slavery in the Global Economy.* Berkley: University of California Press, 2004.

Ball, Helen L., and Hill Catherine M. "Re-evaluating Twin Infanticide." *Current Anthropology* 37, 5 (1996): 856–863.

Barth, Fredrik. *Balinese Worlds.* Chicago: The University of Chicago Press, 1993.

Bartolomé, Miguel A. *El Encuentro de la Gente y los Insensatos.* Mexico City: Instituto Indigenista Interamericano, 2000.

Bateson, Gregory. *Naven: A Survey of the Problems suggested by a Composite Picture of a New Guinea Tribe Drawn from Three Points of View.* Stanford: Stanford University Press, 1958.

Batinder, Elizabeth. *L'Amour en plus.* Paris: Flammarion, 1980.

Beck Kekoe, Alice. *Shamans and Religion: An Anthropological Exploration in Critical Thinking.* Long Grove, IL: Waveland Press, 2000.

Benacerraf, Beryl R. *Ultrasound of Fetal Syndromes.* Philadelphia: Churchill Livingstone, 1998.

Benirschke, Kurt, and Kaufmann Peter. "Multiple Pregnancy," in *Pathology of the Human Placenta,* edited by Kurt Benirschke and Peter Kaufmann. Third Edition, 767–778. New York: Springer Verlag, 1995.

Bernard, Patrick. *Peuples D'Indochine.* Fontenay-Sous-Bois, France: Anako, 1999.

Besinger, Richard E., and Carlson Nancy J. "The Physiology of Preterm Labor," in *Multiple Pregnancy: Epidemiology, Gestation and Perinatal Outcome,* edited by Luis G. Keith, Emile Papiernik, Donald M. Keith, and Barbara Luke, 415–425. New York: The Parthenon Publishing Group, 1995.

Blaffer Hrdy, Sara. *Mother Nature: A History of Mothers, Infants, and Natural Selection.* New York: Pantheon Books, 1999.

Blickstein, Ian. "Maternal Mortality in Twin Gestations." *Journal of Reproductive Medicine* 42, 11 (1997): 679–760.

Blier-Preston, Suzanne. *African Vodun: Art, Psychology, Power.* Berkley: University of California Press, 1995.

Bomsel-Helmreich, Ora, and Widad Al Mufti. "The Mechanism of Monozygosity and Double Ovulation," in *Multiple Pregnancy: Epidemiology, Gestation and Perinatal Outcome,* edited by Luis G. Keith, Emile Papiernik, Donald M. Keith, and Barbara Luke, 25–40. New York: The Parthenon Publishing Group, 1995.

Bonnemère, Pascale, ed. *Women as Unseen Characters.* Philadelphia: University of Pensilvania Press, 2004.

Boswell, John. *The Kindness of Strangers: The Abandonment of Children in Western Europe from Late Antiquity to the Renaissance.* Chicago: Chicago University Press, 1998.

Botting, Beverly, Davies Ian M., and Macfarlane Arthur J. "Recent Trends in the Incidence of Multiple Births and Their Mortality." *Archives of Diseases in Childhood* 62 (1997): 941–950.

Boubacar-Sid, Barry, Creppy Edward G.E., and Estanislao Gacitua-Mario, eds. *Conflict, Livelihoods, and Poverty in Guinea-Bissau.* Washington, DC: World Bank Publications, 2005.

Bowers, Nancy. *The Multiple Pregnancy Sourcebook.* Lincolnwood, IL: Contemporary Books, 2001.

Bowlby, John. *Attachment and Loss: Volume 1, Attachment.* London: Tavistock Institute of Human Relations, 1966.

———. *A Secure Base: Parent-Child Attachment and Healthy Human Development.* London: Basic Books, 1988.

Brand, Roger. "Réalité anthropologique des Jumeaux et Culte Vodun au Sud Bénin," in *Des Jumeaux et des autres,* edited by Claude Savary, 216–233. Geneva: Musée d'ethnographie, 1995.

Brazelton, T. Berry. *Touchpoints.* London: Viking Press, 1992.

Breuer, Joseph, and Sigmund Freud. *Studies on Hysteria.* The Standard Edition 2 (1883–1895). London: The Hogarth Press, 1961.

Bryan, Elizabeth. *The Nature and Nurture of Twins*. London: Ballière Tindall, 1983.

———. *Twins and Higher Multiple Births*. London: Edward Arnold, 1992.

Buckley, Thomas, and Alba Gottlieb, eds. *Blood Magic: The Anthropology of Menstruation*. Berkley: University of California Press, 1988.

Bun Dai Bun, Het, and Hans George Berger. *Laos: Sacred Rituals of Luang Prabang*. London: Westzone, 2000.

Burkert, Walter. *Homo Necans: The Anthropology of Ancient Greek Sacrificial Ritual and Myth*. Berkley: University of California Press, 1986.

———. *The Scapegoat*. Baltimore: The John Hopkins Press, 1989.

Burnett Taylor, Edward. *Religion in Primitive Culture*. First Publication 1871. Gloucester, MA: Peter Smith Publishers, 1970.

Butt-Thompson, Frederick W. *West African Secret Societies*. Berlin: Trubner Press, 2003.

Callewaert, Inger. *The Birth of Religion among the Balanta of Guinea-Bissau*, vol. 12. Lund, Sweden: Lund Studies in African and Asian Religion, 2000.

Campbell, Gwyn, ed. *Slavery, Abolition and Its Aftermath in the Indian Ocean, Africa and Asia*. London: Routledge, 2005.

Carr, Sean P. "Survival Rates of Monoamniotic Twins Do Not Decrease After 30 Weeks' Gestation." *American Journal of Obstetrics and Gynecology* 163 (1990): 719–722.

Castiglioni, Angelo, Castiglioni, Achille and Salvioni, Giovanna. *Babatundé: la vita rinasce*. Varese, Italy: Edizioni Lativa, 1988.

Centers for Disease and Health Control (CDC), *2004 Assisted Reproductive Technology Success Rates*. Atlanta: U.S. Department of Health and Human Services, December, 2006.

Chatwin, Bruce. *On the Black Hill*. New York: Viking Books, 1983.

Churtun, Annette, trans. *Immanuel Kant. Education*. Ann Arbor: University of Michigan Press, 1960.

Clay Wright, Victoria, Chang Jeani, Jeng Gary, Chen Michael, and Macaluso Maurizio. *Assisted Reproductive Technology Surveillance*. U.S. Division of Reproductive Health, 2004.

Collier Paul, *The Bottom Billion: Why the Poorest Countries are Failing and what can Be Done About it*. Oxford: Oxford University Press, 2007.

Conde-Agudelo, Agustin, Belizàn Jose M., and Lindmark Gunilla. "Maternal Morbidity and Mortality Associated with Multiple Gestations." *Obstetrics and Gynecology* 95 (2000): 899–904.

Conrad, Joseph. *Heart of Darkness*. First Edition: Blackwood Magazine, 1902. London: Penguin Classics, 1994.

Corna Pellegrino, Giacomo, and Gianni Morelli. *Enciclopedia Geografica* 8. Milano: Istituto Geografico De Agostani, 2005.

———. *Enciclopedia Geografica* 12. Milano: Istituto Geografico De Agostini, 2005.

Cox, Christopher R. *Chasing the Dragon: Into the Heart of the Golden Triangle*. New York: Henry Holt, 1996.

Cox, Harvey. *Fire from Heaven: The Rise of Pentecostal Spirituality and the Reshaping of Religion in the 21st Century.* Cambridge: Da Capo Books, 2001.

Crave Nussbaum, Martha. *Sex and Social Justice.* New York: Oxford University Press, 1999.

Crittenden, Ann. *The Price of Motherhood: Why the Most Important Job in the World is Still the Least Valued.* New York: Henry Halt, 2001.

Cronenberg David, script writer and director. *Dead Ringers.* Producers, MarcBoyman, and David Cronenberg. Distributed by Twentieth Century Fox, 1988.

De Beauvoir, Simone. *Le Deuxieme Sexe.* Paris: Gallimard, 1963.

De Heush, Luc. *Essais sur le symbolisme de l'inceste royal en Afrique.* Bruxelles: Université de Bruxelles, 1958.

de la Torre, Inès. *Le Vodou en Afrique de L'Ouest.* Paris: L'Harmattan, 1991.

De Mause, Loyd. *The History of Childhood.* New York: Psychohistory Press, 1974.

Denbow, Mark, and Nicholas Fisk, "Twin Pregnancies," in *Fetal Medicine,* edited by Charles H. Roddeck and Martin J. Whittle, 863–877. London: Churchill and Livingstone, 1999.

Derom, Robert, Jacob Orlebeke, Aldur Eriksson, and Evert M. Thiery. "The Epidemiology of Multiple Births in Europe," in *Multiple pregnancy: Epidemiology, Gestation & Perinatal Outcome,* edited by Luis G. Keith, Emile Papiernik, Donald M. Keith, and Barbara Luke, 145–162. New York: Parthenon Publishing Group, 1995.

de Rosny, Eric. *L'Afrique des Guérisons.* Paris: Karthala, 1992.

de Surgy, Albert. *Nature et function des fétiches en Afrique Noire.* Paris: L'Harmattan, 1994.

Dinotshe Tlou, Sheila. *Women and Health.* New York: U.N. Womenwatch, May 11, 2007.

Dostoievskij, Fedor M. *The Double.* First Publication 1846. West Valley City, UT: Waking Lion Press, 2007.

Dundes, Alan. "Wet and Dry, the Evil Eye: An Essay in Indo-European and Semitic Worldview," in *The Evil Eye: A Folklore Casebook,* edited by Alan Dundes, 257–298. New York: Garland Publishing, 1981.

Dyson-Huds, Rada, and Nigel Dyson-Huds. *Turkana Pastoralists.* New York: Rosen Publishing Group, 1996.

Einarsdottir, Jonina. *Tired of Weeping: Mother Love, Child Death, and Poverty in Guinea-Bissau.* Madison, WI: University of Wisconsin Press, 2004.

Eliade, Mircea. *Shamanism: Archaic Techniques of Ecstasy.* First Publication, 1951. Princeton: Princeton University Press, 1994.

Ellison, Hotamisligil, M.A., Lee H., Rich-Edwards J., Pang S., and Hall J. "Psychosocial Risks Associated with Multiple Births Resulting from Assisted Reproduction." *Fertility and Sterility* 83, 5 (2005): 1422–1428.

Evans, Grant, ed. *Laos: Culture And Society.* Bangkog: Silkworm Books, 1998.

Evans, Mark I., Nelson B. Isada, Peter G. Pryde, and John C. Fletcher. "Multifetal Pregnancy Reduction and Selective Second-Trimester Termination," in *Multiple Pregnancy: Epidemiology, Gestation & Perinatal Outcome,* edited by

Luis G. Keith, Emile Papiernik, Donald M. Keith, and Barbara Luke, 359–366. New York: Parthenon Publishing Group, 1995.

Falkner, Frank, and Adam P. Matheny. "The Long-term Development of Twins," in *Multiple Pregnancy: Epidemiology, Gestation and Perinatal Outcome*, edited by Luis G. Keith, Emile Papiernik, Donald M. Keith, and Barbara Luke, 613–624. New York: The Parthenon Publishing Group, 1995.

Feldman-Salvelsberg, Pamela. *Plundered Kitchens, Empty Wombs: Threatened Reproduction and Identity in the Cameroon Grassflieds*. Ann Arbor: The University of Michingan Press, 2002.

Ferguson, Walter F. "Perinatal Mortality in Multiple Geastations." *Obstetrics and Gynecology* 17, 1 (1994): 101–103.

Fonagy Peter, Steele Miriam, Moran George, Steele Howard, and Anna Higgitt. "Measuring Ghosts in the Nursery: An Empirical Study of the Relation Between Parents' Mental Representations of Childhood Experiences and their Infants' Security of Attachment." *Journal of the American Psychoanalytic Association* 41 (1993): 957–989.

Fonseca, Isabel. *Bury Me Standing· The Gypsies and Their Journey*. New York: Vintage Books, 1995.

Former, Nancy. "Older Women in Nonindustrial Cultures. Consequences of Power and Privilege." *Women and Health* 14 (1989): 227–237.

Fraiberg, Selma H., Adelson Edna, and Vivian Shapiro. "Ghosts in the Nursery: A Psychoanalytic Approach to the Problems of Impaired Infant-Mother Relationships." *Journal of the American Academy of Child Psychiatry* 14, 3 (1975): 387–421.

Fraser, Angus. *The Gypsies*. Chichester, West Sussex: Wiley, 1995.

Frazer, James George. *The Golden Bough: A Study in Magic and Religion*. First Publication 1890. London: Dover Press, 2002.

Freud, Anna. *The Ego and the Mechanisms of Defence*. London: Hogart Press, 1937.

Freud, Sigmund. *The Interpretation of Dreams*. (1900–1901). The Standard Edition 5. 2. London: The Hogart Press, 1961.

———. *A Child Is Being Beaten*. (1919). Standard Edition 17. London: Hogart Press, 1961.

———. *Civilization and its Discontent*. (1929). Standard Edition 21. London: The Hogart Press, 1961.

———. *The Question of Lay Analysis*. (1926). Standard Edition 20. London: The Hogart Press, 1961.

Frydman, Renè. *L'Irrésistible désir de naissance*. Paris: Presses Universitaires de France, 1986.

Galton, Sir Francis. "The History of Twins as a Criterion of the Relative Powers of Nature and Nurture." *Journal of the Anthropological Institute of Great Britain and Ireland* 5 (1875): 391–406.

Garcia-Coll, Cynthia, Janet L. Surrey, and Kaethe Weingarten. *Mothering Against the Odds*. London: Guilford Press, 1998.

Gardi, René. *Monti e Popoli Sconosciuti del Camerun*. Milano: Bompiani, 1957.

Geddes, Anne. *Pure*. Kansas City: Andrew Mc Meel Publishing, 2003.

Girad, René. *Violence and the Sacred*. Baltimore: The John Hopkins Press, 1979.

Goodale, Jane C. *To Sing with Pigs Is Human*. Washington, DC: University of Washington Press, 1995.

Goody, Jack. *The Oriental, the Ancient, and the Primitive: Systems of Marriage and the Family in the Pre-Industrial Societies of Eurasia*. Cambridge: Cambridge University Press, 1990.

Goshen-Gottstein, Elizabeth R. "The Mothering of Twins, Triplets and Quadruplets." *Psychiatry* 43, 3 (1980): 189–204.

Graeber, David. *Lost People: Magic and the Legacy of Slavery in Madagascar*. Bloomington, IN: Indiana University Press, 2007.

Griaule, Marcel. *Dieu d'eau: Entretiens avec Ogotemelli*. Paris: Fayard, 1948.

Groothuis, Jessie R., Joyce P. Robarge, and Zelta B. Reynolds. "Increased Child Abuse in Families with Twins." *Pediatrics* 70, 5 (1982): 769–773.

Gulliver, Philip H. *The Family Herds: A Study of Two Pastoral Tribes in East Africa, the Jie and Turkana*. London: Routledge, 1966.

Hancock, Graham. *Lords of Poverty: The Power, Prestige, and Corruption of the International Aid Business*. London: Macmillan, 1989.

Hardacre, Helen. *Marketing the Menacing Fetus in Japan*. Berkley: University of California Press, 1997.

Herdt, Gilbert. *The Sambia: Ritual and Gender in New Guinea*. New York: Holt, Rinehart and Winston, 1987.

Héritier, Fancoise. *Les Deux Sœurs et leur mère. Anthropologie de l'Inceste*. Paris: Odile Jacob: 1994.

Heywood, Colin. *A History of Childhood: Children and Childhood in the West from Medieval to Modern Times*. Cambridge: Cambridge University Press, 2001.

Hobart, Angela, Ruth Rasmeyer, and Albert, Leeman. *The People of Bali*. Malden, MA: Blackwell Publishers, 1988.

Hubert, Henry, and Marcel Mauss. *Sacrifice: Its Nature and Functions*. Berkley: University of California Press, 1986.

Ifemesia, Chieka. *Turkana*. Orlando, FL: Harcourt, 2009.

Inglis, Brian. *Trance a Natural History of Altered States of Mind*. Boulder, CO: Paladin Books, 1990.

Kempadoo, Kamala, ed. *Trafficking and Prostitution Reconsidered: New Perspectives on Migration, Sex Work, and Human Rights*. Boulder, CO: Paradigm Publishers, 2005.

Kennedy, George A. trans. *Aristotle: On Rhetoric*. Oxford: Oxford University Press, 1991.

Kerber, Linda K., and Jane Sherron De Hart. *Women's America: Refocusing the Past*. sixth Edition. Oxford: Oxford University Press, 2003.

Klaus, Marshall H., John H. Kennell, and Phyllis Klaus. *Bonding: Building the Foundations of Secure Attachment and Independence*. New York: Merloyd Lawrence Books, 1982.

Klein, Melanie. *Envy and Gratitude*. London: The Hogart Press, 1946.

———. *Our Adult World and Other Essays*. London: Heinemann, 1963.

Knox, George, and David Morley. "Twinning in Yoruba Women." *British Journal of Obstetrics and Gynecology* 67 (1960): 981–982.

LaFleur, William R. *Liquid Life: Abortion and Buddhism in Japan.* Princeton: Princeton University Press, 1992.

Lainé, Daniel. *African Kings.* Berkley: Ten Speed Press, 2001.

Lallemand, Suzanne. *Grossesse et petite enfance en Afrique noire et à Madagascar.* Paris: L'Harmattan, 1991.

Landy, Helain G., and Luis J. Keith. "The Vanishing Twin: A Review." *Human Reproduction Update* 4, 2 (1998): 177–183.

Leigh, Gillian. *All About Twins.* London: Routledge, 1989.

Lèvi-Strauss, Claude. *The Elementary Structures of Kinship.* Boston, MA: Beacon Press, 1969.

Lewis Paul, and Elaine Lewis. *Peoples of the Golden Triangle.* London: Thames and Hudson, 1984.

Lipset, David. *Mangrove Man: Dialogics of Culture in the Sepik Estuary.* Cambridge: Cambridge University Press, 1997.

Lobo, Eric. *Esprits de Jungle: Irian Jaya l'univers iréel des Papous.* Paris: Romain Pages Editions, 1999.

Lutukeaus, Nancy, Christian Kaufmann, William E. Mitchell, Douglas Newton, Lindo Osmunsen, and Mehinard Schuster, eds. *Sepik Heritage: Tradition and Change in Papua New Guinea.* Durham, NC: Carolina Academic Press, 1990.

MacGillivray, Ian. "Epidemiology of Twin Pregnancy." *Seminars in Perinatology* 10 (1986): 4–8.

Makind, Akin. *African Philosophy, Culture, and Traditional Medicine.* Columbus, OH: Ohio University Press, 1988.

Mark, Mary Ellen. *Twins: Photographs and Interviews.* New York: Aperture Books, 2003.

Marshall, Klaus H., John H. Kennell, and Phyllis H. Klaus. *The Doula Book.* New York: Perseus Group, 2002.

Martin, Joyce A., and Melissa M. Park. "Trends in Twin and Triplet Births: 1980–97." *National Vital Statistics Reports* 47, 24 (September 14, 1999): 1–2.

Matalon Lagnado, Lucette, and Sheila Cohn Dekel. *Children of the Flames. Dr Joseph Mengele and the Untold Story of the Twins of Auschwitz.* New York: Penguin Books, 1991.

Matthews, Thomas J., and Brady E. Hamilton, "Mean Age of Mother, 1970–2000." *National Vital Statistics Reports* 51, 1 (Hyatsville, MD, December 11, 2002): 1–3.

Mauro, Didier, et Raholiarisoa, Emeline. *Madagascar: L'ile essentielle. Etude d'anthropologie culturale.* Paris: Anako, 2000.

Mead, Margaret. *Male and Female.* First Published in 1949. New York: Harper Perennial, 2001.

Meiselas, Susan. *Encounters with the Dani.* Gottingen: Steidl Publishers, 2003.

Menikoff, Barry, ed. "Strange Case of Dr Jekyll and Mr. Hyde," in *The Complete Stories of Robert Luis Stevenson.* First Edition, 1886. New York: Random House Publishing Group, 2002.

Menken, J., Trussell J., and Larsen U. "Age and Infertility," *Science* 23 (1986): 1389.

Miller, Elmer S., ed. *Peoples of the Gran Chaco*. Westport, CT: Greenwood Publisers, 1999.

Morgan Steiner, Leslie. *Mommy Wars: Stay-at-Home and Career Moms Face Off on Their Choices, Their Lives, Their Families*. New York: Random House, 2006.

Musil, Robert. *The Man Without Qualities*. First Publication: 1930–1942. London: Vintage, 1996.

National Organization of Mothers of Twins Clubs Inc. *Fathers only Survey*. Plymouth, MI: NOMOTOC Publications, 2007.

Nelson, Henry B., and Catherine A. Martin. "Increased Child Abuse in Twins." *Child Abuse and Neglect* 9, 4 (1985): 501–505.

O'Connell Davidson, Julia. *Children in the Global Sex Trade*. Cambridge: Polity Press, 2005.

Olivelle, Patrick, trans. *The Law Code of Manu*. Oxford: Oxford University Press, 2004.

Panfilov, Dimitrije E., ed. *Aesthetic Surgery of the Facial Mosaic*. Berlin: Springer-Verlag, 2007.

Parke, Ross D. *Fatherhood*. Cambridge, MA: Harvard University Press, 1996.

Pavitt, Nigel. *Turkana: Kenya's Nomads of the Jade Sea*. New York: Harry N. Abrams, 1997.

Picone, Mary. "Infanticide, the Spirits of Aborted Fetuses, and the Making of Motherhood in Japan," in *Small Wars: The Cultural Politics of Childhood*, edited by Nancy Scheper-Huges, and Carolyn Sargent, 37–57. Berkley: University of California Press, 1998.

Piers, Maria W. *Infanticide Past and Present*. New York: W.W. Norton, 1978.

Piontelli, Alessandra. *Twins: From Fetus to Child*. London: Routledge, 2002.

———. "On the Onset of Human Fetal Behavior," in *Psychoanalysis and Neurosciences*, edited by Mauro Mancia, 391–418. New York: Springer-Verlag, 2006.

Ram, Kalpana, and Margaret Jolly, eds. *Maternities and Modernities*. Cambridge: Cambridge University Press, 1998.

Ramati, Alexander. *And the Violins Stopped Playing: A Story of the Gypsy Holocaust*. London: Hodder and Stoughton, 1986.

Raphael, Dana. *Being Female: Reproduction, Power, and Change*. Chicago: Aldine Press, 1975.

Rich, Adrienne. *Of Woman Born: Motherhood as Experience and Institution*. New York: W.W. Norton, 1985.

Rodham Clinton, Hillary. *It Takes a Village and Other Lessons Children Teach Us*. New York: Simon Schuster, 1996.

Rosenthal, Judy. *Possession, Ecstasy, and Law in Ewe Voodoo*. Charlottesville: University Press of Virginia, 1998.

Rothman, David J.E., Rose T. Awaya, B. Cohen, A. Daar, S.L. Dzemeshkevich, C.J. Lee, R. Munro, H. Reyes, S.M. Rothman, K.F. Schoen, N. Scheper-Hughes, Z. Shapira, and H. Smit. "The Bellagio Task Force Report on Transplantation, Bodily Integrity, and the International Traffic in Organs." *Transplantation Proceedings* 29 (1997): 273–945.

Roudhi-Fahimi, Farzaneh. *Gender and Equity in Access to Health Care Services in the Middle East and North Africa.* Washington, DC: Population Reference Bureau, 2006.

Ruddick, Sara. *Maternal Thinking: Toward A politics of Peace.* Boston: Beacon Press, 1989.

———. "What Do Mothers and Grandmothers Know and Want?" in *What Do Mothers Want?* edited by Sheila Feig Brown, 60–71. London: The Analytic Press, 2005.

Sabini, Meredith, trans. *The Earth Has a Soul: The Nature Writings of C. G. Jung.* Berkley, CA: North Atlantic Books, 2002.

Salvy, Claire. *Jumeaux de sexe différent.* Paris: L'Harmattan, 2000.

Scheper-Huges, Nancy. *Death Without Weeping: The Violence of Everyday Life in Brazil.* Berkley: University of California Press, 1992.

Segal, Nancy L. *Entwined Lives: Twins and What They Tell Us About Human Behavior.* Hialea, FL: Dutton Press, 1999.

Sen, Amartya. *Development as Freedom.* Oxford: Oxford University Press, 1999.

———. "More than 100 Million Women are Missing." *New York Review of Books* 37, 20 (December 20, 1990): 61–63.

Shakespeare, William. "The Comedy of Errors," in *Complete Works of William Shakespeare, 1590–1594.* 166–186. London: Wordsworth Special Editions Paperback, 1997.

——— "Twelfth Night, or What You Will," in *Complete Works of William Shakespeare,1601–1602.* 641–669. London: Wordsworth Special Editions, 1997.

Sharp, Lesley A. *The Possessed and the Dispossessed: Spirits, Identity, and Power in a Madagascar Migrant Town.* Berkley: University of California Press, 1993.

Shorter, Edward. *The Making of the Modern Family.* London: Fontana, 1977.

Shostack, Marjorie. *Nisa.* Cambridge, MA: Harvard University Press, 1981.

Sindiga, Isaac. *Traditional Medicine in Africa.* Nairobi: East African Education Publications, 1997.

Slikkerveer, Jan L. *Plural Medical Systems in the Horn of Africa.* London: Kegan Paul, 1990.

Smith, Rosamond. (alias Joyce Carol Oates). *Lives of the Twins.* New York: Simon and Schuster, 1987.

Snowden, Robert. *The Artificial Family.* St. Leonard, Australia: Unwin and Allen, 1983.

Sorajjakool, Siroj. *Child Prostitution in Thailand.* Binghamton, NY: Haworth Press, 2002.

Spencer, Herbert. *Principles of Biology.* First Publication 1864. Honolulu: University Press of the Pacific, 2002.

Spillman, Jane. "Antenatal and Postnatal Influences in Family Relationships," in *Twin and Triplet Psychology,* edited by Audrey C. Sandbank, 19–34. London: Routledge, 1999.

Spitz, Rene A. *First Year of Life: A Psychoanalytic Study of Normal and Deviant Development of Object Relations.* Madison, CT: International Universities Press, 1966.

Stein, Rebecca, and Philip L. Stein. *Anthropology of Religion, Magic and Witchcraft.* Needham Heights, MA: Alwyn and Bacon, 2007.

Sterling, Robert. *The Book of Doppelgangers.* Rockville, MD: Wildside Press, 2003.

Stewart, Elizabeth A. *Exploring Twins: Towards a Social Analysis of Twinship.* London: Palgrave Macmillan, 1999.

Stone, Lawrence. *Family, Sex and Marriage in England.* London: Penguin Books, 1977.

Strother-Radcliff, Kathrin. *Women and Health: Power, Technology, Inequality and Conflict in a Gendered World.* Needham Heights, MA: Allyn and Bacon, 2001.

Susnik, Branislava. *Los Aborigenes del Paraguay: Approximacion a las Creencias de los Indigenas.* Asuncion, Paraguay: Publicaciones Museo Etnographico Andres Barbero, 1985.

Swadener, Beth Blue, Margaret Kabiru, and Anne Njenga. *Does the Village Still Raise the Child?* Albany, NY: New York State University Press, 2000.

Taffel, Selma M. "Demographic Trends in Twin Births: USA," in *Multiple Pregnancy: Epidemiology Gestation & Perinatal Outcome,* edited by Louis G. Keith, Emile Papiernik, Donald M. Keith, and Barbara Luke, 133–144. New York: The Parthenon Publishing Group, 1995.

Ta-Kuan, Chou. *The Customs of Cambodia.* Bangkok: The Siam Society, 1993.

Tart, Charles T. *States of Consciousness.* Washington, DC (see above): Backinprint, 2001.

This, Bernard, *Naitre... et sourire.* Paris: Flammarion, 1983.

Thorndike, Lynn. *History of Magic and Experimental Science.* New York: Columbia University Press, 1923.

Thornill Wilmsen, Nancy, ed. *The Natural History of Inbreeding and Outbreeding.* Chicago: The University of Chicago Press, 1993.

Thorpe, Keith. "Comparison of Prevalence of Depression in Mothers of Twins and Mothers of Singletons." *British Medical Journal* 302 (1991): 875–878.

Torrés, Dominique. *Esclaves: 200 millions d'esclaves aujourd'hui.* Paris: Phébus, 1995.

UNFPA, "Reproductive Health Fact Sheet." *State of World Population 2005.* New York, 2005.

UNICEF. "Women and Children: The Double Dividend of Gender Equality," in *The State Of The World's Children, 2007.* Geneva: UNICEF, 2005.

United States Department of Agriculture (USDA). *USDA Annual Report on the Cost of Raising a Child.* Washington, DC (2001): 3.

U.S. Census Bureau International Data Base. Population Division. *Country Summaries, Cameroon, 2000.*

U.S. Department of Health and Human Services. *National Child Abuse and Neglect Data System (NCANDS) Child File, 2005.*

U.S. Government. *21st Century Complete Guide to Guinea-Bissau.* White House: CIA Factbook, 2007.

van Gennep, Arno. *The Rites of Passage.* Chicago: Chicago University Press, 1961.

Van Hollen, Cecilia. *Birth on the Threshold.* Berkley: University of California Press, 2003.

van Rouveroy van Nieuwaal, and Adrian B. *L'Etat en Afrique face à la cheferie, Le cas du Togo.* Paris: Karthala, 2000.

Vitebsky, Piers. *Shamanism*. Norman, OK: University of Oklahoma Press, 2001.

Waley, Arthur, trans. *The Book of Songs: The Ancient Chinese Classic of Poetry*. New York: Grove Press, 1996.

Wallace, Marjory. *The Silent Twins*. Harmondsworth, Middlesex: Penguin Books, 1986.

Walsh, Roger. *World of Shamanism: New Views of an Ancient Tradition*. Bristol, UK: Llewellyn Publications, 2007.

Warner, Judith. *Perfect Madness: Motherhood in the Age of Anxiety*. New York: Penguin Books, 2005.

Waterfield, Robin, trans. *Herodotus. The Histories*. Oxford: Oxford World Classics, 1998.

Williams, Melvin D. *Community in a Black Pentecostal Church: An Anthropological Study*. Prospect Heights, IL: Waveland Press, 1984.

Winnicott, Donald. "Transitional Objects and Transitional Phenomena." *International Journal of Psychoanalysis* 34 (1951): 89–97.

Wisntanley, Peter A. "The Approach to Treatment," in *Principles of Medicine in Africa*, edited by Eldryd Parry, Richard Godfrey, David Mabey, and Geoffrey Gill. Third Edition, 1311–1337. Cambridge: Cambridge University Press, 2004.

Wolff, Naomi. *Misconceptions*. Woodston, PE: Anchor Books, 2003.

Wollstonecraft Shelley, Mary. *Frankenstein; or the Modern Prometeus*. First Published in 1818. New York: Simon and Schuster, 2004.

Woodward, Joan. *The Lone Twin: A Study in Bereavement and Loss*. New York: New York University Press, 1998.

World Health Organization (WHO). *Gender and Health Technical Paper 98*. WHO Publications: Geneva, 1998.

———. *Maternal Mortality in 2000: Estimates Developed by WHO, UNICEF, UNFPA*. Geneva: WHO Publications, 2004.

———. Recommendations on exclusive breastfeeding, available at: http//www.who.int/child-adolescent-health/NUTRITION/infant_exclusive.html

———. *World Health Statistics*. Geneva: WHO Press, 2006.

Yoors, Yan. *Gypsies*. Long Grove, IL: Waveland Press, 1987.

Yount, Kathrin M., and Emily M. Agree. "The Power of Older Women and Men in Egyptian and Tunisian Families." *Journal of Marriage and Family* 66 (2004): 126–146.

Zazzo, René. *Les Jumeaux, la couple et la personne*. Paris: Presses Universitaires de France, 1960.

Zelizer, Viviana. *Pricing the Priceless Child: The Changing Social Value of Children*. Princeton: Princeton University Press, 1994.

Zimmer-Tamakoshi, Laura, ed. *Modern Papua New Guinea*. Kirksville, MO: Thomas Jefferson University Press, 1998.

Index